The Complete Guide to

Citing Government Information Resources

THIRD EDITION

A manual for social science & business research

Revised editon by
Debora Cheney, Pennsylvania State University

 LexisNexis

A royalty from the sale of this publication goes to support the activities of the Government Documents Round Table, American Library Association.

ISBN 0-88692-586-X

This manual is the third edition of a work originally published in 1984 as *The Complete Guide to Citing Government Documents: A Manual for Writers and Librarians.*

Printed in U.S.A.

Please inquire for information on discounts for volume purchases for classroom and other uses.

Table of Contents

List of Illustrations

Tables

Figures

Preface

The new edition of *The Complete Guide to Citing Government Information Resources* fills a void in the literature created by the changes in government and organization information production and dissemination since the 1993 revised edition. Although the original edition (1984) was considered a "modest attempt"[1] by its authors, Diane Garner and Diane Smith, no other citation style manual provides the same level of detailed guidance for formulating bibliographic citations to government and organization information in every format. As noted in the 1993 edition, new rules for electronic formats of government information recognized changes occurring then in the "very definition of government *documents*."[2] This edition recognizes that this definition continues to change and expand.

The original purpose of the manual remains the same: "…A bibliographic citation should … *identify* and *differentiate* an item for a reader; …it should give a reader some indication of intellectual *quality* (i.e., a major study as opposed to an information pamphlet); … it should give *credit* to the ideas of other authors; … and it should help the reader *locate* the cited item."[3] What continues to change is the number of formats, the number and variety of information providers (ranging from freely-available government WWW sites to access-controlled commercial databases), and the integration of government and organization information into the information fabric of the WWW. Government and organization information now more visibly exist side-by-side on the WWW, in on-line library catalogs, and in commercial databases.

Two goals guided the preparation of this edition—to expand the rules and examples to address WWW-based resources and to make the manual more accessible to researchers who were not familiar with government and organization information resources and the many challenges they present.

Four major changes were incorporated. First, in an effort to integrate and simplify the manual, the citation rules are now organized by the parts of the bibliographic citation (Issuing Agency, Title, Publishing Information, etc.) illustrated with examples from federal, state, local, regional, and foreign governments and organizations. Second, a new definition of electronic formats distinguishes between those that have a physical electronic form (PEF), such as CD-ROMs and floppy disks, and those that have a virtual electronic form (VEF), such as WWW pages, PDF files, and JPEG images. Part 3 contains new citation rules for VEF sources.[4] Rules for PEF sources are incorporated into Part 2. Third, many new citation examples were included throughout this new edition, including many more from state, local, regional, and foreign government sources and from European Union sources. Most sections include examples from federal and international sources—examples for other governmental units are included as appropriate. Fourth, *Quick Citation Guides* were added that include examples of sources in physical and virtual formats. This edition will allow researchers to see how print and electronic citations are similar and how they differ in form and punctuation. In addition, by integrating both source publications and the format examples, the *Quick Citation Guides* allow researchers to use the elements that will fit their circumstance best. It is my hope that these changes will continue to make the manual accessible to writers, students, teachers, researchers, general reference librarians, and journalists, as well as to government documents specialists.

The current edition remains at its core the work and inspiration of two exceptional government documents librarians—Diane Garner and Diane Smith, authors of the original manual. I have been fortunate to work with and for both of them. I am grateful for their willingness to let me continue to develop this important source. The entire revision was completed during my sabbatical leave from the Social Sciences Library, The Pennsylvania State University Libraries. The staff and librarians there graciously accepted my yearlong absence and made it possible for me to devote all my energies to this project. Professional colleagues and friends have also provided valuable help. Susan Tulis purchased and mailed a copy of the new edition of the Harvard *Bluebook* to me in Oxford and then, adding insult to injury, graciously accepted my "invitation" to read the complete manuscript. My thanks goes to the Committee on Institutional Cooperation (CIC) Librarians who also volunteered to read the final versions of selected chapters, and to Helen Sheehy, who contributed to the revised edition and provided answers to questions —always quickly. My special thanks go to Debbi Schaubman and Dena Hutto who volunteered to read the entire manual under significant time pressure. The manual was supported by a Readex/GODORT/ALA Catherine J. Reynolds Research Award (2000) award. Finally, I thank my family—Patrick, who made it possible for us to come to Oxford during our sabbatical year, and Evan and Kelton, who willingly joined us on our adventure.

Debora Cheney

Kineton Road
Oxford, England
March 2002

_____

[1] Garner, Diane L. and Diane H. Smith, *The Complete Guide to Citing Government Information Resources: A Manual for Writers & Librarians*. Revised ed. Bethesda, MD: Congressional Information Service, 1993, xvi.
[2] Garner and Smith, p. xv.
[3] Garner and Smith, p. xv.
[4] For further explanation and definition of PEF and VEF sources, see Table 1, below.

Introduction

Purposes of a Citation

A citation serves several purposes. The first is a matter of honesty: you should give credit to the people from whom you got your material. A citation can also lend authority to your work, signaling your reader that a great deal of careful research went into your final product. The last, and perhaps most important, function of a citation is to provide a kind of road map for research. This is the function with which most librarians, and the authors of this manual, are primarily concerned.

A good citation should give your readers enough accurate and pertinent bibliographic information to enable them to locate what you have cited. The information required will depend partly on the work cited and partly on the methods of access used by libraries. The problem is that library methods are not absolutely uniform. The best you can do in creating a citation is to provide enough information to accommodate most known situations. The usual elements of a citation--author, title, place, publisher, date--while adequate in most libraries for most books, are not adequate for the publications of governments and organizations.

Government and Organizational Documents: What Are They?

Government documents have never been easy to define, and the rise of electronic formats as media of dissemination has contributed to a blurring of the definition of government and organization publications, prompting many to speak of government "information" rather than government documents. ***In this manual government "documents" or government "information" means information in any format produced by or for a governmental body or by international or intergovernmental organizations (IGO).*** Government information may be a pamphlet on how to quit smoking, a transcript of a congressional hearing, an expert's report on the food needs of a developing country, a floppy disk edition of a civil service test, a magnetic tape containing census data, debates of a parliament in print, or multi-media sources on the WWW; in short, any part of the activities of a governmental body that the government chooses to record and make available in any format.

Why do documents present special citation problems? There are many reasons, but basically they all come down to this: governments and organizations do not always follow standard publishing practices and libraries do not always treat documents as they treat books and other sources published by commercial publishers.

Government Publishing Practices

In the case of commercial publications, certain publishing practices are well-established. You typically can expect to find a page with an obvious title, author, place of publication, and publisher. On the back of that page you can find a copyright date. Governments and organizations, however, do not necessarily follow these "rules."

In the first place, many documents are not meant for publication in the usual sense. Although the government or organization may make every effort to ensure wide distribution, the majority of government and organization documents result from their "business" and not from their desire to publish something. Thus, the publication style is developed independently by each agency with a view to its own needs rather than to a uniform style.

Second, many documents lack, in part or in full, the elements considered necessary for a good citation, such as author, title, and publishing information. Many documents have only anonymous authors--the government is considered to be responsible for the content in most cases. Variations in titles are usually present and the publishing information frequently is missing, although it is implied in many cases. If you follow many other citation styles which often omit what is not given on the document, you may be left with nearly useless bits of information.

Third, governments and organizations are using the WWW heavily as a dissemination medium and are inventing approaches for displaying their publications or for providing access to their information. These electronic formats have introduced new types of "publications" with which citation styles are only just beginning to cope: interactive databases available on the WWW, a "publication" divided into electronic parts accessible via an electronic table of contents, and a wide range of sound and audio formats delivered via the WWW. Given the wealth and diversity of electronic information being produced by governments and organizations, it is necessary to develop a citation style that can evolve to address these changing forms and formats.

Library Document Collections

If government and organization publishing practices have made document citations difficult, library catalogs and indexes have not made them any easier. Recently libraries have begun to include documents in their on-line catalogs, using the same level of cataloging that the library uses for non-government sources. When a library receives a book, it prepares bibliographic records, which typically are indexed in its on-line catalog by author, title, series, subject, and keyword. U.S. documents may also be indexed by Superintendent of Documents (SuDoc) number. This practice is relatively recent and not universal. Many libraries still keep their documents in a separate, uncataloged collection. And many libraries that catalog current U.S. documents have not retrospectively cataloged the documents they received prior to 1976, the year when the U.S. Government Printing Office started cataloging U.S. documents on-line. International and IGO organization publications have fared little better and are frequently even less visible and accessible in on-line library catalogs.

This situation has been relieved somewhat by the appearance of some excellent indexes and abstracts, but the fact remains few libraries have a comprehensive and cumulative list of their documents collections. Furthermore, even in those cases where a library has provided complete cataloging for its documents, those cataloging records are often so complicated that it is only by chance that one ever comes across them in the file.

Given this situation, government document librarians have relied on other methods of making documents accessible. For a document citation to be useful, it must take into account these other methods. These include specific book catalogs, abstracts, and indexes in which bibliographic records may be found by date, by document or report numbers, by names of agencies or committees, by keywords in titles, and so on. In today's electronic environment, libraries are continuing to seek ways to provide access to government and organization sources in electronic formats. For this reason, library catalogs, WWW pages, and sources such as *WorldCat* and *RLIN* and commercial sources such as *LexisNexis* and *Readex/NewsBank* are used to provide bibliographic and virtual access to these electronic sources.

Because there are so many ways to identify and access documents, you and your readers may have to explore many avenues to locate the government information you cite. For this reason, citations to government and organization information need to be as complete as possible and may include more elements than citations to commercial sources.

Government and Organization Information in Electronic Formats--What Are Physical Electronic Formats (PEF) and Virtual Electronic Formats (VEF)?

Electronic media are highly volatile and can be easily altered. In addition, there are also many different Physical Electronic Formats (PEF)—compact disk, video disk, floppy disk, magnetic tapes, and many different Virtual Electronic Formats (VEF) delivered via the WWW in many different file formats—PDF, TXT, .GIF, .XLS, to name only a few. Because of their ability to be copied, a source in one format can be changed from a PEF to a VEF quite easily. For example a CD-ROM's contents can be placed on a WWW server for broader access or a print publication can also be available both in a virtual or physical electronic format (The *Congressional Record* is available in print, on CD-ROM, and via WWW database). Therefore, the medium may not always be a distinguishing characteristic of a government or organization source. However, for purposes of creating citations, it is useful to separate the two types of electronic formats because different rules are needed in some situations.

Table 1: Physical Electronic Formats (PEF) and Virtual Electronic Formats (VEF)

Definition	Example	Citation Rules to follow
Physical Electronic Formats (PEF)—These electronic formats have a physical form which can be held in the hand and is used, viewed, or listened to, using some form of technology—computer, tape recorder, video-recorder, etc.	◦ CD-ROMs ◦ Floppy Disks ◦ Videocassettes ◦ Sound recordings	**Follow the rules of other physical formats (print, microfiche or microfilm, for example) in Part 2: Citation Rules for Physical Formats.**
Virtual Electronic Formats (VEF)—These electronic sources do not have a physical format but rather are accessed via the Internet. They are read, viewed, or listened to via computer or other electronic device. Of course, the researcher can elect to print them out or save them to some other physical format.	◦ WWW files/sources ◦ Data files or extracts from these files ◦ E-mail messages ◦ Webcasts ◦ *RealAudio* files ◦ Image files	**Follow the rules in Part 3: Citation Rules for Virtual Electronic Formats (VEF).**

Note: URLs for government and organization websites and VEF sources can and do change frequently. Thus, the URLs in this book are meant only as examples.

How to Develop a Citation

Researchers must be consistent and plan ahead. ***Remember that the purpose of a citation is to give your reader information.*** The function of a citation's mechanics is to make that information easy to read, and a consistent pattern is easier to read than a random one. This manual strives for consistency in its examples, which should be used as models for your own citations.

If you are unsure which information should be included in a citation for the source you have in hand or on the screen, answer the *Five Basic Questions*. Once the questions have been answered, you will have the information you need to create a bibliographic citation.

Table 2: The Five Basic Questions for a Bibliographic Citation

1. Who is responsible for the content of this source? (Section 1.0 and E1.0)
2. What is the title of the source? (Section 2.0 and E2.0)
3. Is there any additional information to distinguish this source? (Section 3.0 and E3.0)
4. Who is publishing, printing or distributing the source (Section 4.0) or who is the source of information? (Section E4.0)
5. What more can you tell me about this source? (Section 5.0 and E5.0)

You will save yourself a lot of work if you take accurate notes while you are doing your research. When using indexes, take the bibliographic information, such as issuing agency, title, publisher, and date, from the index. Then you will not have to figure out the correct information from a confusing array of candidate items in the work itself. Furthermore, if you take the information from the standard documents indexes (see *Appendix B: Standard Reference Sources for Government and Organization Information*), you can be sure that your reader will be able to find the documents you have cited.

The Quick Citation Guides

The *Quick Citation Guides* include examples of sources in both physical and virtual formats from governments and organizations and cover the wide range of challenges researchers encounter when developing citations for documents.

> ➤ *Quick Citation Guide to Books and Monographs*
> ➤ *Quick Citation Guide to Legislative/Parliamentary Sources*
> ➤ *Quick Citation Guide to Periodical Articles and Statistical Sources*
> ➤ *Quick Citation Guide to Special Cases and Well-Known Sources*

Consult each of these *Quick Citation Guides* for examples similar to the source you have in hand. You will find the examples useful, although in some cases consulting the Rule sections will be necessary. If this is the case, determine which citation element in your document does not fit the examples shown, then go back to the *Index* or consult the *Table of Contents* to identify a section which will discuss the element.

The Recommended Form and Punctuation

The examples throughout this Manual use the *Recommended Form and Punctuation* suggested in each section and illustrated in the *Quick Citation Guides* to organize parts of the citation in a way that will be meaningful to your reader. You may use punctuation described in any style manual (several are included in *Appendix A: Style Manuals*) if preferred. The content of the citation should stay the same no matter which style manual you use—the punctuation may differ.

Above all, do not become excessively concerned with the form and punctuation of the citation. While form and punctuation are important, the anguish caused by the demand for a **correct form** is out of all proportion to its worth. Further, when the quest for correct form causes one to omit necessary content, the integrity of the citation is sacrificed.

Citing Parts: Periodical Articles and Statistical Sources

The most commonly encountered variation is the need to create a citation to periodical articles and statistical sources. Rules and guidance for these and a number of other special cases are covered in the rule sections *Citing Parts: Periodical Articles and Statistical Sources* (Sections 6.0 and E6.0). Examples and recommended form and punctuation are included in the *Quick Citation Guide to Periodical Articles and Statistical Sources*.

Footnote vs. Bibliography

All examples in the text and in the *Quick Citation Guide* are given in bibliographic form. There is no distinction for footnotes, since the differences between these two spring from printing styles rather than from bibliographic needs.

Citing a work in a footnote or in a bibliography depends on the use being made of it. In general you would use a footnote to acknowledge and identify material (quotations, data, ideas) taken directly from another source or material that you need to substantiate your position. Usually, a footnote cites a precise part of a work.

A bibliography, on the other hand, is a list of sources. It may be a list of all the sources consulted in your research, or it may be a selective list of resources, depending on your aims.

When footnotes are printed at the bottom of a page of text, it looks better if you keep the indentations uniform and similar to the paragraph. Also, since footnotes are arranged by a number, there is no need to put an author's last name first as you do in a bibliography. With the modern practice of using end notes rather than footnotes, there is really no reason why the citation form of the two should differ. If you wish to maintain a difference, use the following examples as a guide or consult one of the syle manuals listed in *Appendix A: Style Manuals*. These will provide guidance on form, while this Manual will provide guidance on the content of each citation.

Citation to a Whole Work

BIBLIOGRAPHY

Issuing Agency (in usual order). *Title*. Edition. Place of Publication: Publisher, Date of Publication. (Series). (Notes).

FOOTNOTE

Issuing Agency (in usual order), *Title*. Edition. (Place of Publication: Publisher, Date of Publication. (Series). (Notes).) Page Numbers.

Citation to a Part of a Whole Work

BIBLIOGRAPHY

Author (name inverted). "Title of Part," Page Numbers. In Issuing Agency. *Title*. Edition. Place of Publication: Publisher, Date of Publication. (Series). (Notes).

FOOTNOTE

Author (name in usual order), "Title of Part," Page Numbers. In Issuing Agency, *Title*. Edition. Place of Publication: Publisher, Date of Publication. (Series). (Notes).

<u>Citation to a Periodical Article or Statistical Table</u>

BIBLIOGRAPHY

Author of Article (name inverted). "Title of Article or Table Header," *Title of Periodical* Volume: Issue (Date) Page Numbers. (Notes).

FOOTNOTE

Author (name in usual order), "Title of Article or Table Header," *Title of Periodical* Volume: Issue (Date) Page Numbers. (Notes).

Successive Citations

The *same work* will be cited more than once only in footnotes. How you handle these successive citations will depend on whether you have a bibliography in addition to footnotes. If you have only footnotes, you should give a full citation the first time. After that, an abbreviated form is acceptable. If you have a bibliography, give the complete form in the bibliography and use the short form in the footnotes.

The author's last name, a short title, and a page reference are used in the typical abbreviated book citation. In a government document citation this translates as issuing agency, short title, and page number.

> AID. *Kitale Maize*, p. 3.

Shorten the issuing agency's name only if you can do so without losing its identification. For example, U.S. Department of Housing and Urban Development could safely be shortened to HUD for a second footnote reference, but U.S. House. Committee on Appropriations could not be shortened to Appropriations Committee without confusion, unless there were no other references to documents of an Appropriations Committee.

When abbreviating a document title, make sure that you do not take out so much information that your reader will not be able to distinguish the original source. Once you have decided on a shortened form of both issuing agency and title, be sure to use it consistently.

The use of Latin words and abbreviations (*ibid.*, *op. cit.* and *idem*) for successive citations is NOT recommended because they are too often misused and misunderstood.

In a bibliography when the same issuing agency is listed in successive citations, you may substitute an eight-space underline followed by a period for the issuing agency's name. Be sure that the agency is exactly the same in all its divisions before you use this convention.

> North Atlantic Treaty Organization. *The Eurogroup*. Brussels, [by 1982].
>
> _____. *Financial and Economic Data Relating to NATO Defense* (Press Release M-DPC-2(82)24). Brussels, 1982. (1983 IIS microfiche 2220-SI).

PART 1
Quick Citation Guides

Quick Citation Guide to Books and Monographs

Quick Citation Guide to Books and Monographs

THE BASIC ELEMENTS
    The Recommended Form and Punctuation for Books and Monographs

ISSUING AGENCY AND PERSONAL AUTHOR VARIATIONS
B1.1   Issuing Agency as Author
B1.2   Multiple Issuing Agencies
B1.3   Issuing Agency and Personal Author
B1.4   Issuing Agency and More Than Three Personal Authors
B1.5   Issuing Agency Known in Its Own Right
B1.6   Issuing Agency Name as an Acronym or Abbreviated
B1.7   Issuing Agency Not Named
B1.8   Issuing Agency: Regional Organization
B1.9   No Geo/Political Designation Named
B1.10 No Issuing Agency (Replaced by URL)
B1.11 Issuing Agency as a Personal Author
B1.12 Non-English Language Publications
B1.13 Multi-Lingual Publication in an English Language Bibliography
B1.14 Conference as Issuing Agency

TITLE VARIATIONS
B2.1   Title Includes Date/Edition
B2.2   No Title Given
B2.3   Excessively Long Title
B2.4   Non-traditional Titles
B2.5   Title with a Popular Name
B2.6   Book Chapter
B2.7   Encyclopedia/Yearbook Chapter
B2.8   Paper in a Conference Proceeding

DISTINGUISHING INFORMATION VARIATIONS
B3.1   Publication/Report Numbers
B3.2   Edition
B3.3   Medium or Publication Type

PUBLISHING AND SOURCE INFORMATION VARIATIONS
B4.1   Publishing Information/Source of Information
B4.2   No Publisher, Issuing Agency Assumed
B4.3   No Date of Publication
B4.4   Publisher, Issuing Agency and Personal Author
B4.5   Electronic Source Address (URL) as Source of Information
B4.6   Electronic Version of a Print Publication (Publisher and URL)

SERIES AND OTHER NOTE VARIATIONS
B5.1   Publication in a Series
B5.2   Required Notes

BASIC ELEMENTS

The form as well as the punctuation of your citation organizes the parts in a way that is meaningful to your reader. The following recommended form and punctuation is used throughout this manual. For additional guidance about the content of the citation, consult the rules in Parts 2 and 3. For guidance on footnote vs. bibliography entries, consult the *Introduction*.

Table 3: The Recommended Form and Punctuation for Books and Monographs

For an Organization Publication:

Issuing Agency. *Title Proper: Subtitle* (Medium). (Publication/Report Number). Edition statement. By Personal Author. Place of Publication: Publisher, Date of Publication. (Series). (Notes).

Issuing Agency. *Title Proper: Subtitle* (Medium). (Publication/Report Number). Edition statement. By Personal Author. (Series). (Notes). Available at: [URL]; Accessed: [Date].

For a Government Publication:

Geo/Political Designation. Issuing Agency. *Title Proper: Subtitle* (Medium). (Publication/Report Number). Edition statement. By Personal Author. Place of Publication: Publisher, Date of Publication. (Series). (Notes).

Geo/Political Designation. Issuing Agency. *Title Proper: Subtitle* (Medium). (Publication/Report Number). Edition statement. By Personal Author. (Series). (Notes). Available at: [URL]; Accessed: [Date].

ISSUING AGENCY AND PERSONAL AUTHOR VARIATIONS

B1.1 Issuing Agency as Author (The Recommended Form and Punctuation)

U.S. Dept. of Health and Human Services, National Center for Chronic Disease Prevention and Health Promotion. *CDP File* (CD-ROM). Atlanta, GA: Centers for Disease Control, Apr. 1992. (NCCDPHP CD-ROM, no.2). (HE 20.7616:2/CD).

U.S. General Accounting Office. *Combating Terrorism: Accountability Over Medical Supplies Needs Further Improvement.* Washington, Mar. 2001. (GA1.13:GAO-01-463).

Minnesota. Pollution Control Agency. *MEPA Hazardous Waste Compliance Guide.* St. Paul, 1991.

Cyprus. Ministry of Finance, Dept. of Statistics and Research. *Economic Report, 1989.* n.p.: Printing Office of the Republic of Cyprus, 1991. (General Economic Statistics: Series I. Report no. 34).

United Kingdom. HM Treasury. *Securing Our Future Health: Taking a Long-Term View.* By Derek Wanless. Interim Report. Nov. 2001. Available at: http://www.hm-treasury.gov.uk/Consultations_and_Legislation/wanless/consult_wanless_index.cfm; Accessed: 2/12/02.

U.N. Centre on Transnational Corporations. *Transnational Banks and the International Debt Crisis* (ST/CTC/96). New York, 1991.

B1.2 Multiple Issuing Agencies

U.S. Dept. of Housing and Urban Development. *American Housing Survey: 1985N (National) Core & Supplement Tables & Microdata, 1987N Core Tables & Core & Supplement Microdata, 1989N Core Tables, Microdata, Unpublished Tables, 1988, 1989 MSA's Core Microdata* (CD-ROM). Washington: Nov. 1991. (C 3.214/19:985-89/CD). (With the U.S. Bureau of the Census).

U.S. Dept. of Justice, Bureau of Justice Statistics. *Law Enforcement Management and Administrative Statistics, 1987* (Computer File). Conducted by U.S. Dept. of Commerce, Bureau of the Census. ICPSR ed. Ann Arbor, MI: Inter-University Consortium for Political and Social Research [producer and distributor], 1997. (Study 9222).

Oklahoma. Dept. of Agriculture, Crop and Livestock Reporting Service. *Oklahoma Agricultural Statistics 1981*. Oklahoma City, 1982. (Produced as a cooperative effort with the U.S. Dept. of Agriculture).

Canada. Royal Commission on Electoral Reform and Party Financing. *Interest Groups and Elections in Canada*. Edited by F. Leslie Seidle. (Research Studies, v.2). Toronto: Dundern Press, 1991. (In cooperation with the Canada Communication Group).

U.N. Economic Commission for Latin America and the Caribbean. *Transnational Bank Behaviour and the International Debt Crisis* (LC/G.1553/Rev. 1-P). Santiago, 1989. Estudios e Informes de la Cepal 76). (Joint Publication of ECLAC and United Nations Centre on Transnational Corporations).

B1.3 Issuing Agency and Personal Author

U.S. Library of Congress, The Center for the Book. *The History of Books: A Guide to Selected Resources in the Library of Congress*. By Alice D. Schreyer. Washington: Government Printing Office, 1987. (LC1.6/4: H62).

Hawaii. Dept. of Land and Natural Resources. *The Kalia Burial Site: Rescue Archaeology in Waikiki*. By Earl Neller. Honolulu, 1980.

New Zealand. Cabinet Office. *Honours, Titles, Styles, and Procedure in New Zealand*. Compiled and edited by Phillip P. O'Shea. Wellington: E. C. Keating, 1977.

U.N. Economic Commission for Europe. *How Partners Spend Their Time: A Comparative Study on Time Use by Men and Women*. By Ineke A. L. Stoop and J. Oudhof. Geneva, 1989.

B1.4 Issuing Agency and More Than Three Personal Authors

U.S. Dept. of Education, National Center for Education Statistics. *The 1990 Science Report Card: NAEP's Assessment of Fourth, Eighth, and Twelfth Graders*. By Lee R. Jones et al. Washington, 1992. (ED1.302:Sci1).

Massachusetts. Division of Employment Security. *Occupational Profile of Selected Manufacturing Industries in Massachusetts 1980*. By Richard Subrant et al. Boston, 1981. (Occupation/Industry Research Publication 14).

Organisation for Economic Cooperation and Development. *Japan at Work: Markets, Management and Flexibility*. By Ronald Dore et al. (81-89-01-1). Paris, 1989.

B1.5 Issuing Agency Known in Its Own Right

U.S. Census Bureau. *County and City Data Book, 2000*. Washington: Government Printing Office, 2002.

U.S. Office of Technology Assessment. *Electronic Surveillance in a Digital Age* (OTA-BP-ITC 149; 90 kb). [Washington]: Government Printing Office, July 1995. (OTA Legacy). Available at: http://www.wws.princeton.odu/~ota; Accessed: 2/20/02.

B1.6 Issuing Agency Name as an Acronym or Abbreviated

Southeast Asian Ministers of Education Organization. *Resource Book on SEAMEO* (SEAMES/SPIP-1/1981). Bangkok, 1981.

Organisation for Economic Co-Operation and Development. *Reforming Russian Infrastructure for Competition and Efficiency.* Paris: OECD Publications, 2001. Available at: SourceOECD; Accessed: 12/10/01.

B1.7 Issuing Agency Not Named

U.N. Educational, Scientific, and Cultural Organization. [Secretariat. Sector for Programme Support]. *Organization of UNESCO Secretariat Since 1946* (PRS.79/WS/47). Paris, 1979.

B1.8 Issuing Agency: Regional Organization

Metropolitan Airports Commission, Office of Relations/Communications/Marketing. *Minneapolis/St. Paul International Airport.* Minneapolis, MN, 1997.

Planning Commission of Lehigh-Northampton Counties. *Population Growth Trends, 1980.* Lehigh Valley, PA, 1981.

Tri-City Industrial Development Council. *Tri-Cities Purchasing Behavior.* Kennewick, WA: TRIDEC, 1990.

B1.9 No Geo/Political Designation Named

[Idaho. Dept. of Education.] *Fall Enrollment Report, 1982/83.* Boise, 1982.

B1.10 No Issuing Agency (Replaced by URL)

Site Seeing on the Internet. Available at: http://www.ftc.gov/bcp/conline/pubs/online/-sitesee/; Accessed: 11/20/01.

B1.11 Issuing Agency as a Personal Author

U.S. Dept. of Housing and Urban Development. *Rehabilitation Guidelines 1982: 10 Guidelines on the Rehabilitation of Walls, Windows, and Roofs.* Prepared by National Institute of Building Sciences. Washington: Government Printing Office, 1983. (HH1.6/3:R26/8/982).

U.S. Senate, Committee on Foreign Relations. *Treaties and Other International Agreements: The Role of the United States Senate, A Study* (S. Prt.106-71). Prepared by the Congressional Research Service, Library of Congress. Text from: *Congressional Committee Prints.* Available from: GPO Access, http://www.access.gpo.gov/congress/-cpsrch.html; Accessed: 4/30/01.

Southwestern Pennsylvania Regional Planning Commission. *Directions in Housing Policies for Low and Moderate Income Families . . .* Prepared by the Institute for Urban Policy and Administration, University of Pittsburgh. Pittsburgh, 1972.

Canada. External Affairs Canada. *Studies in Canadian Export Opportunities in the U.S. Market: Telecommunications Equipment.* Prepared by Peat Marwick Consulting Group. Ottawa, 1989. (DSS. Cat. No. E73-7/74-1988).

B1.12 Non-English Language Publications in an English Language Bibliography

Citation to an English Language Title

Cameroon. Ministry of Information and Culture, Dept. of Communication. *Cameroon in Brief.* n.p., n.d.

European Union. *Towards a Freer, Fairer Trade in Industrial Products.* Oct. 2001. Available at: http://trade-info.cec.eu.int/europa/2001newround/goo.htm; Accessed: 12/2/01.

Citation to an French Language Title

Cameroun. Ministère de l'Information et de la Culture, Direction de la Communication. *L'essentiel sur le Cameroun*. n.p., n.d.

Commission Européenne. *Vers des Échanges des Produits Industriels Plus Libres et Plus Équitables*. Oct. 2001. Available at: http://trade-info.cec.eu.int/europa/2001newround/-goo_fr.htm; Accessed: 12/2/01.

Citation to an Spanish Language Title

Bush, George W. *Discurso Radial Del Presidente a la Nacion*. The White House, Office of the Press Secretary, Dec. 8, 2001. (Available in English and Spanish). Available at: http://www.whitehouse.gov/-news/releases/2001/12/20011208-1.es.html; Accessed: 12/10/01.

B1.13 Multi-Lingual Publication in an English Language Bibliography

U.S. National Institutes of Health. *En busca de buena salud fumar: este es el mejor momento para dejarlo*. Bethesda, MD: NIH, 1982. (Available in English).

Texas. Dept. of Health. *Disenteria amibiana*. Austin, 1981. (Available in English).

Canada. Office of the Auditor General. *Report of the Auditor General*. Apr. 2000. (Text available in English or French). Available at: http://www.oagbvg.gc.ca/domino/-reports.nsf/html/00menu_e.html; Accessed: 12/2/01.

U.N. Economic Commission for Latin America and the Caribbean. *Reforma agraria y empresas asociativas* (LC/L.497). Santiago, 1988. (Available in English).

B1.14 Conference as Issuing Agency

U.N. Outer Space Affairs Division. *Seminars of the United Nations Programme on Space Applications, 1992* (A/AC.105/492). Edited by Janet R. Darling. n.p., 1992.

TITLE VARIATIONS

B2.1 Title Includes Date/Edition

U.S. Dept. of Justice, Bureau of Justice Statistics. *Correctional Population in the United States, 1989*. Washington: Government Printing Office, 1991. (J29.17:989).

Indiana. General Assembly, 112th Assembly. House, Regulatory Flexibility Committee. *Meeting Minutes, Aug. 23, 2001*. Available at: http://www.in.gov/legislative/interim/-committee/minutes/RFSC48N.pdf; Accessed: 2/23/02.

Minnesota. Dept. of Economic Development, Research Division. *Minnesota Statistical Profile 1992*. St. Paul, 1992.

European Union. Directorate-General Energy and Transport. *EU Energy and Transport in Figures, 2001*. Last updated Dec. 21, 2001. Available at: http://europa.eu.int/comm/-energy_transport/etif/index.html; Accessed: 2/13/02.

B2.2 No Title Given

Montana. Dept. of Community Affairs, Division of Research and Information Systems. [Profiles: Pondera County] (Computer Printout). 3rd ed. Helena, 1978.

B2.3 Excessively Long Title

U.S. Senate, 100th Congress, 2nd Session. *S.Res. 547, Resolution . . . for a Moratorium on the Commercial Killing of Whales.* Washington: Government Printing Office, 1982. (GPO microfiche no. 24, coordinate A1).

B2.4 Non-Traditional Titles

U.S. Executive Office of the President. *www.whitehousekids.gov/;* Accessed: 12/15/01.

Ben's ABC (K-2). Last updated Feb. 15, 2000. Available at: *Ben's Guide to U.S. Government for Kids,* Superintendent of Documents, U.S. Government Printing Office, http://bensguide.gpo.gov/k-2/alphabet/index.html; Accessed: 2/27/02.

AIDS Economics [Home Page]. Available: http://www.worldbank.org/aids-econ/; Accessed: 12/05/01.

B2.5 Title with a Popular Name

Sharm el-Sheikh Fact-Finding Committee. *Final Report.* [Washington: Meridian International Center], Apr. 30, 2001. (Known as: The Mitchell Report). Available from: U.S. Dept. of State, International Programs, http://usinfo.state.gov/regional/nea/-mitchell.htm; Available: 2/11/02.

Bradford Area (West Yorkshire, United Kingdom). Race Review Panel. *Community Pride, Not Prejudice: Making Diversity Work in Bradford.* [July 2001]. (Known as: The Ouseley Report). Available at: http://www.bradford2020.com/pride/report.pdf; Accessed: 12/11/01.

B2.6 Book Chapter

Steiner, Richard. "Washington Present: Our Nation's Capitol Today," pp. 54-135. In U.S. Capitol Historical Society. *Washington Past and Present.* Washington: U.S. Capitol Historical Society, 1983.

"Panama: Sanitary Conditions on the Isthmus of Panama (no. 91)" pp. 706–708. In *Foreign Relations of the United States, 1904.* Washington: Government Printing Office, 1904. Electronic facsimile. Available at: University of Wisconsin, Madison, Libraries, http://www.wisc.edu/wendt/frus/; Accessed: 2/9/02.

"The Ferguson Township Comprehensive Plan," pp. 201-219. In Centre Regional Planning Commission (PA). *The Planning Document.* State College, 1991.

"Arctic: Barometer of Global Change," pp. 15/1-15/28. In Canada. Environment Canada. *The State of Canada's Environment.* Ottawa: Minister of Supply and Services Canada, 1991. (DSS. Cat. No. EN21-54/1991/E).

Carrion, Alejandro. "Ecuador," pp. 15-24. In Organization of Petroleum Exporting Countries, Public Information Dept. *Not Oil Alone: A Cultural History of OPEC Member Countries.* Vienna, 1981.

B2.7 Encyclopedia/Yearbook Chapter

"Brazil." Text from: *CIA World Fact Book 2001.* Available at: http://www.cia.gov/cia/publications/factbook/index.html; Accessed: 1/12/02.

"Travel Agents." Text from: *Occupational Outlook Handbook.* 2001/02 ed. Available at: http://www.bls.gov/oco/ocos124.htm; Accessed: 11/21/02.

"Children, Youth, and Aging Persons," pp. 809-832. In *Yearbook of the United Nations, 1986.* Boston: Martinus Nijhoff, 1990.

B2.8 Paper in a Conference Proceeding

> Roberts, Steven V. "The Congress, the Press and the Public," pp. 183-198. In U.S. House. *Understanding Congress: Research Perspectives, The Papers and Commentary from "Understanding Congress: A Bicentennial Research Conference,"* 9-10 Feb. 1989 (H. Doc. 101-241). Washington: Government Printing Office, 1991. (Y1.1/7:101-241).

DISTINGUISHING INFORMATION VARIATIONS

B3.1 Publication/Report Numbers

> U.S. Census Bureau. *Inorganic Chemicals (MA325): Summary, 2000.* Issued July 2001. (Current Industrial Reports). Available at: ftp://ftp.census.gov/pub/industry/1/-mq28a005.pdf; Accessed: 12/5/01.

> U.S. Census Bureau. *State & County QuickFacts* (ACSD/01-2060) (CD-ROM). The Bureau, Aug. 2001. (A supplement to the *Statistical Abstract of the United States).*

> United Kingdom. Home Office. *The 2000 British Crime Survey: England and Wales* (18/00). By Chris Kershaw et al. Oct. 17, 2000. (Home Office Statistical Bulletin). Available at: http://www.homeoffice.gov.uk/; Accessed: 2/10/02.

> Council of Europe. Parliamentary Assembly. *Political Prisoners in Azerbaijan.* (2002 Resolution 1272). Provisional ed. Available at: http://stars.coe.fr/index_e.htm; Accessed: 2/14/02.

> European Communities. Commission. *The Old World and the New Technologies: Challenges to Europe in a Hostile World.* By Michael Godet and Olivier Ruyssen (CB-30-80-116-EN-C). Rev. ed. Luxembourg: Office for Official Publications, 1981. (European Perspectives Series).

B3.2 Edition

> U.S. Dept. of State. *Background Notes: China.* Jan. 2002. Available at: http://www.state.gov/r/pa/bgn/2742.htm; Accessed: 2/5/02.

> U.S. Dept. of the Army. *Afghanistan: A Country Study.* Edited by Peter R. Blood. Research completed 1997. (U.S. Library of Congress. Federal Research Division. Country Studies Series). Available at: http://lcweb2.loc.gov/frd/cs/aftoc.html; Accessed: 12/10/01.

> Delaware. Dept. of Natural Resources and Environmental Control. *A Pollution Prevention Guide for General Business Practices: Three "R's" for the 90s—Reduce, Reuse, Recycle.* Last updated 12/17/1996. Available at: http://www.dnrec.state.de.us/del-busi.htm; Accessed: 12/10/01.

> *Everyone's United Nations.* 10th ed. New York: United Nations Dept. of Public Information, 1986.

> U.N. Conference on Trade and Development. *World Investment Report 2001: Promoting Linkages* (UNCTAD/WIR/2001; 222 kb). Internet ed. Available at: http://www.unctad.org/en/docs/wir01ove_a4.en.pdf; Accessed: 12/12/01.

B3.3 Medium or Publication Type

See additional examples in Sections 3.3 and E3.3

> U.S. Dept. of Education, National Center for Education Statistics. *NPSAS: National Postsecondary Student Aid Study, 1986-87* (CD-ROM). Washington: Government Printing Office, n.d. (ED1.333:986-87).

> United Nations. Statistical Office. *United Nations Women's Indicators and Statistics Microcomputer Database: Wistat* (Floppy Disk). (Serial no. 001-2.0-01093). Version 2. New York, 1991. (UN/St/ESA/WISTAT/ver.2).

PUBLISHING INFORMATION VARIATIONS

B4.1 Publishing Information/Source of Information

U.S. Executive Office of the President. *A Blueprint for New Beginnings: A Responsible Budget for America's Priorities*. Washington: Government Printing Office, 2001. (Budget of the U.S. Government, Fiscal Year 2002). Available at: http://w3.access.gpo.gov/usbudget/fy2002/pdf/blueprnt.pdf; Accessed: 12/10/01.

Iowa. Highway Division. *Report on Traffic Control Plan Reviews*. Ames, 1990.

Canadian Advisory Council on the Status of Women. *Women and Labour Market Poverty*. Ottawa: The Council, 1990.

Colombia. Office of the President. *Struggle Against Violence and Impunity: A Democratic Commitment*. Bogota: Imprenta Nacional de Colombia, 1988.

U.N. General Assembly, 56th Sess. *Resolution 56/93: International Convention Against Reproductive Cloning of Human Beings* (A/Res/56/93). Jan. 28, 2002. Available at: UN Documentation Centre, http://www.un.org/documents/ga/res/a56r093.pdf; Accessed: 2/12/02.

Weeks, Julie R., and Danielle Seiler. *Women's Entrepreneurship in Latin America: An Exploration of Current Knowledge*. Washington: Inter-American Development Bank, Sept. 2001. (Sustainable Development Dept. Technical Paper Series, MSM-111).

B4.2 No Publisher, Issuing Agency Assumed

U.S. Bureau of Labor Statistics. *Handbook of Methods*. 1997 ed. Available at: http://www.bls.gov/opub/hom/homtoc.htm; Accessed: 12/11/01.

U.S. Geological Survey. *Digitized Strong-Motion Accelerograms of North and Central American Earthquakes 1933-1998* (CD-ROM). By Linda C. Seekins et al. n.p., 1992. (Digital Data Series, DDS-7). (I19.121:7).

Richmond (VA). Mayor's Office. *Budget for 1992*. 1991.

St. Paul (MN). *Community Development Block Grant Funds: Program Years 1975-78*. Minneapolis, 1979.

B4.3 No Date of Publication

U.S. Bureau of the Census. *Extract* (Software). Release 1.3. n.p., n.d. (C3.277:Ec7/987/floppy 4).

U.S. Energy Information Administration. *State Energy Data System 1960-1989: Census Region 2* (Floppy Disk). (DOE/EIA—0214(89)). n.p., [by 1991]. (E3.42/5:991).

B4.4 Publisher, Issuing Agency and Personal Author

Canada. Federal Provincial Relations Office. *The European Community: A Political Model for Canada?* By Peter M. Leslie. Ottawa: Minister of Supply and Services Canada, 1991. (DSS. Cat. No. CP22-35/1991E).

B4.5 Electronic Source Address (URL) as Source of Information

U.S. Congress, Bipartisan Working Group on Youth Violence. *Final Report*. Nov. 17, 1999. Available at: http://www.house.gov/frost/youthviol.htm; Accessed: 7/25/01.

B4.6 Electronic Version of a Print Publication (Publisher and URL)

U.S. Census Bureau. *County Business Patterns: Oregon, 1995*. Available at: http://www.census.gov/prod/3/97pubs/cbp-9539.pdf; Accessed: 2/5/02.

U.N. Conference on Trade and Development. *World Investment Report, 2001: Promoting Linkages.* New York, 2001. Available at: http://www.unctad.org; Accessed: 2/5/02.

SERIES AND OTHER NOTE VARIATIONS

B5.1 Publication in a Series

U.S. Dept. of the Navy, Naval Historical Center. *On Course to Desert Storm: The United States Navy and the Persian Gulf.* By Michael A. Palmer. Washington: Government Printing Office, 1992. (Contributions to Naval History No. 5). (D207.10/4:5).

Alaska. Dept. of Fish and Game. *Harvest and Use of Fish and Wildlife by Residents of Kake, Alaska.* By Anne S. Firman and Robert G. Bosworth. Juneau, 1990. (Technical Paper 145).

Canada. Environment Canada, Parks Service, National Historic Sites. *A Tenant's Town: Buebec in the 18th Century.* By Yvon Desloges. Ottawa: Supply and Services Canada, 1991. (Studies in Archaeology, Architecture, and History).

The Values of Europeans: Results of "Continuous Tracking" Surveys of European Opinion (Sept. and Oct. 1997), Nov. 1997.(Europinion, #13). Available at: European Commission, *Eurobarometer,* http://europa.eu.int/comm/dg10/epo/eo/eo13/13-txt_en.html; Accessed: 2/21/01.

European Union. Eurostat. *Statistical Yearbook on Candidate and South-East European Countries.* Luxembourg: Office of Official Publications of the European Communities, 2001. (Theme 1: General Statistics; Collection: Panorama of the European Union).

U.N. Dept. of International Social Affairs. *Population Growth and Policies in Mega-Cities: Cairo* (ST/ESA/SER.R/103). New York, 1990. (Population Paper No. 34).

B5.2 Required Notes

U.S. Bureau of the Census. *Tiger/Line Census Files, 1990: Florida (Pinellas-Washington), Idaho* (CD-ROM). Washington, July 1991. (C3.279:F66/2/990/CD).

FEC Reports on Congressional Fundraising for 1997-98: Overall Contributions from Individuals by Size of Contribution, 1997-98, Apr. 28, 1999. (News from the Federal Elections Commission). (1999 ASI Microfiche 9276-1.187).

U.N. Dept. of Public Information. *Basic Facts About the United Nations* (DPI/915). New York, 1987. (UN Sales No. E. 88.1.3).

Quick Citation Guide to Legislative/ Parliamentary Sources

Legislative/Parliamentary Sources

Quick Citation Guide to Legislative/Parliamentary Sources

BASIC ELEMENTS

GOVERNMENTS: LEGISLATIVE BODIES (U.S. AND THE STATES)
L1.1 *Congressional Record* and Other Legislative Debate Sources
L1.2 Committee Hearings
L1.3 Testimony Before a Committee
L1.4 Committee Publications: Reports, Prints, Documents
L1.5 Legislation: Bills, Acts, and Resolutions
L1.6 *U.S. Statutes at Large* and other Session Laws
L1.7 *United States Code* and Other Codified Laws

GOVERNMENTS: PARLIAMENTARY BODIES (CANADA AND THE UNITED KINGDOM)
L2.1 *Hansard* and Other Parliamentary Debate Sources
L2.2 Committee Proceedings
L2.3 Testimony Presented Before a Committee
L2.4 Committee Publications (Parliamentary Papers)
L2.5 Command Papers (White Papers)
L2.6 Legislation: Bills, Acts, and Resolutions
L2.7 Statutes

ORGANIZATIONS: UNITED NATIONS DOCUMENTATION
L3.1 Masthead Documents
L3.2 Official Records
L3.3 U.N. Resolutions

ORGANIZATIONS: THE EUROPEAN UNION DOCUMENTATION

L4.1 *Official Journal of the European Communities*
L4.2 European Parliament Debate
L4.3 Parliamentary Questions
L4.4 COM (Communication) Documents
L4.5 Working Documents/Papers

BASIC ELEMENTS

The publications of the legislative bodies of governments and organizations are as varied as the governments and organizations that produce them. This *Quick Guide* provides examples of the most common variations you will encounter. The examples serve as models that can be modified as needed to document specific publications and the publishing patterns of different governments or organizations.

The citation formats below conform to the rules found in Parts 2 and 3. However, particular guidance in formulating the Issuing Agency statement for legislative/parliamentary bodies is included in Section 1.3: Legislative/Parliamentary Bodies as Authors.

Use the **Recommended Form and Punctuation** for Legislative/Parliamentary materials described in Table 3 (for books and monographs) and Table 10 (for periodical and statistical sources). Many, but not all, legislative/parliamentary citations should include the number of the legislative/parliamentary session.

Table 4: Legislative/Parliamentary Numbering—When Should It Be Included?

Citations to legislative/parliamentary materials can be confusing as to when session numbering and dates are needed and when they are not (Section 1.3e). The main issue is whether the source being cited includes enough detail to distinguish it from other similar sources. Typically, the most reliable way to identify a legislative/parliamentary publication is with the numbered session or date, but that information is not always needed and may lengthen your citation unnecessarily.

Omit Legislative/Parliamentary Numbering:

Rule	Example	Example Citations:
When the source being cited includes consistent volume numbering	➤ *Serial Set* and *Journals of the Continental Congress* ➤ *Legislative Journals* ➤ *Official Gazettes* ➤ *Congressional Record* ➤ *Hansard* ➤ *Official Journal of the European Communities*	S17 and S27 S19 S21 L1.1 L2.1 L4.1
When the source being cited includes sufficient information to identify a specific title without the legislative/parliamentary numbering	➤ Committee Reports (numbered and unnumbered) ➤ Command Papers ➤ White Papers ➤ COM Documents ➤ U.S. Public Laws, *Statutes at Large* (Fig. 1) and other Session Laws	L1.4 L2.5 L2.5 L4.4 L1.6

Include Legislative/Parliamentary Numbering:		
When the source being cited contains materials related to a specific committee, conference, meeting/session and sufficient distinguishing information is not included in the citation	➢ Committee Proceedings ➢ U.N. Official Records (Fig. 2). ➢ U.S. Committee Hearings (Fig. 6) ➢ *Congressional Globe, Register of Debates,* and *Annals of Congress.*	L2.2 L3.2 L1.2 and L1.3 S9
When the source cited includes a number which may be used again in a different Congress	➢ Bill numbers (the U.S. Congress reuses numbers beginning every Congress) (Fig. 7)	L1.5

GOVERNMENTS: LEGISLATIVE BODIES (U.S. AND THE STATES)

L1.1 *Congressional Record* and Other Legislative Debate Sources

The U.S. Congress and many other legislatures provide a nearly verbatim text of debate[1] with each speaker identified and the section containing the debate titled. The *Congressional Record* contains the debate of both the U.S. House and the Senate. The rules for citing the *Congressional Record* can serve as a model for similar publications from state, local, and other national governments.

Historically, the *Congressional Record* has been issued in two editions—the daily edition (issued each day Congress is in session) and the permanent edition (bound volumes that correspond to a specific Congress). Since the 103rd Congress, the daily edition is widely available in electronic format.

Table 5: *Congressional Record* Editions: What's the Difference?

The difference between the Permanent Edition and the Daily Edition of the *Congressional Record* is in the page numbering, not the content. Each Daily Edition issue includes debate from the Senate and the House. The debate is kept separate by having House page numbers begin with an H; the Senate pages begin with an S. There is also a section of pages that begin with E (Extensions of Remarks) and D (the Digest or table of contents for each issue). In the Permanent Edition, specific volumes are devoted to the House and Senate separately so the letter designation for pages is not needed.

One other trick: the date of the daily issue is particularly important for the Daily Edition because page numbering begins with H1 and S1 with every Congress.

Electronic versions of the *Congressional Record* are the equivalent of the Daily Edition. However, different vendors present the page in different formats.[2]

> **Include This Information:**
>
> - Speaker's last name, and home state abbreviated; honorary titles can be omitted (Section 1.4a)—if citing a general debate, begin with the title of the topic/section.
> - *Title of the debate topic/section.
> - Unique identifying numbers (applies to some electronic sources, primarily) (Section 3.0).
> - *Congressional Record, edition, volume, issue no.
> - *Date of the debate/issue (Section 4.3 and 6.4a).
> - Pages (if known) (Section 6.4b and E6.4b).
> - *The source information (VEF sources) (Section E4.0).
>
> **Related Sections:**
>
> ➢ Citing Parts: Periodical Articles and Statistical Sources (Sections 6.0 and E6.0).
>
> ***Required**

"Religion and Schools," *Congressional Record* 20, Pt. 1 (Dec. 21, 1888) pp. 433-434.

Rep. Anderson (CA). "Legislation for the Care of Vietnamese Refugees," *Congressional Record* 121:10 (Apr. 25, 1975) pp. 12-52.

Sens. Hawkins (FL), Grassley (IA) and Packwood (OR). "Radio Marti," *Congressional Record* (Sept. 12, 1983). Daily ed. pp. S11970-11981.

Rep. Lee (CA). "Authorizing Use of Armed Forces Against Those Responsible for Recent Attacks Against the United States" (DOCID:cr14se01-82), *Congressional Record* (Sept. 14, 2001) pp. H5642. Available at: GPO Access, http://www.access.gpo.gov/-su_docs/aces/aces150.html; Accessed: 11/7/01.

Rep. Lee (CA). "Authorizing Use of Armed Forces Against Those Responsible for Recent Attacks Against the United States," *Congressional Record* 147:120 (Sept. 14, 2001) p. H5642. Available at: Congressional Universe, LexisNexis; Accessed: 11/7/01.

"Consideration of the Energy Bill," *Congressional Record* (Feb. 5, 2002) p. S314. Available at: *Thomas* (Library of Congress), http://thomas.loc.gov/; Accessed: 2/10/02.

L1.2 Committee Hearings

Hearings are particularly likely to be accessible in a variety of sources because many hearings are open to the public and to stenographic firms. Once transcribed, they can be distributed by these printers and stenographic firms via print and electronic avenues frequently more quickly than the official printed version or the official government electronic source (Fig. 6).

➢ **Official hearings** may include a transcription of verbal testimony, the question and answer (Q&A) period for each witness, and submitted written testimony. All of these are cited frequently.

➢ **Unofficial hearing** sources include the transcribed testimony and selected submitted written testimony. A wide range of databases provide the transcribed text of testimony available from Federal News Service and Federal Document Clearinghouse. Government WWW sites often provide the testimony key government administrators present to Congressional committees. Increasingly webcasts are being used to make hearings more "visible."

It is important to always include the exact name of the witness as well as the date the testimony was presented, so that researchers can locate the same text in alternative sources which may be more accessible to them.

Include This Information:

* *Legislative/Parliamentary Body (Section 1.3).

* *Title—The titles of a U.S. hearing will usually be found at the head (top) of the title page.

* Date of hearing/testimony (if applicable and not part of title) following the word "Hearing" (Section 2.1g).

* Unique identifying numbers (if present) (Section 3.0).

* *Publishing information (if print or PEF source) (Section 4.0).

* *The source information (VEF source) (Section E4.0).

Related Sections:

➢ Citing Parts: Periodical Articles and Statistical Sources (Sections 6.0 and E6.0).
➢ *Quick Citation Guide to Special Cases and Well-Known Sources*, Legislative Journals, S19.

*Required

U.S. House, Committee on Energy and Commerce. *Disapproving the FTC Funeral Rule*, Hearing, May 4, 1983 (Serial No. 98-18). Washington: Government Printing Office, 1983. (Y4.En2/3:98-18).

U.S. Senate, Committee on Banking, Housing, and Urban Affairs. *Gold and Silver Coinage Proposals*, Apr. 15, 1983 (S. Hrg. 98-113). Washington: Government Printing Office, 1983. (Y4.B22/3: S.Hrg.98-113).

U.S. House, Select Committee on Children, Youth, and Families. *Babies and Briefcases: Creating a Family-Friendly Workplace for Fathers*, Hearing, June 11, 1991. Washington: Government Printing Office, 1991. (Y4.C43/2:B11/2).

U.S. House, Committee on Commerce. Subcommittee on Energy and Power. *Electric Utility Industry Restructuring: The California Market*, Hearing, Sept. 11, 2000. Washington: Government Printing Office, 2001. (2000 CIS Microfiche H271-22).

U.S. House, Committee on Government Reform. *Protecting American Interests Abroad: U.S. Citizens, Business, and Nongovernmental Organizations*, Hearing, Apr. 3, 2001. (DOCID: f:75955.wais). Washington: Government Printing Office, 2001. Text from: *107th Congress House Hearings*. Available from: GPO Access, http://www.access.gpo.gov/congress/cong017.html; Accessed: 2/11/02.

U.S. House, Committee on Ways and Means. Subcommittee on Human Resources. *H.R. 7: The Community Solutions Act*, Hearing, June 14, 2001 (Serial 107-34). Available at: http://waysandmeans.house.gov/humres/107cong/6-14-01/107-34final.htm; Accessed: 11/15/02.

U.S. Senate, Judiciary Committee, Subcommittee on Technology, Terrorism, and Government Information. *Germs, Toxins, and Terror: The New Threat to America*, Hearing, Nov. 6, 2001. [Transcript of Healthcast/Webcast]. Available at: http://www.kaisernetwork.org/-health_cast/transcript_110601.pdf; Accessed: 2/12/02.

U.S. Senate, Judiciary Committee, Subcommittee on Technology, Terrorism, and Government Information. *Germs, Toxins, and Terror: The New Threat to America*, Hearing, Nov. 6, 2001. [Healthcast/Webcast]. Available at: http://www.kaisernetwork.org/health_cast/hcast_index.cfm; Accessed: 2/12/02.

L1.3 Testimony Before a Committee

"Testimony from McLeodUSA," p. 2. In Indiana. General Assembly, 112th Assembly. House, Regulatory Flexibility Committee. *Meeting Minutes, Aug, 23, 2001*. Available at: http://www.IN.gov/legislative/interim/committee/minutes/RFSC48N.pdf; Accessed: 11/15/01.

Collins, Jeremiah. Statement to the House, Committee on Education and the Workforce. *Open Shops in the 21st Century Workplace,* Hearing, May 3, 2000 (Serial 106-105). Available: http://commdocs.house.gov/committees/edu/hedo&i6-105.000/hedo&i6-105.htm; Accessed: 11/15/01.

MacCarthy, Mark. "Online Fraud and Crime: Are Consumers Safe?" prepared testimony, May 23, 2001, before the U.S. House, Energy and Commerce Committee, Subcommittee on Commerce, Trade, and Consumer Protection (Federal News Service). Text from: *Testimony*. Available on: Congressional Universe, LexisNexis; Accessed: 11/12/01.

Siller, Bobby L. "Banning Amateur Sports Gambling," testimony, June 13, 2000, before the U.S. House, Committee on the Judiciary (Federal Document Clearinghouse Congressional Testimony). Text from: *Testimony*. Available on: Congressional Universe, LexisNexis; Accessed: 11/12/01.

"Statement: Advanced Medical Technology Association," pp. 54-57. In U.S. House. *President Bush's Trade Agenda,* Hearing, Mar. 7, 2001 (Serial 107-2). Washington: Government Printing Office, 2001. Text from: *Congressional Hearings*. Available at: GPO Access, http://www.access.gpo.gov/-congress/cong017.html; Accessed: 1/15/02.

L1.4 Committee Publications: Reports, Prints, Documents

Committees produce a wide range of publications. The following provide some common examples and variations to be used as models. For information about, and examples of, joint committee and conference committee publications, consult Section 1.3b.

Table 6: Types of Committees

Most Legislative/Parliamentary bodies divide their chambers into committees and subcommittees where much of the work is accomplished and from which many publications are generated (Section 1.3).

The following types of committees exist in the U.S. Congress:

Committees—bills are assigned to a committee. Hearings are held usually in a subcommittee. A report with information on the bill's merits (and with minority views from committee members) is submitted for legislation which the committee, typically, is recommending for passage.

Conference Committees—temporary committees formed from members of the House and Senate to negotiate the differences in the bill when two different (yet similar) versions have passed the House and Senate. The conference committee agrees to wording, then submits the bill back to both the House and Senate for a vote.

Joint Committees—permanent committees composed of members of both the House and Senate (for example, the Joint Committee on Printing).

Consult Section 1.3b for rules on how to develop citations for conference committees and joint committees.

Include This Information:

- *Legislative/Parliamentary Body (Section 1.3).

- *Title (Section 2.0).

- Unique identifying numbers (if present) (Section 3.0).

- *Publishing information (if print or PEF source) (Section 4.0).

- *The source information (VEF sources) (Section E4.0).

Related Sections:

➢ Omitting Levels in the Legislative/Parliamentary Organization Hierarchy (The Rule of Three) (Section 1.3b).

➢ *Quick Citation Guide to Special Cases and Well-Known Sources*, Serial Set, S27.

*Required

North Carolina. Legislative Research Commission. *Capital Punishment: Mentally Retarded and Race Bias: Report to the 2001 General Assembly.* Available from: http://www.ncga.state.nc.us/LegislativePublications/legislativestud_/legislativerese_/capitalpunish me/default.htm; Accessed: 2/11/02.

Oklahoma. Legislature, House of Representatives, Research Division. *Legislator's Guide to Oklahoma Taxes.* Edited by Alicia Ramming Emerson. Revised ed. Oklahoma City, 1990.

U.S. House, Committee on the Judiciary. *Shipping Act of 1983* (H. Rpt.98-53, Pt. 2). Washington: Government Printing Office, 1983. (Y1.1/8:98-53/Pt.2).

U.S. House. *Columbus in the Capitol: Commemorative Quincentury Edition* (H. Doc. 102-319). Washington: Government Printing Office, 1992. (Y1.1/7:102-319).

U.S. House, Committee on the Judiciary. *Jacob Wetterling Crimes Against Children and Sexually Violent Offenders Registration Improvements Act of 1997* (H. Rpt. 105-256). Text from: *Committee Reports.* Available from: *Thomas* (Library of Congress), http://thomas.loc.gov; Accessed: 2/11/02.

U.S. Senate. *History of the Committee on Finance* (S. Doc. 95-27). Washington: Government Printing Office, 1977. (1977 CIS microfiche S360-1).

U.S. Senate, Committee on Foreign Relations. *Treaties and Other International Agreements: The Role of the United States Senate, A Study* (S. Prt. 106-71). Prepared by the Congressional Research Service, Library of Congress. Text from: *Congressional Committee Prints.* Available from: GPO Access, http://www.access.gpo.gov/-congress/cpsrch.html; Accessed: 4/30/01.

U.S. Senate, Committee on Governmental Affairs. *Phony Identification and Credentials via the Internet* (S. Rpt.133), Feb. 4, 2002. Text from: *Publications (Reports).* Available from: Congressional Universe, LexisNexis; Accessed: 2/11/02.

L1.5 Legislation: Bills, Acts, and Resolutions

Most proposed legislation (bills, acts or resolutions) goes through different versions as the bill (or act) moves through the complete legislative process. In order to keep track of the legislation, each piece of legislation is assigned a number when it is first introduced. Because most legislatures have more than one chamber, an abbreviation is used to indicated whether the bill originated in the House or Senate (in the U.S. Congress, bills originating in the House are given the abbreviation H.R.; Senate bills are given S., for example). In addition, there are many different types of legislation—bills, resolutions, etc. For this reason, citing legislation requires the attention to bill numbering (Fig. 7).

In most legislatures bill numbers are reused each legislative session. Therefore, identifying the exact legislation requires that you provide the numbered session as part of the Issuing Agency Consult Section 1.3e and Table 4.

Include This Information:

* *Legislative Body, including legislative session/number (Section 1.3).

* *Bill number –most descriptive feature—each legislature has a numbering system: use the information as it appears on the document. (Section 2.1f).

* *Title (may use the popular name title if appropriate), may be abbreviated (Section 2.0 and 2.1j).

* *Version (a printers number, for example, if known)—if the source provides a date, a version may not be required (Section 3.2c).

* *Publishing information (if print or PEF source) (Section 4.0).

* *The source information (VEF sources) (Section E4.0).

*Required

California. Legislature, 1991/92 Regular Sess. Assembly. *AB 2541 Earthquake Safe Building Construction.* Sacramento, 1992.

Michigan. Legislature, 2001-01 Sess. House. *House Bill No. 4002, Use Tax Act.* As passed by the Senate. Available at: http://198.109.172.10/pdf/house.bills.intro/2001-2002/4002hhhh.pdf; Accessed: 11/15/01.

U.S. House, 96th Congress, 1st Sess. *H.R. 2, A Bill To Require Authorization for Budget Authority. . ..* Washington: Government Printing Office, 1979.

U.S. House, 101st Congress, 1st Sess. *H.R. 1216, An Act to Provide Federal Assistance and Leadership to. . .Renewable Energy and Energy Efficiency Technologies. . ..* Version 3, Sept. 23, 1989. Text from: *Bills.* Available on: Congressional Universe, LexisNexis; Accessed: 11/15/01.

U.S. House, 101st Congress, 1st Sess. *H.R. 1946, An Act to Reinstate and Validate . . . Oil and Gas Lease. . . OCS-P-0218 and OCS-P-226.* Washington: Government Printing Office, 1990. (GPO microfiche no. 393, coordinate C13).

U.S. House, 102nd Congress, 2nd Sess. *H.R. 5983, Government Printing Office Electronic Information Access Enhancement Act of 1992.* As passed by the House. Text from: *Bill Text.* Available on: *Thomas* (Library of Congress), http://thomas.loc.gov; Accessed: 11/15/01.

U.S. House, 107th Congress, 1st Sess. *H.R. 3162, Uniting and Strengthening America Act...to Obstruct Terrorism* (DOCID: f:h3162enr.txt). Enrolled bill. Text from: Congressional Bills. Available on: GPO Access, http://www.access.gpo.gov/-su_docs/legislative.html; Accessed:11/15/01.

U.S. House, 107th Congress, 1st Sess. *H.R. 3310, A Bill to Improve the Ability of the United States to Prepare for and Respond to a Biological Threat or Attack.* As introduced in the House. Text from: Bills. Available from: Congressional Universe, LexisNexis; Accessed: 2/28/02.

U.S. Senate, 94th Congress, 1st Sess. "S.Res.55, To Establish Legislative Review Subcommittees," *Congressional Record* 121:2 (Feb. 3, 1975) p. 2078.

L1.6 *U.S. Statutes at Large* and Other Session Laws

Once a bill has become law, most states assign it a law number. The laws passed in a legislative session are collected into a set generally referred to as "session laws." Laws are frequently cited as part of these session laws.

Table 7: How Laws Are Numbered

Governments use various systems for numbering their enacted laws, and these systems often differ from their bill numbering systems. Recognizing these numbering systems will help you determine what information to include in your citation. A U.S. Congress example:

P.L. 103-40—Government Printing Office Electronic Information Access Enhancement Act of 1993

Laws passed by the U.S. Congress are consecutively numbered (this was the 40th act to become law) and preceded by the number of the Congress (the 103rd). Most laws have a popular name title as well as a rarely cited more formal title. (The formal title for the bill above is: "To Establish in the Government Printing Office a Means of Enhancing Electronic Public Access to a Wide Range of Federal Electronic Information") (Section 2.1j) (Fig. 1).

There is no common title pattern for the compilations of session laws. For example, *U.S. Statutes at Large* and the *Laws of Pennsylvania* are both session law compilations. The numbering systems will also vary from state to state; the following examples can serve as models.

Include This Information:

* *Title abbreviated (if necessary) or popular title (Section 2.0 and 2.1j).
* Date of passage.
* *Title of the session laws (e.g. *U.S. Statutes at Large*).
* Volume, chapter, year, pages (as appropriate).
* *Source information (VEF sources) (Section E4.0).

Related Sections:

➢ Citing Parts: Periodical Articles and Statistical Sources (Sections 6.0 and E6.0).

*Required

"An Act Relating to Charitable Organizations…." (Chapter 45; Apr. 24, 2001). Text from: *Minnesota Session Laws 2001.* Available at: http://www.revisor.leg.state.mn.us/slaws/2001/c045.html; Accessed 11/15/01.

"An Act Amending the Public School System" (Act 38, May 4, 1990), *90 Laws of Pennsylvania*, p. 164.

"Americans with Disabilities Act of 1990" (P.L. 101-336, July 26, 1990). Text from: *Laws (Statutes at Large).* Available from: Congressional Universe, LexisNexis; Accessed: 2/11/02.

"Intermodel Surface Transportation Efficiency Act of 1991" (PL 102-240, Dec. 18, 1991), *United States Statutes at Large*, 105 (1991) pp. 1914-2207.

"Higher Education Amendments of 1992" (PL 102-325, July 23, 1992). Text from: *Public Laws by Law Number.* Available from: *Thomas* (Library of Congress), http://thomas.loc.gov; Accessed: 2/11/02.

"Uniting and Strengthening America by Providing Appropriate Tools Required to Intercept and Obstruct Terrorism (USA Patriot Act) Act of 2001" (P.L. 107-56, Oct. 26, 2001). Text from: *Public and Private Laws*. Available from: GPO Access, http://www.access.gpo.gov/nara/nara005.html; Accessed: 2/11/02.

L1.7 *United States Code* and Other Codified Laws

Every government creates a codified (subject arrangement) of its laws. Because laws are passed and amended frequently, you should provide an edition statement or the date accessed. When citing a print version, provide the date of last update—this will tell your reader how up-to-date the text you cited was. (For example, a *U.S. Code* edition printed at the end of 1999, will not include laws passed in 2000). When in doubt about citing a code section, consult *The Bluebook: A Uniform System of Citation* (Consult App*endix A: Style Manuals* for complete bibliographic information).

Table 8: The U.S. Code Annotated (USCA), the U.S. Code Service (USCS) and the U.S. Code (USC)—What's in a Name?

The *U.S. Code* (officially published by the Government Printing Office and made accessible via GPO Access), is also published and made available by a surprising number of print and electronic sources—for example, the *U.S. Code Service* (USCS) is published by Lawyer's Co-Operative Publishing Co. and is available electronically from LexisNexis' Congressional Universe and Academic Universe (and other sources) while the *U.S. Code Annotated* (USCA) is published by West Publishing Company and is made available electronically on WestLaw.

The main difference between these versions (in print and electronically) is in the "bells and whistles" the private publishers add to the official text (e.g., citations to related case law, periodical articles, regulations, encyclopedia articles and other research aids) and more frequent updating by inclusion of the most recently passed laws. The *U.S. Code,* on the other hand, is only updated once each year, in a separate Supplement volume, and is reprinted in its entirety every six years. The USCA and USCS are updated much more frequently (daily on some systems, and monthly on others).

You should cite the particular version of the code you have, if you know it. If not, use the generic *U.S. Code* but include any "last updated" information you can locate, or at least the date you accessed the database.

Include This Information:

* Section heading (for example, "Misbranded Foods")—can be located in the header for each entry.

* *The title number/name—corresponds to a broad subject area (for example, title 49 *U.S. Code* contains transportation laws, while California uses titles for its 29 codes or 29 subject areas within the code.

* *Title of the code (*U.S. Code*, for example).

* *Section number (within title number)—"Parts" and "Chapters" should be omitted.

* Edition/date last update (if known).

* *Publishing information (if print or PEF source) (Section 4.0).

* *The source information (VEF sources) (Section E4.0).

Related Sections:

➢ Quick Citation Guide to Legislative/Parliamentary Sources, *Code of Federal Regulations* (CFR) and the *Federal Register* (FR), S7.
➢ Statutes, L2.7.

*Required

"Vocational Rehabilitation Services," Title 29 *U.S. Code*, Pts. 720 et seq. 1976 ed. Supp. V, 1981.

"Screening Passengers and Property," Title 49 *U.S. Code*, Pt. 44901. 1994 ed. Supp. V, 1998. Available at: GPO Access, http://www.access.gpo.gov/su_docs/legislative.html; Accessed: 12/2/01.

"Misbranded Food," 21 *U.S. Code Service*, Pt. 343 (1996). Current through 12/21/01. Text from: *Laws (United States Code)*. Available from: Congressional Universe, LexisNexis; Accessed: 12/15/02.

"Title 42 *U.S. Code Service*, Pt. 13701. Text from: *U.S. Code Service*. Current through 10/4/01. Text from: *Legal Research (Federal Code)*. Available from: Academic Universe, LexisNexis; Accessed: 11/15/01.

States publish their laws in a manner similar to the *U.S. Code*. The titles and subject arrangements vary.

"Bulk Sales," *California Commercial Code*, Pts. 6101, et seq. Available at: http://www.leginfo.ca.gov/calaw.html; Accessed: 11/15/01.

When citing code sections, use the title as given in the source. This includes using any abbreviations for the title of the code set (e.g., Cal U Com). These abbreviations are readily identified in legal abbreviation source books. The "Text from:" element should provide adequate identification for your reader to return to this source and may, as in the examples below, also provide the complete title for the abbreviated form. Follow the Rule of Three for identifying the "Text from:" statement (Section 6.2a and E6.2a).

"Commercial Code: Bulk Sales," Cal U Com Code § 6101 (2001). Text from: *Deering's California Codes Annotated*. Current through 2002 Supp. Text from: *Statutes*. Available from: State Capital Universe, LexisNexis; Accessed: 11/15/01.

"Stalking in the Fourth Degree," NY CLS Penal § 120.45 (2001). Text from: *New York Consolidated Law Service*. Current through 11/28/01. Text from: *Legal Research (State Codes)*. Available from: Academic Universe, LexisNexis; Accessed: 2/10/02.

"Labeling," Title 3 *Pennsylvania Statutes*, Pt. 132-4 (2001). Text from: *Statutes*. Available from: State Capital Universe, LexisNexis; Accessed: 1/15/01.

GOVERNMENTS: PARLIAMENTARY BODIES (CANADA AND THE UNITED KINGDOM)

Governments with parliamentary bodies use a variety of sources to record the work of their committees and chambers. The following examples refer to Canada and the United Kingdom sources. These examples use some of the most frequently encountered titles and will provide models that can be adapted for different publishing patterns in other parliamentary systems.

L2.1 *Hansard* and Other Parliamentary Debate Sources

Many parliamentary bodies record their debates in a publication typically called *Hansard*.

Include This Information:

* Last name of the speaker and district represented, if available; honorary titles can be omitted (Section 1.4a)—if citing a general debate, begin with the title of the topic/section.
* *Title of the debate topic/section.
* *Parliamentary body (Section 6.5a).
* *Hansard* (use title as given), edition, series, volume, issue no. (Section 4.3 and 6.4a).
* Pages (if known) (Section 6.4a and E6.4a).
* *The source information (VEF sources) (Section E4.0).

Related Sections:

➤ Citing Parts: Periodical Articles and Statistical Sources (Sections 6.0 and E6.0).

*Required

"Question Period: National Defence, United States-Terrorist Attacks of September 11, 2001—Possible Retaliatory Measures—Contribution by Armed Forces," Canada. Parliament. *Debates of the Senate (Hansard),* 139: 51 (Sept. 20, 2001) p.1410. Available at: http://www.parl.gc.ca/; Accessed: 2/11/02.

King, Tom. "Army (Restructuring)," United Kingdom. Parliament. House of Commons. *Parliamentary Debates, Official Report (Hansard)* 6th Series, 195 (Feb. 22, 1991) pp.1031-1034.

Spelman, Caroline (Meridien). "Adoption Bill," United Kingdom. Parliament. *Hansard—House of Commons Debate,* 365: 63 (Mar. 30, 2001) col. 1203. Available at: http://www.parliament.the-stationery-office.co.uk/pa/cm/cmhn0301.htm; Accessed: 11/13/01.

Symons, Baroness. "International Terrorism," United Kingdom. Parliament. *Hansard—House of Lords Debate,* 627: 29 (Oct. 18, 2001) col. 751. Available at: http://www.parliament.thestationeryoffice.co.uk/pa/ld199900/ldhansrd/pdvn/lds01/index/11018-x.htm#contents; Accessed: 2/22/02.

L2.2 Committee Proceedings

Some legislative/parliamentary bodies (for example, the Canadian Parliament) publish their committee proceedings as a serial publication.

Table 9: Canada's Committee Proceedings: A Model

Each committee publishes its own proceedings in a separately titled series, which may change over time.

* Each separate issue corresponds to a committee meeting; occasionally more than one meeting may be included in an issue.

* Each issue may also deal with more than one topic or legislative matter.

* Each issue may contain minutes, reports, transcripts (evidence of proceedings), and orders of reference. The topic of discussion may be descriptive and may be omitted—any one of these may be cited individually or the entire issue may be cited as a whole.

Include This Information:

* *Legislative/Parliamentary body (Section 1.3), including session numbering.
* Title of the topic/legislative matter (if necessary).
* *Title of the proceedings; may be shortened if title includes committee name (Section 2.1c).
* *Issue number and date (Section 4.3 and 6.4a).
* Publishing information (if shown for print or PEF sources) (Section 4.0).
* *The source information (VEF sources) (Section E4.0).

Related Sections:

➢ Citing Parts: Periodical Articles and Statistical Sources (Sections 6.0 and E6.0).

*Required

Canada. Parliament, 34th Parl., 3rd Sess. 1991-92. Senate, Standing Committee on Foreign Affairs. *Proceedings of the Standing Committee . . .* Issue no. 10 (May 5, 1992).

Canada. Parliament, 34th Parl., 3rd Sess. 1991-92. Senate, Standing Committee on Foreign Affairs. "Sixth Proceedings on the Examination of Negotiations for a North American Free Trade Agreement...," *Proceedings of the Standing Committee. . .*, Issue no. 10 (May 5, 1992) pp. 234-40.

Canada. Parliament, 37th Parl., 1st Sess., 2001-02. House of Commons, Standing Committee on Industry, Science, and Technology. *Minutes of Proceedings*, Meeting No. 48 (Nov. 6, 2001). Available at: http://www.parl.gc.ca/; Accessed: 11/15/01.

L2.3 Testimony Presented Before a Committee

Plekanov, Sergei M. "Transcript (Evidence) of Proceedings: Emerging Political, Social, Economic and Security Developments in Russia & Ukraine and Canada's Policy and Interests in the Region and Other Related Matters," Canada. Parliament, 37th Parl., 1st Sess., 2001. Senate, Standing Committee on Foreign Affairs. *Proceedings of the Standing Committee. . ..* Issue no. 11 (June 6, 2001) pp. 71-73.

"Minutes of Evidence for Wednesday 31 October 2001...The Impact of Foot and Mouth Disease," United Kingdom. Parliament, 2001-02 Sess. House of Commons, Environment, Food, and Rural Affairs Committee. *First Report*, Ordered printed, Jan. 16, 2002 (Publication on the Internet). Available at: http://www.publications.parliament.uk/pa/-cm200102/cmselect/cmenvfru/323/1103101.htm; Accessed: 2/11/02.

L2.4 Committee Publications (Parliamentary Papers)

Parliamentary bodies issue reports as part of their committee proceedings and also as separate reports. In addition, a wide range of committee and legislative materials are collected in series called *The Parliamentary Papers* and *Command Papers* (Section L2.6). When the reports are published separately, they should be cited by the individual report title since many libraries will provide access in this manner.

Include This Information:

* *Legislative/Parliamentary Body (Section 1.3).

* *Title (Section 2.0).

* Unique identifying numbers (if present) (Section 3.0).

* *Publishing information (if print or PEF formats) (Section 4.0).

* Series note—if the report also includes information about the committee proceedings (issue number and date), include this as a Series note. (Section 5.1).

* *The source information (VEF sources) (Section E4.0).

*Required

British Columbia. Legislative Assembly, Select Standing Committee on Public Accounts. *Review of Auditor General Reports* (C2002-960038-3). Feb. 2002. Available at: http://www.legis.gov.bc.ca/CMT/37thParl/2nd-session/pac/reports/pafeb02report.htm; Accessed: 2/28/02.

Canada. Parliament. House of Commons, Standing Committee on Foreign Affairs and International Trade. *Crossing the Atlantic: Expanding the Economic Relationship Between Canada and Europe.* Ottawa, 2001. (DSS. Cat no. XC11-3731-1-1-02).

Canada. Parliament. Senate, Standing Committee on Energy, the Environment, and Natural Resources. *Canada's Nuclear Reactors: How Much Safety Is Enough?* Interim Report. June 2001. Available at: http://www.parl.gc.ca/37/1/parlbus/commbus/senate-/com-e/enrg-e/rep-e/repintjun01-e.htm; Accessed: 11/15/01.

Canada. Parliament. Senate, Standing Committee on Social Affairs, Science and Technology. *The Health of Canadians: The Federal Role*, Vol. 4, *Issues and Options.* Sept. 2001. Available at: http://www.parl.gc.ca/37/1/parlbus/commbus/senate/com-E/SOCI-E/rep-e/repintsep01-e.htm; Accessed: 1/15/02.

United Kingdom. Parliament, House of Commons, Culture, Media, and Sport Committee. *Unpicking the Lock: The World Championships in the UK* (First Report). Ordered printed Nov. 13, 2001. (HC264) (Publications on the Internet). Available at: http://www.-publications.parliament.uk/pa/cm200102/cmselect/cmcumeds/264/26402.htm; Accessed: 2/1/02.

United Kingdom. Parliament, House of Commons. *Industrial Development Act 1982: Annual Report . . .* London: HMSO, 1991. (House of Commons Paper 593). (Readex British Parliamentary Papers, 1990/91).

L2.5 Command Papers (White Papers)

Command Papers (frequently called "white papers") generally originate outside Parliament but are "presented" to Parliament at the "command" of the monarch. They are then issued by Parliament and printed in various "Command Papers" series.

Include This Information:

- *Legislative/Parliamentary Body (Section 1.3).

- *Title (Section 2.0).

- Unique identifying numbers (if present) (Section 3.0).

- *Publishing information (if print or PEF formats) (Section 4.0).

- Series note for Command Paper number (Section 5.1).

- *The source information (VEF sources) (Section E4.0).

                                                                  *Required

---

United Kingdom. Parliament. *Britain's Army for the 90's*. London: HMSO, 1991. (Command Paper 1595).

United Kingdom. Parliament. *Your Right to Know: The Government's Proposals for a Freedom of Information Act*. London: Stationer's Office, 1997. (CM 3818). Available at: http://www.official-documents.co.uk/document/caboff/foi/foi.htm; Accessed: 11/13/01.

L2.6 Legislation: Bills, Acts, and Resolutions

Bills are very often numbered on introduction to a country's parliamentary body. These numbers are retained until a bill becomes law and are often useful in tracking the progress of legislation. Because the numbers are often used again in subsequent years, you should include the year and/or session number as well as the bill number in your citation. Consult Table 4 for additional explantation.

Include This Information:

- *Parliamentary body, including legislative session/number, inclusion of a regnal year is optional (Section 1.3).
- *Bill number—its most descriptive feature—each legislature has a numbering system; use the information as it appears on the document (Section 2.1f).
- *Title (may use the popular name if appropriate), may be abbreviated (Section 2.1j).
- *Version (a printers number, for example, if known)—if the source provides a date, a version may not be required (Section 3.2c).
- *Publishing information (if print or PEF source) (Section 4.0).
- *The source information (VEF sources) (Section E4.0).

Related Sections:

➢ Citing Parts: Periodical Articles and Statistical Sources (Sections 6.0 and E6.0).

                                                                    *Required

---

Ontario. Legislative Assembly, House, 37th Legislature, 2nd Sess. *Bill 143: Gravesites of Former Premiers Act, 2001* (Private Members Bill). First reading, Nov. 28, 2001. Available at: http://www.ontla.on.ca/documents/Bills/37_Parliament/Session2/-b143_e.htm; Accessed: 2/28/02.

Canada. Parliament, House of Commons, 35th Parl. 2nd Sess. (45-46 Elizabeth II, 1996-97). *Bill C-84: An Act to Amend the Citizenship and Immigration Act*. First Reading, Feb. 20, 1997).

Available at: http://www.parl.gc.ca/bills/government/C-84/C-84_1/C-84_cover-E.html; Accessed: 11/16/01.

"Bill C-4: Civil International Space Station Agreement Implementation Act," *Canada Gazette,* Pt. III, 22:4 (Jan. 31, 2000). (*Statutes of Canada,* 2000, Chpt. 35). Available at: http://canada.gc.ca/gazette/part3/pdf/g3-02204.pdf; Accessed: 11/15/01.

United Kingdom. Parliament, House of Lords. 1989/1990 Sess. *Human Fertilization and Embryology Bill, No. 1.* (Elizabeth II, 1989). London: HMSO, 1989.

United Kingdom. Parliament, House of Lords, 2000-01 Sess. *European Communities (Amendment) Bill.* As introduced Oct. 18, 2001. Available at: http://www.parliament.the-stationery-office.co.uk/pa/ld200102/ldbills/014/2002014.htm; Accessed: 11/13/01.

L2.7 Statutes

Many parliamentary governments publish laws in one form or another. The two most common arrangements are by date of passage and by general topic. The subject compilations consolidate laws currently in force and, therefore, may omit laws found in the chronological collections.

Include This Information:

* *Parliamentary body, session number; inclusion of a regnal year is optional—if the parliamentary body is included in the title, it can be omitted as an issuing agency.
* The title or popular name of the statute, abbreviated, if necessary.
* *Date of passage.
* *Title of the source containing the laws (e.g., *Acts of Parliament* or *Revised Statutes of Canada*).
* Volume, chapter, section, year (as appropriate).
* Publishing information (if appropriate).
* *The source information (VEF sources) (Section E4.0) or required notes (microfiche) (Section 5.3a).

Related Sections:

➤ *Quick Citation Guide to Special Cases and Well-Known Sources*, Official Gazettes, S21.
➤ *United States Code* and Other Codified Laws, L1.7.

*Required

China. National People's Congress. Standing Committee. Legislative Affairs Commission. *The Laws of the People's Republic of China, 1979-1982.* Beijing: Foreign Languages Press, 1987.

"Children Act 1989." In United Kingdom. *Public General Acts and Measures,* Chpt. 41. (Elizabeth II, 1989). London: HMSO, 1989.

"Criminal Justice and Police Act." *Acts of the UK Parliament.* (2001, Chpt. 16). Available at: http://www.hmso.gov.uk/acts/acts2001/20010016.htm; Accessed: 11/13/01

"Northwest Territories Act." *Revised Statutes of Canada* (1985, V. 6, Chpt. N-27). Ottawa: Queen's Printer for Canada, 1985.

"Canadian Environmental Protection Act: Part II, Toxic Substances, Fuels," *Revised Statutes of Canada* (1985, c. 16, s. 47). Updated Nov. 10, 2001. Available at: Academic Universe, LexisNexis; Accessed: 11/15/01.

"Export Act." Canada. *Consolidated Statutes (R.S.* 1985, c. E-16, sec.1). Updated to Apr. 30, 2001. Available at: http://laws.justice.gc.ca/en/E-18/text.html; Accessed: 11/15/01.

ORGANIZATIONS: UNITED NATIONS DOCUMENTATION

Official Records constitute a final edition of many U.N. masthead documents (Section 53d) including resolutions and other parliamentary documents. When available, cite the Official Record rather than the masthead document version.

L3.1 Masthead Documents

Formerly called "Mimeos," masthead documents are printed and distributed in small quantities for U.N. officials and not meant for public distribution. Despite being printed and distributed in small quantities, they are readily available in many libraries and in electronic form. Masthead documents may include: conference proceedings, resolutions, and meeting agendas.

Masthead documents may become part of the *Official Record* (Section L3.2), or be included in the Readex microfiche collection (Section 5.3a), and may be available electronically (Fig. 10).

Include This Information:

* *Name of main U.N. body, session (if one) and subsidiary body, session (if one) (Section 1.2).

* *Title—may be shortened (Section 2.1c) or may need to be enhanced (Section 2.1d).

* *Unique identifying number (Section 3.0).

* *Publication date (Section 4.3 and 6.4a).

* *Required note: masthead documents (Section 5.3d).

* *Required note: microfiche collections, if applicable (Section 5.3a).

* *The source information (VEF sources) (Section E4.0).

Related Sections:

➢ Table 15: Is it AccessUN or the UN Documentation Centre? (Section E4.1a).
➢ *Quick Citation Guide Special Cases and Well-Known Sources*, U.N. Conferences, S31.

*Required

U.N. Economic and Social Council. *Human Rights Questions: Allegations Regarding Infringements of Trade Union Right* (E/1992/70). June 10, 1992. (Masthead).

U.N. General Assembly, 45th Sess. [Peace Process in El Salvador] *Note Verbale dated 19 October 1990 from the Permanent Representative of El Salvador . . . to the . . . Secretary-General* (A/45/667; S/21906). Oct. 24, 1990. (Masthead; issued jointly with the U.N. Security Council, 45th Year). (Readex Microfiche 1990).

U.N. General Assembly, 56th Sess. *Children and Armed Conflict: Report of the Secretary-General* (A/56/342). Sept. 7, 2001. (Masthead). Text available on the Internet. Available via: AccessUN, Readex/NewsBank; Accessed: 2/12/02.

U.N. General Assembly 56th Sess. *Women in Development: Access to Financial Resources, a Gender Perspective, Report of the Secretary-General* (A/56/321). Aug. 23, 2001. (Masthead). Available from: UN Documentation Centre, http://www.un.org/documents/ga/docs/56/a56321.pdf; Accessed: 1/31/02.

L3.2 Official Records

The following categories are issued:

* Meeting records—verbatim or summary records.

* Supplements—contain reports of various bodies to the session.

* Annexes—usually come in groups and may contain material such as a list of agenda items.

* Unassigned—documents that don't fall into any of the above categories (e.g., list of delegations, resolutions and decisions of the Security Council) (Fig. 2).

Include This Information:

* *Name of main U.N. body, session (if one) and subsidiary body, session (if one) (Section 1.2).

* *Title may be shortened (Section 2.1c) or may need to be enhanced (Section 2.1d).

* *Unique identifying number (Section 3.0).

* *Publication date (Section 4.3 and 6.4a).

* *Official Record (include Supplement or Annex number)—Note: although the source includes the title Official Records, the singular form may be used when citing a single number.

* Publishing information, if available (print and PEF sources only) (Section 4.0).

* *Required note: Microfiche Collection (Section 5.3a), if applicable.

* *The source information (VEF sources) (Section E4.0).

Related Sections:

➢ Table 15: Is it AccessUN or the UN Documentation Centre? (Section E4.1a).
➢ *Quick Citation Guide Special Cases and Well-Known Sources*, U.N. Conferences, S31

*Required

U.N. General Assembly. 34th Sess., 107th Plenary Meeting. *Agenda Item 75: Draft Convention on the Elimination of the Discrimination Against Women* (A/34/PV.17), Dec. 18, 1979. Available at: http://www.un.org/Depts/dhl/landmark/pdf/a34pv107e.pdf; Accessed: 11/2/01.

U.N. General Assembly, 46th Sess. *Report of the Human Rights Committee* (A/46/40). Official Record, Supp. No. 40. New York, 1991.

U.N. General Assembly, 46th Sess. Special Political Committee. *Summary Record of the the 29th Meeting* (A/SPC/46/SR.29). Official Record. Dec. 4, 1991. (Readex Microfiche 1991).

U.N. General Assembly, 55th Sess. *Report of the Commissioner General of the United Nations Relief and Works Agency for Palestine Refugees in the Near East, 1 July 1999-30 June 2000* (A/55/13). Official Record, Supp. No. 13. New York, 2000. Available at: UN Documentation Centre, http://www.un.org/documents/ga/docs/55/a5513.pdf; Accessed: 2/12/02.

U.N. General Assembly, 55th Sess. Committee on the Rights of the Child. *Report of the Committee. . .* (A/55/41). Official Record, Supp. No. 41. May 8, 2000. Available from: AccessUN, Readex/NewsBank; Accessed: 2/12/02.

U.N. General Assembly, 55th Sess., 74th Plenary Meeting. *Agenda Item 38: Zone of Peace and Cooperation of the South Atlantic, Draft Resolution A/55/L.39*, Nov. 29, 2000. (A/55/PV.74). Official Record. Available from: AccessUN, Readex/NewsBank; Accessed: 1/30/02.

U.N. Security Council, 49th Year. *Resolutions and Decisions of the Security Council, 1994* (S/INF/50). Official Record. New York, 1996.

<u>Meeting Record</u>

U.N. General Assembly, 46th Sess. Special Political Committee. *Summary Record of the 29th Meeting*, Nov. 29, 1991 (A/SPC/46/SR.29). *Official Record*. Dec. 4, 1991.

U.N. General Assembly, 51st Sess. *94th Plenary Meeting, Mar. 27, 1997* (A/51/PV.94). Official Record. Available from: AccessUN, Readex/NewsBank; Accessed: 2/12/02.

U.N. General Assembly, 56th Sess., 1st Plenary Meeting. *[Verbatim Record of the Plenary Meeting]*, Sept. 12, 2001 (A/56/PV.1). Official Record. Available at: UN Documentation Centre, http://www.un.or/documents/ga/docs/56/pv/a56pv1.pdf; Accessed: 2/12/02.

U.N. Security Council. 10th Year. *707th Meeting: 16 December 1955* (S/PV.707). New York, 1955. (Readex Microfiche 1955).

<u>Unassigned documents</u>

U.N. Security Council, 32nd Year. *Resolutions and Decisions of the Security Council 1977* (S/INF/33). *Official Record*. New York, 1978. (Readex Microfiche 1977).

U.N. Security Council, 45th Year. *Resolutions and Decisions of the Security Council 1990* (S/INF/46). *Official Record*. New York, 1991.

L3.3 U.N. Resolutions

For information to include in each citation, consult Section L3.1 (Masthead Documents) and L3.2 (Official Records).

<u>As a Masthead Document</u>

U.N. General Assembly, 40th Sess. *Resolution Adopted by the General Assembly, 40/19: Return or Restitution of Cultural Property to Countries of Origin* (A/RES/40/19). Nov. 27, 1985. (Masthead). Available from: AccessUN, Readex/NewsBank; Accessed: 2/12/02.

U.N. General Assembly, 55th Sess. *Resolution Adopted by the General Assembly, 55/243: The Destruction of Relics and Monuments in Afghanistan* (A/RES/55/243). May 1, 2001. (Masthead) (Readex Microfiche 2001).

U.N. General Assembly, 56th Sess. *Resolution 56/93: International Convention Against Reproductive Cloning of Human Beings* (A/Res/56/93). Jan. 28, 2002. Available at: UN Documentation Centre, http://www.un.org/documents/ga/res/a56r093.pdf; Accessed: 2/12/02.

U.N. Security Council, 2288th Meeting. *Resolution 487 (1981) [On the Israeli Air Attack on Iraqi Nuclear Installations]* (S/Res/487). June 19, 1981. (Masthead).

<u>As an Official Record</u>

U.N. Economic and Social Council. *Commission on Human Rights Resolution 1998/79. Situation of Human Rights in Bosnia and Herzegovina, The Republic Of Croatia and the Federal Republic of Yugoslavia*. (E/1998/23). Official Record, Supp. No. 3, 1998. (Readex Microfiche 1998).

U.N. Security Council, 43rd Year. "Resolution 612 [The Situation between Iran and Iraq]," May 9, 1988, p. 10. In *Resolutions and Decisions of the Security Council* (S/INF/44). Official Record. New York, 1989.

<u>As Part of a Collection</u>

For information to include, consult Section 2.3.

> U.N. General Assembly, 24th Sess. "Resolution 2603 Question of Chemical and Bacteriological (Biological) Weapons," Dec. 16, 1969, pp. 226-227. In *United Nations Resolutions, Series I General Assembly*, Vol. XII. Dobbs Ferry, NY: Oceana, 1975.

ORGANIZATIONS: EUROPEAN UNION DOCUMENTATION

L4.1 *Official Journal of the European Communities*

The *Official Journal* is published daily in 11 languages. Since 1967, the *Official Journal* has been divided into four series—the L series (legislation), the C series (information, communication and preparatory legislative acts of the European Union), supplements, and an annex. Although the title on the European Union WWW site is: *Official Journal*, it is recommended that the full title, *Official Journal of the European Communities,* be used in the citation. Before 1972 there was no official English version; therefore, you will be citing an edition in French or in some other official language.

Include This Information:

* *Title—may be shortened (Section 2.1c) or may need to be enhanced (Section 2.1d).

* *Unique identifying numbers (Section 3.0).

* *Official Journal of the European Communities*, Section, date, pages. (Section 4.3 and 6.4a).

* *Required note: Microfiche Collections, if applicable (Section 5.3a).

* *The source information (VEF sources) (Section E4.0).

Related Sections:

➢ Citing Parts: Periodical Articles and Statistical Sources (Sections 6.0 and E6.0).
➢ *Quick Citation Guide to Special Cases and Well-Known Sources*, Treaties, S30.

*Required

For citations to pre-1967 material, the citation will be much like a periodical citation with title, volume/issue number, date, and pages:

> "Résolution portant avis du Parlement Européen sur la proposition de directive concernant les problèmes sanitaires dans les échanges de produits à base de viandes," *Journal Officiel des Communautes Européennes* 7:109 (9 July1964) p.1710.

<u>Post-1967 citations:</u>

> "Commission Regulation (EEC) No. 71/80 of 15 Jan. 1980, Altering the Import Levies on Products Processed from Rice or Cereal," *Official Journal of the European Communities* L 11 (Jan. 16, 1980) pp. 12-13.

> "Commission Decision of 1 Dec. 1999 Declaring a Concentration Compatible With the Common Market and the Functioning of the EEA Agreement," *Official Journal of the European Communities* L 152/1 (6 July 2001) pp. 1-23. Available from: CELEX, http://europa.eu.int/eur-lex/en/search/search_oj.html; Accessed: 2/12/02.

> "Council Regulation (EC) No. 2156/2001 of 5 Nov. 2001, Repealing Regulation (EC) No. 926/98 Concerning the Reduction of Certain Economic Relations With the Federal Republic of Yugoslavia" (32001R2156). *Official Journal of the European Communities* L 289 (11/6/2001) p. 5.

"Agreement Between the European Community and the Republic of Slovenia on the Reciprocal Recognition, Protection and Control of Designations for Spirit and Aromatised Drinks" (Dec.3, 2001), *Official Journal of the European Communities* L 342 (Dec. 27, 2001) pp. 92-97. Text from: *CELEX Database (Legislation)*. Available from: Academic Universe, LexisNexis; Accessed: 2/13/02.

L4.2 European Parliament Debate

For information to include in each citation, consult Section L4.1 (*Official Journal of the European Communities*).

"Allocution de M. le President de L'Assemblée," *Assembles Parlementaire Européenne: Debats* (1 Mars 1958) pp. 30-32. (1958-59 *Journal Officiel: Débats* microfiche 1).

"Organ transplants," *Official Journal of the European Communities, Annex: Debates of the European Parliament* 297 (11-15 Apr. 1983) pp. 268-269.

"Promoting Innovation with New Technologies; Teaching and Learning: Towards the Learning Society; E-Learning: Designing Tomorrow's Education; Future Objectives of Education and Training Systems (Debate, May 14, 2001)," *Official Journal of the European Communities* C34E (7 Feb. 2002) p. 14. Text from: CELEX, http://europa.eu.int/eur-lex/en/search/search_oj.html; Accessed: 2/13/02.

L 4.3 Parliamentary Questions

For information to include in each citation, consult Section L4.1 (*Official Journal of the European Communities*).

"Written Question No. 190/76 . . . 21 May 1976 [on Birth Grants]," *Official Journal of the European Communities* C 7 (9 Jan. 1978) pp. 1-2. (1978 O.J. microfiche no. 3).

"Written Question E-1155/01 by Daniel Varela Suanzes-Carpegna (PPE-DE) to the Commission (10 Apr., 2001). Tuna Steaks." *Official Journal of the European Communities* C 364 E (Dec. 20, 2001) pp. 51-52. Text from: Eur-Lex, Parliamentary Questions, http://europa.eu.int/eur-lex/en/search/search_epq.html; Accessed: 2/12/02.

"Written Question E-3383/00 by Piia-Noora Kauppi (PPE-DE) to the Commission. Planned Directive with Harmful Effects on Regional Airlines," *Official Journal of the European Communities* C 174 E (June 19, 2001) pp. 42-43. Text from: *CELEX Database (Parliamentary Questions)*. Available from: Academic Universe, LexisNexis; Accessed: 2/13/02.

"Oral Question H-0756/01… by Laura González Álvarez to the Commission, Subject: The Mont Blanc Tunnel and the European Transport System Management" (Part Sess., Oct. 1, 2001; 5th Parliamentary Term, 1999-2004). Text from: Eur-Lex, Parliamentary Questions, http://europa.eu.int/eur-lex/en/search/search_epq.html; Accessed: 2/13/02.

L4.4 COM (Communication) Documents

For information to include, consult the Citation rules in Parts 1 and 2.

European Communities. Commission. *Financial Situation of the European Communities on 30 June 1981* (COM(81)400). n.p., [by 1981].

European Communities. Commission. *Proposal for a Council Directive on Procedures for Harmonizing the Programs for the Reduction and Elimination of Pollution . . . from the Titanium Dioxide Industry* (COM(83)189 final; CB-CO 83 058-EN-C). Luxembourg: Office for Official Publications, 1983. (Microfiche EN-83-11).

European Communities. Commission. *Designing Tomorrow's Education: Promoting Innovation with New Technology* (COM(2000)23 Final). Report from the Commission to the Council and the European Parliament. Brussels, Jan. 27, 2000. Available at: http://europa.eu.int/comm/education/elearning/rapen.pdf; Accessed: 2/13/02.

European Communities. Commission. *Proposal for a Directive of the European Parliament and the Council on Public Access to Environmental Information.* (COM(2000 402). Text from: Eur-Lex, http://europa.eu.int/eurlex/en/com/pdf/2000/-en_500PC0402.pdf; Accessed: 2/13/02.

L4.5 Working Documents/Papers

Cite the title of the individual document (shortened, if necessary) and cite *Working Documents* as a series with the document number. Give the full publication date; no other Publishing Information (Section 4.0) is usually provided.

European Communities. European Parliament. *Report Drawn Up. . .on Persons Missing in Argentina.* Oct. 24, 1983. (1983-1984 Working Documents No. 902).

European Communities. European Parliament. Directorate-General for Research. *The Work of the Committee on Women's Rights, 1994-1999.* Manuscript completed, Mar. 1999. (Working Paper; Women's Rights Series; FEMM 105 EN). Available at: Europarl, http://www.europarl.eu.int/workingpapers/femm/105/default_en.htm; Accessed: 2/12/02.

---

[1] Wines, Michael, "Word for Word: In the House—How the *Record* Tells the Truth Now," *New York Times*, Late Edition, Final (Jan. 22, 1995) p. 7. Available from: Academic Universe, LexisNexis; Accessed: 2/28/02.

[2] GPO Access provides both a PDF and TEXT version of every page, for example. Between these two formats, it is fairly easy to identify the exact page on which a speaker's text begins even though the text is grouped into sections. It is more difficult to locate the volume number (it's back on the database selection screen) and an issue number (not easily found without additional searching). LexisNexis's *Congressional Universe* also provides a TEXT version, but it provides a header that includes the volume and issue numbering. Each issue is grouped into sections. As a result, citing a single speech can mean looking for the exact page number (page number 5642 displays as [*5642]) buried in the text. The bottom line is that you will need to sleuth out this information in each source, in order to provide citations that provide your readers with enough information to locate the same text, regardless of which system or format they use.

Figure 1: *U.S. Statutes at Large*

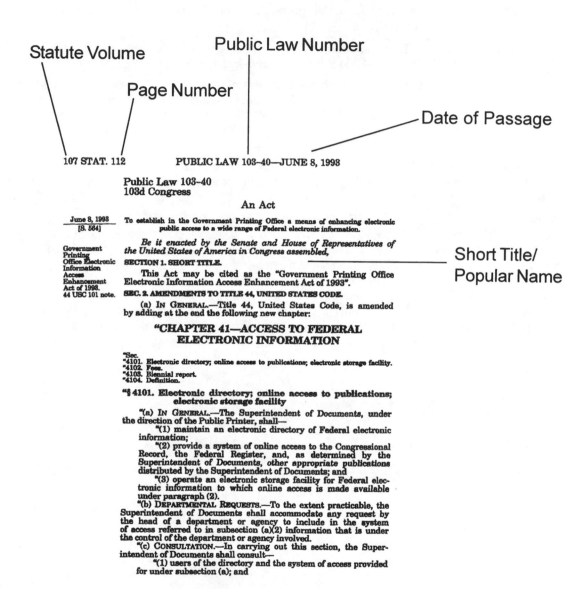

Figure 2: U.N. Official Records

Issuing Agency
and Logo

Title of Official Record Issue

United Nations

Report of the Commissioner-General of the United Nations Relief and Works Agency for Palestine Refugees in the Near East

1 July 1999-30 June 2000

Additional Issuing
Agency Information

General Assembly
Official Records
Fifty-fifth session
Supplement No. 13 (A/55/13)

Series/Symbol Number

Official Record Supplement Number

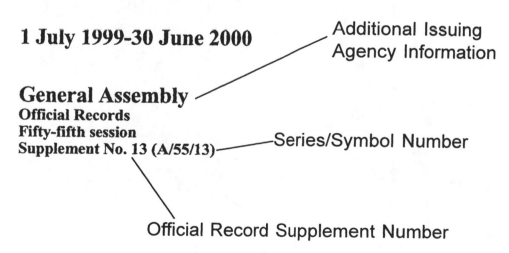

Quick Citation Guide to Periodical Articles and Statistical Sources

Quick Citation Guide to Periodical Articles And Statistical Sources

BASIC ELEMENTS

The Recommended Form and Punctuation For Periodical Articles and Statistical Sources

PERIODICAL CITATIONS
P1 Periodical Article With One Author
P2 Periodical Article With More Than One Author
P3 Periodical Article With No Author
P4 VEF Periodical Article With a Print Equivalent
P5 Periodical Article with No Print Equivalent
P6 Periodical Article from a Commercial Database Vendor

STATISTICS CITATIONS (RECOMMENDED FORM AND PUNCTUATION)
P7 Statistical Volume
P8 Data Table in a Statistical Volume
P9 Data Table in a Periodical
P10 VEF Data Table With No Print Equivalent

STATISTICS SOURCES (BY TITLE)
P11 Annual Survey of Manufactures
P12 Census of Population and Housing—1790-1980
P13 Census of Population and Housing—1990-2000
P14 County and City Data Book
P15 County Business Patterns
P16 Crime in the U.S. (Uniform Crime Reports)
P17 Demographic Yearbook (United Nations)
P18 Digest of Education Statistics
P19 Economic Censuses (U.S.)
P20 Eurostat (European Union)
P21 International Financial Statistics
P22 National Statistical Compendia
P23 Sourcebook of Criminal Justice Statistics
P24 State and County QuickFacts (U.S. Census Bureau)
P25 Statistical Abstract of the United States
P26 Stat-USA/Internet
P27 State Statistical Compendium
P28 Survey of Current Business
P29 UNESCO Statistical Yearbook
P30 USA Counties
P31 World Development Indicators
P32 World Investment Report
P33 Yearbook of the United Nations

BASIC ELEMENTS

Citations of periodical articles and statistical tables should distinguish between the information about the article or table being cited and the title of the periodical or statistical source for that table (Figs. 13 and 14). For guidance on footnote vs. bibliography entries, consult the *Introduction*.

Table 10: Recommended Form and Punctuation for Periodical Articles and Statistical Sources

---

A Print Periodical or Statistical Table

Author of Article (name inverted). "Title of Article or Table Header," *Title of Periodical* Volume: Issue (Date) Page Numbers. (Notes).

A VEF Periodical or Statistical Table

Author of Article (name inverted). "Title of Article or Table Header," *Title of Periodical or Statistical Source* Volume:Issue (Date) Page Numbers. (Notes). Available at: [URL]; Accessed: [Date].

PERIODICAL SOURCES

P1 Periodical Article With One Author

May, Michael M. "Nuclear Weapons in the New World Order," *Disarmament* 15:3 (May 1992) pp. 18-45. (Publication of the United Nations).

Meadows, Michelle. "Why Drugs Get Pulled Off the Markets," *FDA Consumer Magazine* (Jan.-Feb. 2002). Available at: http://www.fda.gov/fdac/features/-2002/102_drug.html; Accessed: 1/15/02.

P2 Periodical Article With More Than One Author

Greenburg, Martin A., and Ellen C. Wertleib. "The Police and the Elderly (Pt. II)," *FBI Law Enforcement Bulletin* 52:9 (Sept. 1983) pp. 1-6. (J1.14/8:52/9).

Lappé, Frances, et al. "Hope's Edge: Finding Our Path in Uncertain Times," *UN Chronicle Online* 38:3 (2001). Available at: http://www.un.org/Pubs/chronicle/2001/-issue3/0103p52.html; Accessed: 2/15/02.

P3 Periodical Article With No Author

"Common European Security and Defence Policy," European Commission. *Bulletin of the European Union* (Bull. EU 9-2001). Available at: http://europa.eu.int/abc/-doc/off/bull/en/200109/sommai00.htm; Accessed: 1/15/02.

"Former College Will Become State's Newest Prison," *Correctional Newsfront* 17:1 (Winter 1991) p.1. (Publication of the Pennsylvania Dept. of Corrections).

"Progress and Challenges: Looking at EPA Today," *EPA Journal* 16:5 (Sept./Oct. 1990) pp.15-29. (EP1.67:16/5).

"AIDS Cases and Annual Rates..., United States," *HIV/AIDS Surveillance Report* 12:2 (Yearend 2000 edition). Available at: http://www.cdc.gov/hiv/stats/hasrlink.htm; Accessed: 2/20/02.

P4 VEF Periodical Article With a Print Equivalent

Hettiarachchy, Tilak, and Stephen L. Schensul. "Risks of Pregnancy and the Consequences Among Young Unmarried Women Working in a Free Trade Zone in Sri Lanka" Economic and Social Commission for Asia and the Pacific. *Asia-Pacific Population Jounal* 16:2 (June 2001): pp. 125-40. (2001 IIS microfiche 3170-P9.5).

McDaniel, Lynda. "Ecotourism Takes Off in the Heart of Appalachia," *Appalachia Magazine Online* (May-Aug. 2001). Available at: Appalachian Regional Commission (Washington, D.C.), http://arc.gov/infopubs/appalach/mayaug01/ecointro.htm; Accessed: 1/15/02.

Breler, Nicole. "European Eco-Label: The Flower in Full Bloom," *Environment for Europeans* no. 8 (Oct. 2001) p. 14. Available at: http://europa.eu.int/comm/-environment/news/efe/index.htm; Accessed: 1/15/02.

Hoang, Francis Q. "Addressing School Violence: Prevention Planning Practice," *FBI Law Enforcement Bulletin* 70:8 (Aug. 2001) pp.18-22. Available at: http://www.fbi.gov/publications/leb/2001/aug01leb.pdf; Accessed 1/15/02.

P5 Periodical Article With No Print Equivalent

Baucus, Max. "Doha and Beyond: The Role of Congress in a New Trade Round," *Economic Perspective* 7:1 (Jan. 2002) pp. 18-20. (An Electronic Journal of the U.S. Dept. of State). Available at: http://info.state.gov/journals/ites/0102/-ijee/ijee0102.pdf; Accessed: 2/15/02.

"No One Wants to Wear this Yellowjacket: OUCH!" *Sci4Kids*, Last updated 2/8/02. Available from: U.S. Dept. of Agriculture. Agricultural Research Service, http://www.ars.usda.gov/is/kids/bigcity/story2/yjtrap.htm; Accessed: 2/15/02.

P6 Periodical Article From a Commercial Database Vendor

"Green Taxation: 73% of Europeans in Favour of Eco-Taxes" *Europe Environment* 480 (June 27, 1996) (387 words). Text from: *General News (Newsletters)*. Available from: Academic Universe, LexisNexis; Accessed: 1/16/02.

Lenain, Patrick. "What is the Track Record of OECD Economic Projections?" *OECD Economic Outlook* no.70 (Dec. 2001). Available from: SourceOECD; Accessed: 2/15/02.

STATISTICS CITATIONS

P7 Statistical Volume

U.S. Energy Information Administration. *Annual Energy Review, 1999* (DOE/EIA-0384(99)). Washington: Government Printing Office, 2001. Available from: http://ww.eia.doe.gov/aer; Accessed: 2/15/02.

Demographic Yearbook, 1990. New York: United Nations, 1992.

OECD Information Technology Outlook, 1999. Paris, 1999. Available from: SourceOECD; Accessed: 2/1/02.

P8 Data Table in a Statistical Volume

"Unemployment Rate of Women," p.15. In *100 Basic Indicators from Eurostat Yearbook, 2000*. Available at: http://www.europa.eu.int/comm/eurostat/; Accessed: 2/15/02.

"Table 385: Unemployment Rate of Persons 16 Years Old and Over, by Age, Sex, Race/Ethnicity, and Highest Degree Attained: 1996, 1997, and 1998" (PDF file; 13 kb). In *Digest of Education Statistics, 1999*. Available at: http://nces.ed.gov/pubs2000/-Digest99/tables/PDF/Table385.pdf; Accessed: 11/25/01.

"SD-1.5: Television Viewing Habits," p. 194. In U.S. Dept. of Health and Human Services. *Trends in the Well-Being of America's Children and Youth, 2000*. Produced by Westat. [Washington, D.C., 2000] (2001 ASI microfiche 4004-37) (HE1.63:2000).

"Boy Scouts and Girl Scouts—Membership and Units: 1970 to 1989," No. 410, p. 241. In *Statistical Abstract of the United States, 1991*. 111th ed. Washington: Government Printing Office, 1991.

P9 Data Table in a Periodical

"Table 2: Pediatric Aids Cases by State of Residence, and Size of Place of Residence, Reported in 1999 and Cumulative," U.S. Centers for Disease Control and Prevention. *HIV/AIDS Surveillance Supplemental Report* 6 (no. 2) p. 5. (2001 ASI microfiche 4206-

"Table 28: Consumer Price Index: U.S. City Average by Expenditure Category and Commodity and Service Groups" (GIF 148 kb), *Monthly Labor Review* (Apr. 2000) pp. 73-75. Table from: *Power Tables*. Available from: Statistical Universe, LexisNexis; Accessed: 2/15/02.

"Real Inventories, Sales, and Inventory-Sales Ratios for Manufacturing and Trade, 2001:III," *Survey of Current Business* (Jan. 2002) pp. 7-8. Available at: http://www.bea.doc.gov/bea/pubs.htm; Accessed: 2/5/02.

P10 VEF Data Table With No Print Equivalent

"Sports Involvement, by Sex." Table from: Canadian Statistics (Culture, Leisure and Trade). Available at: Statistics Canada, http://www.statcan.ca/english/Pgdb/-People/Culture/arts18.htm; Accessed: 2/15/02.

"*QT-P3: Race and Hispanic or Latino: 2000—Union County, NC.*" Data Set: *Census 2000* (SF1).Available at: American FactFinder (Census Bureau), http://factfinder.census.gov/; Accessed: 1/25/01.

Forstall, Richard L., comp. and ed. *Population of Counties by Decennial Census: 1900 to 1990: Connecticut*. Washington: Bureau of the Census. Population Division, 3/27/95. Available at: http://www.census.gov/population/cencounts/ct190090.txt; Accessed: 2/5/02.

"Table 10.-U.S. International Transactions, by Area—Western Europe." Release Date: Dec. 12, 2001; Earliest Year Revised on Dec. 12, 2001: No Revision. Data from: Bureau of Economic Analysis, *U.S. International Accounts Data*. Available at: http://www.bea.doc.gov/; Accessed: 1/15/02.

STATISTICS SOURCES (BY TITLE)

P11 Annual Survey of Manufactures

"SIC 372: Aircraft and Parts: U.S." Data from: U.S. Census Bureau. *Annual Survey of Manufactures [1987-1996]*. Available at: http://tier2.census.gov/asm/asm.htm; Accessed: 2/1/02.

P12 Census of Population and Housing—1790-1980

The U.S. Census is extremely complex and most citations require several parts for a complete citation. Citing a census volume is complicated because the Census Bureau has organized the volumes differently with nearly every census as size, need, and changing delivery media have demanded. The key is to include enough information so that your reader can locate the specific volume or part of the Census set.

U.S. Census, 1790: Heads of Families. Washington: Government Printing Office, 1908.

U.S. Census, 1850: Statistical View of the United States. . . Compendium of the Seventh Census. By J. D. B. DeBow. Washington: A. O. P. Nicholson, Public Printer, 1854.

"N[umber]. Slaveholders Holding 200-299 Slav[es]." Data from: *U.S. Census, 1860*. Available at: United States Historical Census Browser, http://fisher.lib.virginia.edu/-census/; Accessed: 2/5/02.

U S. Census of Population, 1970: Subject Reports: American Indians (PC(2)-IF). Final Report. Washington: Government Printing Office, 1973.

U.S. Census of Population and Housing, 1980: Final Population and Housing Unit Counts. Pennsylvania (PHC 80-V-40). Advance Report. Washington: Government Printing Office, 1982.

U.S. Census of Population and Housing, 1980: Block Statistics: Minnesota, Selected Areas (PHC 80-1-25; microfiche). Washington: Government Printing Office, 1982. (C3.229/5:PHC80-1-25).

P13 Census of Population and Housing—1990-2000

U.S. Census of Population and Housing, 1990: Summary Social Economic, and Housing Characteristics, Virginia 1990 (CPH-5-48). Final Report. Washington: Government Printing Office, 1992.

Census of Population and Housing, 1990: Block Statistics, Middle-Atlantic Division (New Jersey, New York, Pennsylvania) (CD90-1B-2) (CD-ROM). Reissued. Washington: Bureau of the Census, Sept. 1992. (C3.282:CD90-1B-2).

Census of Population and Housing, 1990: Summary Tape File 3A (CD90-3A) (CD-ROM). Washington: Bureau of the Census, Sept. 1992. (C3.282/2:CD90-3).

Census of Population, 1990: Special Tabulation on Aging. Washington, Bureau of the Census Data User Services Div., 1994. (C3.281/2:CD90-0A0A).

Census Data Tables:

"Commuting to Work (1990 QT)—State College, PA" Part of: *Quick Table: DP-3—Labor Force Status and Employment Characteristics: 1990.* Data Set: *Census of Population and Housing, 1990* (STF 3). Available at: American FactFinder (Census Bureau), http://factfinder.census.gov; Accessed: 1/28/01.

"Detailed Race" (040 Pennsylvania, 161 Columbia Borough). Data from: *Census of Population and Housing, 1990: Summary Tape File 1C, United States Summary* (CD90-1C) (CD-ROM). Washington, Feb. 1992. (C3.282:990-1C).

"General Profile for Pennsylvania." Taken from: *Census of Population and Housing, 1990.* Available at: Government Information Sharing Project, http://govinfo.library.orst.edu; Accessed: 11/18/92.

"White Alone Population in Households and Group Quarters by Sex and Selected Age Groups, for the United States 2000" (PDF format; 6 kb). Data from: *Census, 2000.* Internet release date. 3/20/2001. Available at: http://www.census.gov/population/www/-cen2000/tablist.html; Accessed: 1/25/02.

"PHC-T-12: Population in Selected Group Quarters for the United States, States, Counties with 100 or More People in Emergency and Transition Shelters, and Census Tracts … and for Puerto Rico" (Excel format; 83 kb). Data from: *Census, 2000: Population and Housing Tables (PHC-T Series).* Release Date Oct. 30, 2001. Available at: http://www.census.gov/population/www/cen2000/phc-t12.html; Accessed: 1/28/02.

"PCT5. *Sex by Age: 2000—Race or Ethnic Group: Black or African American—Rhode Island.*" Data Set: *Census, 2000* (SF2). Available at: American FactFinder (Census Bureau), http://www.factfinder.gov; Accessed: 1/28/02.

"GCT-P5. *Age and Sex: 2000—Rhode Island—Place and County Subdivisionl.*" Data Set: *Census, 2000* (SF 1). Available at: American FactFinder (Census Bureau), http://factfinder.census.gov; Accessed: 1/26/02.

P14 County and City Data Book

"State Data: Arkansas" (dBase format). Data from: U.S. Census Bureau. *County and City Data Book.* 1994 ed. Available at: University of Virginia, Geospatial and Statistical Data Center, http://fisher.lib.virginia.edu/ccdb/; Accessed: 1/28/02.

U.S. Census Bureau. *County and City Data Book,* 2000. Washington: Government Printing Office, 2002. (C3.134/2:C83/2002).

P15 County Business Patterns

"Metal Mining (SIC 1000): Pennsylvania, State Totals, 1988" (dBase format). Available at: U.S. Bureau of the Census. *County Business Patterns, 1988 & 1989* (CD-ROM). Washington, Mar. 1992. (C3.204/4:1988/89).

U.S. Census Bureau. *County Business Patterns: Oregon, 1995.* Available at: http://www.census.gov/prod/3/97pubs/cbp-9539.pdf; Accessed: 2/5/02.

"SIC07: Agricultural Services, Forestry and Fishing" (Pennsylvania, Centre County). Data from: *County Business Patterns, 1997.* Available from: CenStats, http://tier2.census.gov/cbp/index.html; Accessed: 2/15/02.

P16 Crime in the U.S. (Uniform Crime Reports)

"Table 2.36: Agency Hate Crime Reporting, by State, 2000," p. 63. In: U.S. Federal Bureau of Investigation. *Crime in the United States: Uniform Crime Report.* 2000 ed. Washington: Government Printing Office, 2000. Available at: http://www.fbi.gov/ucr/-00cius.htm; Accessed: 12/5/01.

P17 Demographic Yearbook (United Nations)

Demographic Yearbook, 1990. New York: United Nations, 1992.

"Kazakstan: Population of … Cities of Over 100,000… Inhabitants," Table 8. Data from: *Demographic Yearbook, 1995.* Available from: U.N. Statistics Division, http://www.un.org/Depts/unsd/demog/index.html; Accessed: 2/15/02.

P18 Digest of Education Statistics

"Table 385: Unemployment Rate of Persons 16 Years Old and Over, by Age, Sex, Race/Ethnicity, and Highest Degree Attained: 1996, 1997, and 1998" (PDF file; 13 kb). In *Digest of Education Statistics, 1999.* Available at: http://nces.ed.gov/pubs2000/-Digest99/tables/PDF/Table385.pdf; Accessed: 11/25/01.

P19 Economic Censuses (U.S.)

U.S. Census, 1890: Mineral Industries. New York: Norman Ross Publishing, [1993]. (Reprint of original edition published: Washington, 1892-97).

U.S. Census of Manufactures, 1967: Vol. II, Industry Statistics: Pt. I Major Groups 20-24. Final Report. Washington: Government Printing Office, 1971.

Economic Censuses, 1987 (CD-ROM). Volume 1, Report Series. Release 1D. Washington: Bureau of the Census, Nov. 1991. (C3.277:Ec7/987/v.1/Release 1D).

Economic Census, 1992. Survey of Minority-Owned Business: Black (MB92-1). Washington: Government Printing Office, 1996. (C 3.277/3:97-4).

Economic Census, 1997: Accommodation and Food Services, California . Washington: Government Printing Office, 2000.

Economic Census, 1997. Arts, Entertainment, Recreation (EC97S71S-SZ). Washington: Bureau of the Census, Oct. 2000. Available at: http://www.census.gov/epcd/-www/97EC71.HTM; Accessed 1/19/02.

Economic Census, 1997: Vol. 1, NAICS Report Series (CD-EC97-1) (Disc 1E). Washington: Census Bureau, Nov. 2001.

Citing a Data Table

"Economic Census, 1997: ZIP Code Statistics, United States Total." Last modified: 10/22/02. Available at: http://www.census.gov/epcd/ec97zip/us/US00000.HTM; Accessed: 1/25/02.

"Table 3: Statistics by Economic Sector, Subsector, and Industry Group—Bellefonte, PA" (Geography Quick Report). Data based on the: *Economic Census, 1997*. Available at: American Factfinder (Census Bureau), http://factfinder.census.gov; Accessed: 1/26/02.

"Monetary Authorities—Central Bank (NAICS: 521110), Selected Industry Statistics by State: 1997 and 1992" (Industry Quick Report). Data based on the: *Economic Census, 1997*. Available at: American FactFinder (Census Bureau), http://factfinder.census.gov; Accessed: 2/22/02.

P20 Eurostat (European Union)

Tourism Trends in Mediterranean Countries. Luxembourg: Office for Official Publications of the European Union, 2001. (Cat. No: KS-40-01-666-EN-C) (Theme 4: Industry, Trade and Services).

"High-tech Employment (% of Total Employment)" (5.21 kb). Last updated: 10/12/2001, Release 1.61. (Theme: Science and Technology; Collection: Key Indicators). Available from: Eurostat, http://europa.eu.int/eurostat; Accessed: 2/15/02.

P21 International Financial Statistics

Data from: *International Financial Statistics* (CD-ROM). Washington: International Monetary Fund, July 2001.

P22 National Statistical Compendia

Belize. Ministry of Finance. Central Statistical Office. *Abstract of Statistics, 1999*. Belmopan, Belize: The Office, [2000]. (CIS National Statistical Compendium Microfiche).

"Population Changes," Table 1, p.12. In Denmark. Danmarks Statistik. *Monthly Review of Statistics,* No. 6, June 1992. Copenhagen: Danmarks Statistik, 1992.

Abejo, Socorro. "Comparative Analysis of Population Age-Sex Distribution from Sample and Complete Enumeration: 1970 and 1980 Census Data," *Journal of Philippine Statistics* 42:1 (1991) pp. 23-25.

P23 Sourcebook of Criminal Justice Statistics

"Table 427—Arrests for Alcohol-Related Offenses and Driving Under the Influence, United States, 1972-99" (WK1; 2 kb). Data from: U.S. Dept. of Justice. Bureau of Justice Statistics. *Sourcebook of Criminal Justice Statistics Online, 2000*. 28th ed. Available at: http://www.albany.edu/sourcebook/; Accessed: 1/29/02.

P24 State and County QuickFacts (U.S. Census Bureau)

"People Quick Facts: Middlesex County, Connecticut." Data from: U.S. Census Bureau. *State & County QuickFacts*. Available at: http://quickfacts.census.gov/-qfd/states/09/09007.html; Accessed: 1/28/02.

P25 Statistical Abstract of the United States

Statistical Abstract of the United States, 1991. 111th ed. Washington: Government Printing Office, 1991.

"Boy Scouts and Girl Scouts—Membership and Units: 1970 to 1989," No. 410, p. 241. In *Statistical Abstract of the United States, 1991*. 111th ed. Washington: Government Printing Office, 1991.

"No. 938—Magazine Advertising Revenue by Category: 1998 and 1999." In *Statistical Abstract of the United States, 2000.* 121st ed. Available at: http://www.census.gov/prod/-2001pubs/statab/sec18.pdf; Accessed 12/25/01.

P26 Stat-USA/Internet

"Argentina: Telecommunications Equipment" (5/1/2000). Text from: *NTDB.* Feb. 5, 2002 ed. (Industry Sector Analysis Reports). Available at: Stat-USA/Internet, http://www.stat-usa.gov; Accessed: 2/5/02.

"Consumer Confidence, From the Survey of Consumers, University of Michigan" (umcc200201.txt; Released 2/4/02, 8:30 a.m. EST). Text from: *State of the Nation.* Available at: Stat-USA/Internet, http://www.stat-usa.gov; Accessed: 2/5/02.

P27 State Statistical Compendium

Most states produce an annual statistical abstract. Although these documents are usually prepared and issued by a state agency, sometimes universities or private organizations become involved in the production of the volume. A citation to such reference sources should specify the issuing agency or group, title, edition, and imprint data (Fig. 3).

"Table 59: Total State Taxes Per Capita, Fiscal Year 1994-95." In California. *Economic Report of the Governor, 1997.* Sacramento: Dept. of Finance, Financial, Economic, and Demographic Research, 1998. (1997 SRI Microfiche S0840-3).

Minnesota. Dept. of Economic Development. Research Division. *Minnesota Statistical Profile 1992.* St. Paul, 1992.

"New and Expanded Manufacturing Industries, by Name, Location, Product, Employment, and Investment: Mississippi, 1998" (GIF; 26 kb) p. 242. In *Mississippi Statistical Abstract, 1999.* n.p.: Office of Business Research Services, Dec. 1999. Table from: *Power Tables.* Available from: Statistical Universe, LexisNexis; Accessed: 2/15/02.

P28 Survey of Current Business

"Real Inventories, Sales, and Inventory-Sales Ratios for Manufacturing and Trade, 2001:III," *Survey of Current Business* (Jan. 2002) pp. 7-8. Available at: http://www.bea.doc.gov/bea/pubs.htm; Accessed: 2/5/02.

P29 UNESCO Statistical Yearbook

UNESCO Statistical Yearbook, 1999 [Selected Tables]. Available at: http://www.uis.unesco.org/en/stats/stats0.htm; Accessed: 1/25/02.

"Table IV.10: Newsprint and Other Printing and Writing Paper: Production, Imports, Exports and Consumption (Total and per 1,000 Inhabitants)." In *UNESCO Statistical Yearbook,* 1999 (Selected Tables). Available at: http://www.uis.unesco.org/-en/stats/stats0.htm; Accessed: 1/25/02.

P30 USA Counties

"Centre County, Pennsylvania: General Profile." Data from: U.S. Census Bureau. *USA Counties.* 1998 ed. Available at: Government Information Sharing Project, http://govinfo.library.orst.edu/; Accessed: 1/30/02.

P31 World Development Indicators

Data from: *World Development Indicators, 2001* (CD-ROM). 5th ed. Washington: World Bank, 2001.

"Belarus at a Glance." Taken from: *World Development Indicators 2001 Database.* As of July 2001. (Country-at-a-Glance Tables). Available at: http://www.worldbank.org/data/countrydata/countrydata.html; Accessed: 1/28/02.

P32 World Investment Report

United Nations Conference on Trade and Development. *World Investment Report 2001: Promoting Linkages* (UNCTAD/WIR/2001). Available at: http://www.unctad.org/wir/contents/wir01content.en.htm; Accessed: 12/12/01.

P33 Yearbook of the United Nations

Yearbook of the United Nations, 1998. New York: Dept. of Public Information, 2001.

Figure 3: State Statistical Compendium

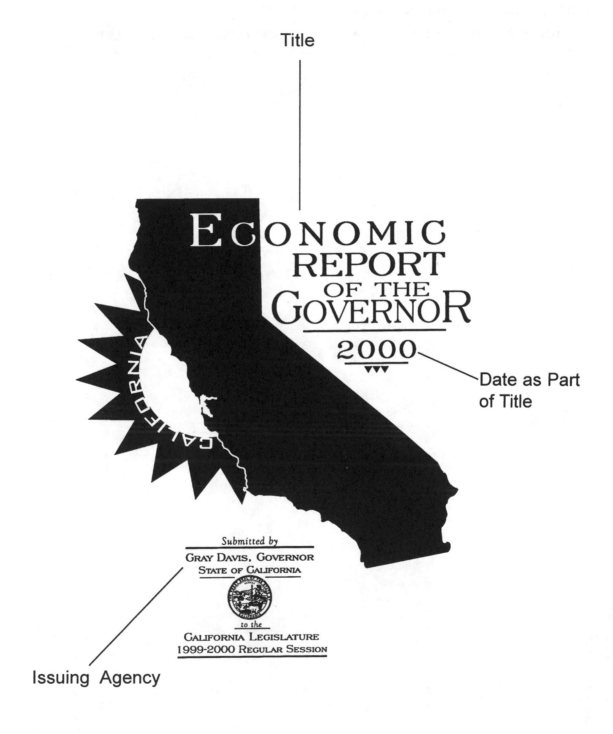

Title

Date as Part
of Title

Issuing Agency

Quick Citation Guide
to Special Cases
and Well-Known Sources

Quick Citation Guide to Special Cases and Well-Known Sources

BASIC ELEMENTS

SPECIAL CASES AND WELL-KNOWN SOURCES

S1 **Agricultural Experiment and Extension Publications**
S2 **American State Papers**
S3 **Archival Documents**
S4 **Blue Books**
S5 *Budget of the United States*
S6 **Clearinghouse Documents**
S7 *Code of Federal Regulations* **(CFR) and the** *Federal Register* **(FR)**
S8 **Congressional Directory**
S9 *Congressional Globe, Register of Debates,* **and** *Annals of Congress*
S10 **Constitutions**
S11 **Court Cases**
S12 **E-Mail Messages and List-Serv Messages**
S13 *Economic Report of the President*
S14 **Embassy, Consulate, and Information Agency Publications**
S15 *Foreign Relations of the United States* **(FRUS)**
S16 **Freedom of Information Documents**
S17 *Journals of the Continental Congress*
S18 **League of Nations**
S19 **Legislative Journals**
S20 **Loose-leafs**
S21 **Official Gazettes**
S22 **Organization of American States (OAS)**
S23 **Patents and Trademarks**
S24 **Presidential Documents**
S25 **Press Releases**
S26 **Securities and Exchange Commission (SEC) Reports**
S27 *Serial Set*
S28 **Software**
S29 **Translations of Non-English News Sources**
S30 **Treaties**
S31 **U.N. Conferences**
S32 *U.S. Government Manual*

BASIC ELEMENTS

Certain titles and some types of government and organization documents are so frequently cited or present unique challenges for researchers. For your convenience some of the most frequently cited and best-known sources are shown separately in this section. These sources often appear in many editions and formats. If a citation contains complete information, your readers will be able to locate a source that is most accessible to them.

These citation formats conform to the rules found in Parts 2 and 3.

Use the **Recommended Form and Punctuation** described in Table 3 (for books and monographs) and Table 10 (for periodical and statistical sources).

SPECIAL CASES AND WELL-KNOWN SOURCES

S1 Agricultural Experiment and Extension Publications

The U.S. government has established throughout the country cooperative inter-governmental organizations which deal with agriculture and home economics. These agencies are known generally as "ag extension services" and "agricultural experiment stations." Any citation to documents produced by these agencies should list the standard citation elements of issuing agency, title, edition, imprint, series, and notes.

> Connecticut. Agricultural Experiment Station. *Quality of Chip Dip.* By Lester Hankin, Donald Shields, and J. Gordon Hanna. New Haven, 1981. (Bulletin 794).

S1a Many universities serve as agricultural extension services and experiment stations. Citations to publications issued directly by these organizations should identify the university as the Issuing Agency, and include personal authors in the title statement.

> Montana State University. Cooperative Extension Service. *Farm and Home Security.* By Roy Linn. Bozeman, 1982. (Circular 1017).

> Athens (GA) Experiment Station. Dept. of Agricultural and Applied Economics. *An Analysis of Foreign Direct Investment in the U.S. Fruit and Vegetable Industry.* By J. C. Burnham and J. E. Epperson. n.p.: The Georgia Agricultural Experiment Stations, College of Agricultural and Environmental Sciences, The University of Georgia, 1999. (Research Bulletin no. 436). Available at: http://www.ces.uga.edu/ES-pubs/RB436.html; Accessed: 2/9/02.

S2 American State Papers

The *American State Papers (ASP)* is a compilation of the publications of the early Congresses, arranged in broad categories. With the *Serial Set* (Section S27) it forms the most complete collection available of Congressional reports and documents. Since the documents in *ASP* are not chronologically arranged, it is necessary to cite subject area, volume, report number, and page numbers.

> "Naval Register for 1832," *American State Papers: Naval Affairs*, Vol. IV (Doc. 461) pp. 48-63.

S3 Archival Documents

Some government documents are not published in the traditional sense and are available only in archives. To cite such documents, follow the general rules outlined in Parts 2 and 3 and include a note informing your reader about the collection, box number and the location of the document.

> John A. Garfield. Correspondence to Lucretia Garfield. Sept. 14, 1868. (John A. Garfield Papers; Box 3; Library of Congress Manuscript Division, Washington, DC).

> U.S. Census of Population, 1900. Schedule No. 1: Allen Township, Northampton County, Pennsylvania. In U.S. National Archives and Records Service. *Twelfth Census of the United States, 1900*. Washington: NARS, 1973. (Reel 1446).

S3a Frequently archival material is microfilmed as part of a subject-based collection. In citing such a document, you must cite the microform collection as well as the document, since it is unlikely that your reader would ever find it except in that specific microform collection. This is in contrast to a republication of a popular or current title on microform by a private publisher, such as CIS, which would be included in a Note (Section 5.3a). Give the Issuing Agency, Title (shortened if necessary), and Publisher Information, place, and date of issuance for the original document. Then give the title and Publisher Information of the collection and whatever number (e.g., reel number, microfiche number) is used to locate the document.

MICROFICHE COLLECTION OF A COMMERCIAL PUBLISHER

> U.S. Joint Chiefs of Staff. *Memorandum for the Deputy Director for Intelligence . . . [on] Development of U.S. Position on Zones of Occupation for Germany, 1943-44.* Washington: 1952. In *Declassified Documents Reference System, 1980.* Washington: Carrolton Press, 1980. (Microfiche 42A).

MICROFILM COLLECTION OF A COMMERCIAL PUBLISHER

> U.S. Library of Congress, Congressional Research Service. *Do We Really Need All Those Electric Plants?* by Alvin Kaufman and Karen K. Nelson. 1982. In *Major Studies and Issue Briefs of the Congressional Research Service, 1982-83 Supp.* Frederick, MD: University Publications of America, 1983. (Reel IV, frame 278).

> Ireland. Central Statistical Office. *Census of Population of Ireland, 1981. Vol. 3, Household Composition and Family Units.* Dublin: Stationary Office, 1985. (*International Population Censuses*: Ireland, Reel 1, 1981).

S4 Blue Books

State "blue books" are government documents which cover various types of information. Usually they provide background data about a state and its government. To cite "blue books" provide the Issuing Agency; Title; Personal Author, if any; and any relevant Publisher Information.

> Oklahoma. Dept. of Libraries. *Directory of Oklahoma: State Almanac 1989-1990.* Oklahoma City, 1989.

> *Oregon Blue Book.* 2001/02 ed. Secretary of State, Archives Division. Available at: http://bluebook.state.or.us/; Accessed: 2/9/02.

S4a Some blue books are not written or published by the state but by a private individual or group. Credit should then be given to the private group or publisher.

> Arizona. Dept. of State. *Bill Turnbow's 1977-78 Arizona Political Almanac.* Edited by Mrs. Bill Turnbow. Phoenix, 1977.

S5 *Budget of the United States*

The *Budget of the United States* appears in two editions: Congressional and executive branch. To differentiate between the two, look for the Congressional numbering scheme on the document.

CONGRESSIONAL VERSION

> *Budget of the United States Fiscal Year 1993* (H. Doc. 102-178). Washington: Government Printing Office, 1992.

EXECUTIVE BRANCH VERSION

> *Budget of the United States Fiscal Year 1993.* Washington: Government Printing Office, 1992.

> *Budget of the U.S. Government, Fiscal Year 2003.* Washington: Government Printing Office, 2002. Available at: GPO Access, http://w3.access.gpo.gov/usbudget/index.html; Accessed: 2/9/02.

S6 Clearinghouse Documents

The U.S. government has established more than 300 clearinghouses that gather and distribute information on various topics. Clearinghouse documents may be unpublished reports, contract reports, or reports previously published by non-governmental and governmental organizations at all levels. These documents are generally known as "technical reports," although their subject matter is frequently neither scientific nor technical.

S6a A citation to a contract report should include, as applicable: Issuing Agency; Title; Personal Author, Institutional Affiliation, and Location; Publication/Report number; Date; and a Note including the abbreviated clearinghouse name and the report identification number. If the medium is other than paper, it should be noted (Section 3.3).

> U.S. Environmental Protection Agency, Office of Research and Development. *Evaluation of Solid Sorbents for Water Sampling* (EPA-600/2-80-193). By J. C. Harris et al. of Arthur D. Little, Inc., Cambridge, MA, 1980. (NTIS PB 81-106585).

> U.S. Dept. of Energy, Office of Energy Assessments. *Emerging Energy Security Issues: Natural Gas in the Gulf Nations, An Overview of Middle East Resources, Export Potentials, and Markets* (DOE/EP/10050—T8). By R. D. Ripple and R. E. Hagen of East-West Center, Honolulu, HI (United States). Sept. 1995. (Program on Resources: Energy-Minerals; Report Series No. 4). Text from: DOE Information Bridge, http://www.osti.gov/servlets/purl/110228-TsSuRr/webviewable/110228.pdf; Accessed: 2/9/02.

> U.S. Environmental Protection Agency, Office of Pollution Prevention and Toxics. *Enhancing Supply Chain Performance With Environmental Cost Information: Examples from Commonwealth Edison, Andersen Corporation, and Ashland Chemical* (EPA 742-R-00-002). Apr. 2000. (Environmental Accounting Project, USEPA). Available at: http://www.epa.gov/oppt/acctg/eacasestudies.pdf; Accessed: 2/10/02.

S6b A citation to a government report should include, as applicable: Issuing Agency; Title; Personal Authors, if any; Publisher Information; Series; and a Note including the abbreviated clearinghouse name and the report identification number. If the medium is other than paper, it should be noted.

> Pennsylvania. Governor's Justice Commission. *Comprehensive Plan for the Improvement of Criminal Justice in Pennsylvania.* Harrisburg, 1978. (NTIS microfiche PB 284 551).

> U.S. Dept. of Health, Education and Welfare, Bureau of Occupational and Adult Education. *Counseling Implications of Re-Entry Women's Life Experiences.* By Ruth Ekstrom et al. Washington: DHEW, 1980. (ERIC microfiche ED 209 600).

> U.S. Dept. of Justice, Office of Juvenile Justice and Delinquency Protection. *Reducing Youth Gun Violence: An Overview of Programs and Initiatives—Program Report* (NCJ no. 154303). Washington, May 1996. Available from: NCJRS Abstracts Database, http://www.ncjrs.org/pdffiles/redyouth.pdf; Accessed: 2/9/02.

> U.S. National Bureau of Standards, Center for Fire Research. *Effect of Ventilation on the Rates of Heat, Smoke and Carbon Monoxide Production in a Typical Jail Cell Fire.* By B. T. Lee. Washington, 1982. (U.S. National Criminal Justice Reference Service *Microfiche Collection,* NCJ-84592).

S6c A citation to a non-governmental report should include, as applicable: Personal Author, Title, Publisher Information, Series, and a Note including the abbreviated clearinghouse name and the report identification number. If the medium is other than paper, it should be noted.

> Greeley, Andrew M. *The Rediscovery of Diversity.* Chicago: National Opinion Research Center, 1971. (ERIC microfiche ED 068 602).

Powell, Margaret S. *The U.S. Federal Depository Library Program and U.S. Government Information in an Electronic Environment: Issues for the Transition and the Millenium.* Presented at the 65th IFLA Council and General Conference, Bangkok, Thailand, Aug. 20-28, 1999. (ERIC Document ED 441 448; 911 kb). Available at: ERIC Document Reproduction Service, http://www.edrs.com/; Accessed: 2/13/02.

S6d A citation to an unpublished report should include, as applicable: personal author, Title, Date, and a Note including the abbreviated clearinghouse name and report identification number. If the medium is other than paper, it should be noted.

Basefsky, Stuart. *Bibliographic Citations and U.S. Government Publications.* 1979. (ERIC microfiche ED 223 251).

S6e Some contract reports are distributed both by the GPO and by clearinghouses. If you have a document distributed by the U.S. Government Printing Office which also has a clearinghouse "availability statement, " you should alert your reader in a note about this dual distribution.

U.S. National Aeronautics and Space Administration. *Environmental Exposure Effects on Composite Materials for Commercial Aircraft.* By Martin N. Gibbons and Daniel J. Hoffman of Advanced Structures, Boeing Commercial Airplane Co., Seattle, WA (NASACR-3502; microfiche). Washington: Government Printing Office, 1982. (NAS1.26:3502; also available NTIS microfiche NASA-CR-3502).

S7 *Code of Federal Regulations* (CFR) and the *Federal Register* (FR)

Executive branch agencies of the federal government create regulatory law. These regulations typically guide the details for implementing laws passed by Congress. Typically, the regulations are issued first in draft form for public comment in a daily publication called the *Federal Register*. The final forms of the regulations are later codified in the *Code of Federal Regulations* (CFR).

S7a To cite the *Code of Federal Regulations* give the name of the section, title number, *Code of Federal Regulations*, Title and part numbers, and edition. Since the CFR is reissued annually and substantial regulatory changes may be enacted, inclusion of the edition statement is essential. Page numbers are not necessary, but can be included. Publishing Information is not necessary.

"Product Noise Labeling," Title 40 *Code of Federal Regulations*, Pt. 211. 1991 ed.

Most electronic forms of regulations are updated more frequently than the update cycle for the print version. For this reason it is very important to include a date indicating the last changes made to the electronic version. The source of this information will vary among electronic sources. The following examples show two different ways each electronic source provides this information.

"Temporary Employment of Aliens in the United States," Title 20 *Code of Federal Regulations*, Sec. 655. Revised as of 4/1/01. Available from: GPO Access, http://www.gpo.gov/nara/cfr/; Accessed: 2/10/02.

"Minimum Wage Determinations," Title 41 *Code of Federal Regulations*, Sec. 50-202.2. (Current Through 1/24/2002). Text from: *Regulations*. Available from: Congressional Universe, LexisNexis; Accessed: 2/10/02.

S7b A citation to the *Federal Register* should allow the reader to find the exact section cited without having to search the entire text of a daily issue; that is, it should be cited in the manner of a periodical (Section 6.0). In addition, include the type of action represented (e.g., final rule, proposed rule to amend, notice, etc.).

To cite the *Federal Register* give the name of the section, any identifying agency report numbers, volume of the *Federal Register*, issue, date, and pagination. You should also include as part of the section name an indication of what action is represented (e.g., final rule, proposed rule to amend executive order, proclamation).

"Air Contaminants; Proposed Rule," *Federal Register* 57:114 (12 June 1992) pp. 26002-26601.

Most systems have developed a unique identifier for each section. This identifier should be included in parentheses immediately following the section title:

"Security Considerations in the Design of the Flightdeck on Transport Category Airplanes" (Final Rule; DOCID:fr15ja02-14), *Federal Register* 67:10 (Jan. 15, 2002) pp. 2117-2128. Available from: GPO Access, http://frwebgate2.access.gpo.gov; Accessed: 2/10/02.

"National Vaccine Injury Compensation Program: Revisions and Additions to the Vaccine Injury Table—II" (Final Rule; RIN 0905-AE52), *Federal Register* 62:34 (Feb. 20, 1997) pp. 7685-7690. Available from: Academic Universe, LexisNexis; Accessed: 2/10/02.

S7c States publish regulations in patterns similar to the U.S. sources: there is usually a codified version as well as a weekly or daily source for current changes and notices. Titles vary from state to state.

"Physical Education and Athletics," Title 22 *Pennsylvania Administrative Code* (Matthew Bender), Sec. 4.27. Contains all activity through 30 PA.B. 4886, Sept. 16, 2000. Text from: *Regulations*. Available from: State Capital Universe, LexisNexis; Accessed: 2/10/02.

"Required Immunizations," Title 25 *Texas Administrative Code* Sec. 97.63. Rules in effect as of 1/31/02. Text from: *Regulations*. Available from: State Capital Universe, LexisNexis; Accessed: 2/10/02.

S8 Congressional Directory

The *Congressional Directory* is published once every Congress and is updated by a paper supplement. Since the title implies the Issuing Agency, it is not necessary to repeat the agency.

Congressional Directory, 1991-92. 102nd Congress. Washington: Government Printing Office, 1991.

Congressional Directory, 106th Congress. Oct. 2000 online revision. Available at: GPO Access, http://www.access.gpo.gov/congress/browse-cd-oct00.html; Accessed: 2/6/02.

S9 *Congressional Globe*, *Register of Debates*, and *Annals of Congress*

The *Congressional Globe*, the *Register*, and the *Annals* are cited much like the *Congressional Record*. Consult the *Quick Citation Guide to Legislative/Parliamentary Sources*, L1.1, for additional examples. Since there are no consistent volume numbers, the number of the Congress, the session number, and the part, if applicable, must be given. If there is no title, a descriptive statement can be used in its place.

ANNALS OF CONGRESS

"Trial of Samuel Chase," *Annals of Congress* 8th Congress, 2nd Session (1804-1805) pp. 81-676.

CONGRESSIONAL GLOBE

Sen. Polk (MO). Speech on the State of the Union, *Congressional Globe* 36th Congress, 2nd Sess., Pt. 1 (Jan. 14, 1861) pp. 355-360.

Sen. Polk (MO). Speech on the State of the Union, *Congressional Globe* 36th Congress, 2nd Sess. (Jan. 14, 1861) pp. 355-360. (Library of Congress, American Memory). Available at: *A Century of Lawmaking for a New Nation*, http://memory.loc.gov/-ammem/amlaw/lwcg.html; Accessed: 2/9/02.

CONGRESSIONAL GLOBE, APPENDIX

Sen. Smith (CT). "Claims for French Spoliations," *Congressional Globe, Appendix* 31st Congress, 2nd Session (Jan. 16, 1851) pp. 115-126.

REGISTER OF DEBATES

"Gratitude to Lafayette," *Register of Debates* 18th Congress, 2nd Sess. (Dec. 21, 1824) pp. 28-35.

S10 Constitutions

Constitutions can be published as separate publications, within yearbooks or legislative manuals, or as part of a commercially produced collection of constitutions. Where you locate the constitution will determine how you cite the material.

S10a If citing a whole constitution, give your source and its date. Since most constitutions have been amended over time, it may be important for the reader to know which version is being cited. If necessary, examine any prefatory material or notes to determine the dates of amendments. If this information is taken from anywhere other than the title page, include it.

> Australia. Parliament. *The Constitution of the Commonwealth of Australia, as Altered to 30 June 1987.* Canberra: Australian Government Publishing Service, 1990.

> *The Constitution of the United States of America: Analysis and Interpretation* (S. Doc. 99-16). Washington: Government Printing Office, 1987. (Serial Set 13611).

> *The Constitution of the United States of America: Analysis and Interpretation* (S. Doc.106-8). 1998 Suppl. Available at: http://www.access.gpo.gov/congress/-senate/constitution/index.html; Accessed: 2/9/02.

S10b It is more likely you will want to cite a part or section from a constitution. Examine the constitution to determine its organization. The format of a constitution varies greatly from country to country. The object in developing your citation is to unambiguously identify the section of the constitution you are citing. Look for designations such as parts, titles, sections, and articles. Determine the hierarchy within the structure and construct your citation using as many pieces of the hierarchy as may be necessary to identify that portion of the document. It is not necessary to use the name of each part or title, unless it seems necessary to clarify your citation.

> Australia. Parliament. *The Constitution of the Commonwealth of Australia, as Altered to 30 June 1987.* Chpt. I, Pt. II Sec.15(a). Canberra: Australian Government Publishing Service, 1990.

> U.S. Constitution. Art. 1, Sect. 1.

S10c When a constitution is found in a larger work, cite as in *Titles of Chapters and Other Book Parts* (Section 2.3).

> Australia. "The Constitution, as Altered to 1 December 1977 . . . ." pp. 592-654. In *Parliamentary Handbook of the Commonwealth of Australia.* 25th ed., 1991. Canberra: Australian Government Publishing Service, 1991.

S10d When the constitution is part of a collection of constitutions published by a commercial publisher, give information on both the constitution and the collection in your citation.

> *Constitution of Belize, 1981.* Text from: Georgetown University/Organization of American States. *Political Database of the Americas,* http://www.georgetown.edu/-pdba/Constitutions/Belize/belize.html; Accessed: 2/9/02.

> Vietnam. "Constitution of the Socialist Republic of Vietnam [as amended through July 15, 1989]." In *Constitutions of the World.* Dobbs Ferry, New York: Oceana Publications, 1992.

S11 Court Cases

The *Bluebook: A Uniform System of Citation* (17th ed.) provides the most detailed and extensive description developed for the legal profession of how to cite court cases and other legal sources. This section is based on the citation rules described in *Rule 18 –Electronic Media and Other Nonprint Resources.* "This rule requires the use and citation of traditional printed sources, except when the information is not available in a printed source…" Simply stated, VEF sources for court cases are still considered less authoritative and should be considered "parallel" citations to the traditional print source.[1] Thus, the following examples include, when possible, a parallel citation (same case in a different publication or source) to the print source for a case, as well as the citation to the VEF source.

Although the parallel print source can be omitted, this information allows users who may not have access to commercial sources additional avenues for locating a case. In addition, as long as the print sources are considered "authoritative" by the legal profession, these standards should be maintained in other disciplines as well.

U.S. REPORTS (Supreme Court)

Include the full name of the case (plaintiff v. defendant); court (if not included in database or file name) and all identifying case citations, docket number or order numbers (this may be listed in some finding tools); date of the decision; a parallel citation to the print source (if provided).

> Brown v. the Board of Education of Topeka, Shawnee County, Kansas, 347 *U.S. Reports* (17 May 1954) pp. 483-500.

Some VEF sources will not show inclusive paging and will not provide the complete name of the case reporter set. In short, they will give a citation in the *Bluebook* form. Use this citation, when necessary.

> Radio Corp. v. U.S., 341 US 412. Available at: <u>www.fedworld.gov/supcourt/index.htm</u>; Accessed: 2/9/02.

A CASE IN WHICH THE PAGE NUMBERS HAVE NOT YET BEEN SET

> National Cable and Telecommunications Assoc., Inc. v. Gulf Power Co. et al. 534 U.S. ___ (2002). Available at: <u>http://www.supremecourtus.gov/opinions/opinions.html</u>; Accessed: 2/10/02.

STATE COURTS

> Commonwealth of Pennsylvania v. Warren Peterson, Aug. 19, 1991 (408 Pa. Super. 22, 596 A.2d 172). Text from: *State Case Law: Pennsylvania*. Available from: Academic Universe, LexisNexis; Accessed: 2/10/02.

ADMINISTRATIVE COURTS

> Goodless Electric Co. v. and Local Union No. 7, International Brotherhood of Electrical Workers, AFL-CIO, 321 NLRB no. 18, Apr. 30, 1996. Available at: <u>http://www.nlrb.gov/bound321.html</u>; Accessed: 2/10/02.

UNPUBLISHED DECISIONS

> Emma C. et al., v. Delaine Eastin et al. (United States District Court for the Northern District of California) 2001 U.S. Dist. LexisNexis 16099 (Oct. 4, 2001). Text from: *Federal Case Law*. Available from: Academic Universe, LexisNexis; Accessed: 2/22/02.

> Christopher Roche v. Kenneth Pettibone (B137341, Court of Appeal of California, Second Appellate District, Division One) 2001 Cal. App. LEXISNEXIS 974 (Oct. 11, 2001). Text from: *State Case Law (California)*. Available from: Academic Universe, LexisNexis; Accessed: 2/22/02.

ATTORNEY GENERAL OPINIONS

> Re: State Departments (Office of the Attorney General of the State of Kansas) Opinion no. 2001-53, 2001 Kan. AG LexisNexis 53. Text from: *Tax Law (State Tax Cases)*. Available from: Academic Universe, LexisNexis; Accessed: 2/22/02.

INTERNATIONAL COURT OF JUSTICE

> Continental Shelf (Libyan Arab Jamahiriya/Malta) Order of 26 Apr. 1983, *International Court of Justice Reports 1983*, pp. 3-4.

EUROPEAN COMMUNITIES COURT OF JUSTICE REPORTS

The year on the cover should be used as the volume number; the issue number need not be used since the pagination is continuous throughout the year.

Pierre Favre v. Commission of the European Communities, Order of Feb. 7, 1983 *European Communities Court of Justice Reports 1983*, pp. 199-201.

Mary Carpenter v. Secretary of State for the Home Department (Case C-60/00) Sept. 13, 2001. European Court of Justice, Text from: Eur-Lex (Case Law). Available at: http://europa.eu.int/eur-lex/en/search/search_case.html; Accessed: 2/10/02.

REPORTS OF THE EUROPEAN COMMISSION AND COURT OF HUMAN RIGHTS

Citations to cases reported in the *Yearbook of the European Convention on Human Rights* should include, after the type of agreement, whose decision (the Commission's or the Court's) is being reported.

Max von Sydow v. Sweden (Decision of the Commission, May 12, 1987), *Yearbook of the European Convention on Human Rights 1987*, pp. 55-72.

Citations to cases reported in *Publications of the European Court of Human Rights* present special problems because this publication is not organized like other court reports. It has two series judgments and pleadings. The same case may appear in either series a number of times over a number of years. For these reasons you should include the series and the publishing information. You can omit pages because each volume is devoted to a single case.

Case of Young, James, and Webster (Judgment of Oct. 18, 1982), *Publications of the European Court of Human Rights: Series A: Judgments and Decisions* Vol. 55. Strasbourg: Council of Europe, Registry of the Court, 1983.

Affaire H.L. c. France (REF00003161) (Requête n° 42189/98). Decided: Février 7, 2002. (French Language only). Text from: *Judgments and Decisions.* Available at: European Court of Human Rights, http://www.echr.coe.int/Eng/Judgments.htm; Accessed: 2/10/02.

For Series B there will be a range of dates instead of a date of decision. Include this after the series name.

Sunday Times Case, *Publications of the European Court of Human Rights: Series B: Pleadings, Oral Arguments and Documents (1977-1980)* Vol. 28. Strasbourg: Council of Europe, Registry of the Court, 1982.

S12 E-Mail Messages and List-Serv Messages

Correspondence and information in e-mail and list-serv messages are frequently cited. Include the following information: name of the sender, including e-mail address, if available; subject or title of the message followed by qualifier; name of the intended recipient, preceded by "Message to:" and followed by e-mail address, if available; original date of the message; date message was accessed; length of message, if provided by the system; name of Electronic Bulletin Board (EBB) or discussion group containing the message (if appropriate).

Cheney, Debora (DLC@PSULIAS). Subject: Citing Electronic Formats (E-Mail). Message to: Elizabeth Montgomery (EBM@HARVARDA), Dec. 5, 1992. Accessed: Dec. 6, 1992).

Davis, J. Mike. Subject: *Chronic Disease Prevention CD-ROM* (E-Mail). Message to: GOVDOC-L Discussion List (Govdoc-L@psuvm.psu.edu), Mar. 2, 1992. Accessed: Mar. 3, 1992).

S13 *Economic Report of the President*

The *Economic Report of the President* appears in two editions each year: the Congressional and the executive branch version. The Congressional version will have a House document number.

CONGRESSIONAL VERSION

Economic Report of the President February 1992 (H. Doc.102-177). Washington: Government Printing Office, 1992.

EXECUTIVE BRANCH VERSION

> *Economic Report of the President February 1992.* Washington: Government Printing Office, 1992.

ELECTRONIC EDITIONS

> *Economic Report of the President, 2002* (PDF; 3.2 mb). Available at: GPO Access, http://w3.access.gpo.gov/eop/; Accessed: 2/9/02.

S14 Embassy, Consulate, and Information Agency Publications

Citations to publications of embassies and information agencies should include the city, state and country (if necessary) in which the embassy or agency is located. Include this information in parentheses following the name of the embassy. If, for alphabetization purposes, it is desirable to keep all publications related to a country together in your bibliography, the Embassy name (Issuing Agency) can begin with the country name. For example, Embassy of Madagascar would become Madagascar, Embassy. See also Press Releases, S25.

> Argentine Consulate (Hong Kong). *Traders in Hong Kong.* The Embassy, n.d. Available at: http://home.netvigator.com/~consarhk/; Accessed: 3/7/02.

> German Information Center (New York, NY). *Germany's Contribution to the Gulf Effort* (Fact Sheet). New York: German Information Center, 1991.

> Embassy of Madagascar (Washington, D.C.). Madagascar: *Tourism Information: Arts and Crafts.* Available from: Electronic Embassy, http://www.embassy.org/-madagascar/index.html; Accessed: 3/7/02.

> Royal Embassy of Saudi Arabia (London). *Saudi Justice Through British Eyes* [Home Page]. The Embassy, n.d. Available at: http://www.saudiembassy.org.uk/index2.htm; Accessed: 3/7/02.

> Embassy of the Republic of Slovenia (Washington, D.C.). *Reasons to Invest in Slovenia.* The Embassy, n.d. Available from: Electronic Embassy, http://www.embassy.org/-slovenia/econ2.htm; Accessed: 3/7/02.

S15 *Foreign Relations of the United States* (FRUS)

Foreign Relations of the United States is a compilation of diplomatic papers of the U.S. published since 1861. The set is arranged by year and within the year, by volumes (and occasionally parts) which cover various geographic areas or policy issues. Due to official rules regarding classification and secrecy, these papers are not released for publication for many years; thus, the publication date will differ considerably from the year covered. Therefore, it is vital to your reader that you include both dates: one for locating and one for informational purposes.

> *Foreign Relations of the United States, 1914.* Washington: Government Printing Office, 1914. Electronic facsimile. Available at: University of Wisconsin Libraries, http://www.wisc.edu/wendt/frus/; Accessed: 2/9/02.

> *Foreign Relations of the United States, 1949, Vol. VIII, Pt. 2: The Far East and Australia.* Washington: Government Printing Office, 1976.

> *Foreign Relations of the United States, Kennedy Administration, Vol. I, Vietnam, 1961.* Washington: Government Printing Office, 1988. Available at: http://www.state.gov/-r/pa/ho/frus; Accessed: 2/15/02.

S15a To cite a single document within *Foreign Relations of the United States*:

> "Panama: Sanitary Conditions on the Isthmus of Panama (no. 91)" pp. 706–708. In *Foreign Relations of the United States, 1904.* Washington: Government Printing Office, 1904. Electronic facsimile. Available at: University of Wisconsin, Madison, Libraries, http://www.wisc.edu/wendt/frus/; Accessed: 2/9/02.

> "The Secretary of State to the Embassy in Greece," pp. 533-534. In *Foreign Relations of the United States, 1951, Vol. V: The Near East and North Africa.* Washington: Government Printing Office, 1982.

S15b Some volumes fall outside the annual series. These are compilations devoted to a single subject (Japan 1931-1941; Paris Peace Conference, 1919; etc). In citing these documents include the individual volume titles to distinguish them from the annual compilations.

> *Foreign Relations of the United States: The Conferences at Washington, 1941-42, and Casablanca, 1943.* Washington: Government Printing Office, 1968.

S16 Freedom of Information Documents

For documents obtained under the federal Freedom of Information Act (FOIA), you should try to identify the documents as precisely as possible. The element used will depend on the nature of the document and the amount of information given.

Some elements which should be included are: personal author and agency affiliation; title or subject; type of document, including identifying numbers or other information; date; and number of pages.

You should also name the agency from which you obtained the document, the nature of your request, the date of your request, and the date of receipt. With this information your reader could (theoretically) get the same documents.

LETTER

> Hamilton, Donald R. U.S. Embassy, El Salvador. [Subject: Roatan Island]. Letter to Stephen Dachi, U.S. Information Agency; Mar. 2, 1983. 2 pp. Obtained under the Freedom of Information Act from U.S. Information Agency; requested as "Materials on Radio Marti" May 1983; received June 1983.

FORM (contract, requisition, etc.)

> 50 KW Antenna Design and Proposed Site Evaluation, Antigua, W.I. Request for Supplies/Service; Order No. A226842; May 24, 1982. 7 pp. Obtained under the Freedom of Information Act from U.S. Information Agency; requested as "Materials on Radio Marti," May 1983; received June 1983.

MEMORANDUM

> Fernandez, John. Conference by High-Ranking State Department Officials on Radio Marti and the Hawkins Bill (S. 602). Memorandum to Shay, Rodriguez and Briss; Mar. 4, 1983. 3 pp. Obtained under the Freedom of Information Act from U.S. Information Agency; requested as "Materials on Radio Marti" May 1983; received June 1983.

PAPER (no author given, no date)

> Assessment of the Effect of Radio Free Cuba (RFC) on the Second Session, Region 11 Medium Frequency Broadcasting Conference, Rio de Janeiro, Nov. 1981. Working paper. n.d. 2 pp. Obtained under the Freedom of Information Act from U.S. Information Agency; requested as "Materials on Radio Marti," May 1983; received June 1983.

PAPER (no author, omissions noted; date implied by text)

> VOA Requirements in the Caribbean. Position Paper No. 5C [missing pages]. [1981?]. 6 pp. Obtained under the Freedom of Information Act from U.S. Information Agency; requested as "Materials on Radio Marti," May 1983; received June 1983.

TELEGRAM (include, if given, reference numbers, time, sender, and receiver)

> International Telecommunications Union. Plenipotentiary Conference Nairobi . . . 952Z 5 Nov. 1982, 10322 (incoming telegram NAIROB28119). 3 pp. Obtained under the Freedom of Information Act from U.S. Dept. of State; requested as "Materials on Radio Marti," May 1983; received June 1983.

REPORT (include identifying number)

> Castro on Radio Marti. Aug. 19, 1982 (Correspondent Rpt. #2-8806). 1 p. Obtained under the Freedom of Information Act from U.S. Information Agency; requested as "Materials on Radio Marti," May 1983; received June 1983.

> U.S. Federal Bureau of Investigation. *Communist Infiltration—Motion Picture Industry (COMPICS) (Excerpts)*—Part 1a (File Number 100-138754; Serial: 4; Part 1/15). (Freedom of Information Act). Available at: http://foia.fbi.gov/compic.htm; Accessed: 2/9/02.

S16a Most states have statutes similar to the federal Freedom of Information Act through which citizens can request unpublished state documents. The citation elements for such documents are similar to those for FOIA material: personal author, state, and agency affiliation, if applicable; title or subject; document type; any identifying numbers; date; pagination; agency from which the material was requested; nature of the request; date of request; and date of receipt.

> LaVine, William. Pennsylvania. Dept. of Environmental Resources. Kepone Levels in Spring Creek. Report and Data Gathered from Last Fish Kill, May 1981. 7 pp. Obtained under the Pa. Open Records Act; requested as "Spring Creek Kepone Levels," June 1981; received Dec. 1981.

S17 *Journals of the Continental Congress*

There have been many editions of the *Journals*. How you cite them will depend upon the organization of the edition used. In every case the Publisher Information should be given. The Library of Congress edition is the most complete and most widely available. Its volumes are numbered consecutively; therefore, the volume number will locate an item precisely. However, it is a good idea to include the date of the Continental Congress in parentheses for your reader's convenience.

SINGLE ENTRY OR DOCUMENT WITHIN A VOLUME

> "Address to the People of Great Britain," pp. 81-90. In U.S. Library of Congress. *Journals of the Continental Congress 1774-1789*, Vol. I (1774). Washington: Government Printing Office, 1904.

> "…Respecting Sundry Passages in the… *Pennsylvania Packet or General Advertiser* [newspaper], " pp. 29-31. In *Journals of the Continental Congress* Vol. XIII (Jan. 6, 1779). (Library of Congress, American Memory). Available at: *A Century of Lawmaking for a New Nation* http://memory.loc.gov/ammem/amlaw/lwjc.html; Accessed: 2/9/02.

INDIVIDUAL VOLUME

> U.S. Library of Congress. *Journals of the Continental Congress 1774-1789*, Vol. I (1774). Washington: Government Printing Office, 1904.

THE WHOLE SET

> U.S. Library of Congress. *Journals of the Continental Congress 1774-1789*. Washington: Government Printing Office, 1904.

S18 League of Nations

League of Nations documents fall into two classes: "official publications" and documents which were issued by League agencies, such as the Information Section, but which are not considered official.

Official documents carry the official publication number, usually in the upper right-hand corner of the title page. The number designates to whom the document was distributed, in what sequence, in what year, and in what subject category. Put it after the title in parentheses. This number is used for classification in many League documents collections. You may also find series numbers which you should include in the appropriate place.

League of Nations. *How to Make the League of Nations Known and to Develop the Spirit of International Cooperation* (C.515.M. 174.1927.XIIA). Geneva, 1927. (Publications of the League of Nations XIIA Intellectual Cooperation C.I.C.I. 190).

League of Nations. Conference for the Reduction and Limitation of Armaments. *Co-Operation of the Press in the Organisation of Peace* (Official Number: Conf. D.143). Geneva, Nov. 1, 1932. Available at: League of Nations Statistical and Disarmament Documents, Northwestern University Libraries, http://digital.library.northwestern.edu/-league/le000039.pdf; Accessed: 2/10/02.

S18a For some conference documents the official publication number may not be indicated on the document. In that case, give as much information as you can find on the document including the meeting dates, conference number, and sales number (if any).

League of Nations. Conference for the Reduction and Limitation of Armaments. *Verbatim Record (Revised) of the 18th Plenary Meeting . . .* July 23, 1932 . . . (Conf.D/PV.18). n.p., 1932. (Sales No. 1932.IX.60).

S18b If you are citing a League document from a microform collection, cite the document and then the collection, giving the location of the document in the collection.

League of Nations. *Protection of Minorities in Poland: Petition and Annexes*, 23 June 1931 (C.306.1932.IB and C.306(I).1932.IB). Geneva, 1932. In *League of Nations Documents, 1919-1946*. New Haven, CT: Research Publications, 1975. (Reel 1B-18).

S18c When citing an unofficial publication, be as specific as you can about the Issuing Agency. You will not find League numbers on unofficial publications.

League of Nations. Secretariat. *The Aims, Methods and Activities of the League of Nations*. Rev. ed. Geneva, 1938.

S18d The League of Nations produced several periodicals over its existence. Cite these as you would any periodical.

Anigstein, Ludwik. "Malaria and Anophelines in Siam," *Quarterly Bulletin of the Health Organisation* 1:2 (June 1932) pp. 233-308. (Published by the League of Nations).

Be sure to cite special editions as such.

"The Appeal of the Finnish Government to the League of Nations," Special Supplement to the *Monthly Summary of the League of Nations*, December 1939.

S19 Legislative Journals

Many governments publish an official legislative journal recording legislative action. They may include submitted committee reports, messages from the governor and other executive branch department heads, bill readings (versions), and votes. In the absence of a verbatim record of debate, these journals provide the supporting materials related to the legislative process. Other governments, particularly local governments are more informal and may publish their committee minutes, agendas, and reports separately, rather than as a "legislative journal." In both situations, these sources are increasingly accessible via the WWW.

Since titles are not usually given to sections of the *Journals*, give the speaker, state, and subject. Then include Congress/legislative body, session, date, and page numbers.

Oxford City (U.K.). Council, Economic and Social Wellbeing Overview and Scrutiny Committee. *Minutes and Agenda. Mar. 6, 2002*. Available at: http://www.oxford.gov.uk/-oxford/minutes.nsf/search?Openform; Accessed: 3/5/02.

"S.B. no. 67, Of Marriage and Solemnization Thereof, Third Reading and Roll Call Vote, no. 132," pp. 526-27. In the Michigan. Legislature, House. *Journal*. No. 36 (May 3, 2001). Available at: http://argus.mileg.org/documents/20012002/journal/house/pdf/2001-HJ-05-03-036.pdf; Accessed: 11/15/01.

Albert, Carl (OK). Remarks, *Journal of the House of Representatives* 94th Congress, 1st Session (Jan. 14, 1975) pp. 2-4.

S20 Loose-leafs

Some government publications come in loose-leaf format so that they can be easily updated. These are usually the procedural documents of the government bureaucracy—manuals, guidelines, regulations, standards, etc. They are often massive and their internal organization may be complicated.

In citing these publications, you will usually be citing a specific part rather than the whole. The information to include will depend on the organization of the loose-leaf and will usually be the name of the part, the internal filing numbers, and a date. The date of the part to which you are referring is important, since it is entirely possible that the part you are citing will be superseded later by an amendment with the same number and name. The date will usually be printed at the top or bottom of each page.

Information about the volume or set should include: Issuing Agency, title, agency report number (if any), place, publisher, series number (if any), and "loose-leaf" in a note. You will note that the date of the main volume is omitted. If you can find an edition date for the whole publication, you may include it. However, it will be simply the date for the reprinted whole edition and the edition will likely include later changes.

Loose-leafs may be organized in many ways—by part number, by page number, or by some other system especially adapted to the contents of the loose-leaf. You must look at the publication and give the information that best locates the part you are citing.

S20a Parts of a Loose-leaf (Common Variations)

"Sampling for Inspection and Testing" (Method 1022; Feb. 1, 1980). In U.S. General Services Administration. *Paint, Varnish, Lacquer and Related Materials: Methods for Sampling and Testing.* Washington: Government Printing Office. (Federal Test Method Standard Number 141B). (Loose-leaf; GS2.8/7:141B).

"Chapter 5-1300: Fire Exits" (Supp. 4, 1975). In Philadelphia (PA). *Philadelphia Code.* (Loose-leaf).

"Reducing, Suspending, or Cancelling Food Stamp Benefits" (Sect. 543, Mar. 9, 1981). In Pennsylvania Dept. of Public Welfare. Office of Family Assistance. *Public Assistance Eligibility Manual.* Harrisburg. (Loose-leaf).

"Agreement in the form of an exchange of letters between the European Economic Community and Turkey on imports into the Community of untreated olive oil . . . Nov. 1, 1977 to Oct. 31, 1978" (Sect. Gen. 1, p. 1; June 30, 1979). In European Communities. Council. *Collected Acts: Association Between the European Economic Community and Turkey*, Vol. 2. n.p.: Secretariat of the Council of the European Communities. (Loose-leaf).

"Performance Funding System" (pp. 1-10; Feb. 1977). In U.S. Dept. of Housing and Urban Development. *Performance Funding System Handbook* (HUD Handbook 7475.13). Washington: HUD. (Loose-leaf; HH1.6/6:7475.13).

"Telegraphic Bids" (Sect. 1-2.202-2 FPR Amendment 229; Mar. 1983). In U.S. General Services Administration. *Federal Procurement Regulations.* 2nd ed.; reprinted 1981. Washington: Government Printing Office. (Loose-leaf; GS1.6/5:964/rep.5).

"Federal Employees Required to File Financial Disclosure Reports" (FPM Letter 734-1; 4 Nov. 1982). In U.S. Office of Personnel Management. *Federal Personnel Manual.* Washington: Government Printing Office, 1993. (Loose-leaf; PM1.14/2).

S21 Official Gazettes

A common method used by foreign governments to inform the public of new laws, regulations, and other items of government business is to issue an official gazette. The format of a gazette will vary considerably from country to country. As with other legal documents, look for identifying numbers that should be included in a citation. Include the title (short title if available), volume and part numbers, source, and pagination.

"Disclosure of Charges (Banks) Regulation," *Canada Gazette*, Pt. II, 126:12 (June 3, 1992) pp. 2256-2258. (Registration: SOR/92-324).

"Regulations Amending the United Nations Suppression of Terrorism Regulations" (SOR/2002-42), *Canada Gazette,* Pt. II, Extra 136, no. 1 (Jan. 11, 2002) pp. 1-3. Available at: http://canada.gc.ca/gazette/part2/pdf/g2-136x1.pdf; Accessed: 2/10/02.

The name of an agency issuing a regulation or notice may be included to clarify a citation.

Canadian Radio-Television and Telecommunications Commission. "Public Notice 1992-54. Private French-Language Television. Preamble to Decisions 1992-544 to 1992-565," *Canada Gazette,* Pt. I, 126:34 (Aug. 22, 1992) pp. 2624-2629.

Regulations are similar to laws in that they are often published in both chronological forms and subject compilations. The rules for citing them are similar to rules for citing laws. Examine the format of the document. Determine the title, use the short title if there is one, and any identifying numbers attached to the regulation.

"Foreign Investment Review Regulations," *Consolidated Regulations of Canada, 1978.* v. 9, chpt. 872, pp. 6397-6412. Ottawa: Queen's Printer for Canada, 1978.

"Quarantine Act: Regulations" *Consolidated Statutes of Canada* R.S.C. 1985, c. Q-1, s. 21. Current through Vol. 136 *Canada Gazette* No. 5, Pt. 1. Text from: *Legal Research* (*Canadian Statutes and Regulations*). Available from: Academic Universe, LexisNexis; Accessed: 2/10/02.

S22 Organization of American States (OAS)

To cite official records of the Organization of American States you should give, as applicable: the full name of the issuing body (including the number, date, and place for meeting records); the title and date of the document; its OAS classification number; official record; and the place and year of publication (if known).

Organization of American States. Inter-American Nuclear Energy Commission, 10th Meeting, 11-15 July 1977, Lima, Peru. *Final Report* (OEA/Ser.C/VIII.10). Official Record. Washington, 1977.

Organization of American States. General Assembly, 31st Regular Session, 3rd Plenary Session, San José, Costa Rica, June 2001. *Resolution: The Human Rights of All Migrant Workers and Their Families* (AG/RES. 1775 XXXI-O/01). June 5, 2001. Available at: http://www.oas.org/; Accessed: 2/10/02.

S22a If you are citing an official document in the microfiche collection, you must add the year, the name of the collection, and the microfiche filing number. You can omit "Official Record" as an edition since it will be given as the title of the collection.

Organization of American States. Ministers of Foreign Affairs, 17th Meeting of Consultation, Sept. 21, 1978, Washington, D.C. *Note from the Ambassador . . . of Nicaragua Requesting Distribution of the Note . . . Concerning Document OAS/Ser L/V/II.45 . . . "Report on . . . Human Rights in Nicaragua"* Feb. 15, 1979 (OEA/Ser.F/II.17; Doc. 27/19). Washington, n.d. (1979 OAS Official Records microfiche 79-00002).

S23 Patents and Trademarks

To cite a patent granted by the U.S. government, you will probably have in hand either the patent itself or its abstract in the *Official Gazette*. In either case it is recommended that you give your reader the name of the invention, the inventor, the patent number, and the date granted. A citation to the abstract will also include a citation into the correct volume of the *Official Gazette*.

PATENT

>   "Implement Wheel" by William Schumacher. U.S. Patent 4,376,554 (Mar. 15, 1983). Available at:
>   United States Patent and Trademark Office, *Patent and Full-Text Image Database*,
>   http://www.uspto.gov/patft/index.html; Accessed: 2/10/02.

OFFICIAL GAZETTE

>   "Implement Wheel" by William Schumacher. U.S. Patent 4,376,554 (Mar. 15, 1983), *Official
>   Gazette of the United States Patent and Trademark Office* 1028:3 (Mar. 15, 1983) p. 517.

For trademark images, include the title of the trademark; status (registered, pending, etc.); date
published; owner; unique identifying number, such as the serial number, database accession
number, etc.

>   "PennState 1855" (Registered, Nov. 17, 1992; Serial number 74-081-576). Published, Aug. 25,
>   1992. Pennsylvania State University. Text and Image from: U.S. Patent and Trademark Office,
>   *Trademark Electronic Search System (TESS)*, http://www.uspto.gov/-web/menu/tm.html;
>   Accessed: 2/10/02.

S24 Presidental Documents

Presidential statements and other materials are issued in a current weekly edition and in a
permanent edition. Either source can be cited. Presidential materials are now widely available on
the WWW. Consult rules in Sections E1.0-E6.0 for help citing these sources.

>   Bush, George W. *State of the Union Address*. Jan. 29, 2002. Available at: GPO Access:
>   http://www.access.gpo.gov/congress/sou/sou02.html; Accessed: 2/12/02.

S24a The *Weekly Compilation of Presidential Documents* can be cited like a typical periodical.
The title should include the president name in reverse order, title of the article, nature of the
document (e.g., speech, executive order, proclamation), and the date of the document.

>   Clinton, William J. "Introduction of Illegal Aliens" (Executive Order 12807, May 29, 1992), *Weekly
>   Compilation of Presidential Documents* 28:22 (June 1, 1992) pp. 923-924.

If the nature of the document and its date are given in the title, they do not need to be repeated.

>   Reagan, Ronald W. "The President's News Conference of October 19, 1983." *Weekly
>   Compilation of Presidential Documents* 19:42 (Oct. 24, 1983) pp. 1465-1472.

>   Bush, George W. "Remarks on Signing the USA Patriot Act of 2001" (Oct. 26, 2001). Text from:
>   *Weekly Compilation of Presidential Documents* (size: 7486; DocID: pd29oc01_txt-26). Available
>   at: GPO Access, http://www.access.gpo.gov/-nara/nara003.html; Accessed: 1/16/02.

S24b The *Public Papers of the Presidents* are bound permanent editions and compilations of
Presidential documents. The volumes are arranged by President, year, and volume number (if
there is more than one volume in the year). Include the title followed by the President's name.
Since there are other non-governmental editions of *The Public Papers*, it is necessary to include
Publisher Information.

CITING A PART WITHIN A VOLUME

>   "Inaugural Address" (Jan. 20, 1961) pp. 1-3. In *Public Papers of the Presidents of the United
>   States: John F. Kennedy, 1961*. Washington: Government Printing Office, 1962.

>   "Remarks to the Community in Pittsburgh" (Apr. 17, 1993) pp. 450-53. In *Public Papers of the
>   Presidents of the United States: William Jefferson Clinton, 1993* (Vol. 1). Available at: GPO
>   Access, http://www.gpo.gov/nara/pubpaps/srchpaps.html; Accessed: 1/16/02.

ALL THE VOLUMES OF A PRESIDENT

>   *Public Papers of the Presidents of the United States: John F. Kennedy*. Washington: Government
>   Printing Office, 1962-1964.

A SINGLE VOLUME OF A PRESIDENT

> *Public Papers of the Presidents of the United States: John F. Kennedy, 1961.* Washington: Government Printing Office, 1962.

A NON-GOVERNMENT EDITION

> *The Public Papers and Addresses of Franklin D. Roosevelt.* New York: Random House, 1938-1950.

S25 Press Releases

Citations to press releases and other informational notices from states, governments, and organizations should include an Issuing Agency and Geo/Political Designation, if appropriate, the date of the press release, and a medium/publication type (e.g., Press Release). See also Embassy, Consulate, and Information Agency Publications, S14.

> Virginia. Dept. of Alcoholic Beverage Control. *ABC Education Highlights the Positive with "Social Norms" Marketing Campaign* (Information/News Release). VA ABC Education Section, Nov. 19, 2001. Available at: http://www.abc.state.va.us/-newsrel/press135.html; Accessed: 1/19/02.

> "Consumer Price Index: December 2001" U.S. Dept. of Labor, Bureau of Labor Statistics. *News* (Jan. 16, 2002) pp. 3. Available at: http://www.bls.gov/news:release/-pdf/cpi.pdf; Accessed: 2/5/02.

> Ireland. Consulate General of Ireland (New York, NY). *Government Statement on the Maguire Case* (Press Release). New York: The Consulate, 16 June 1991.

> Uruguay Embassy (Washington, D.C.). *Uruguay: Free from "Mad Cow" Illness.* Release date: Aug. 7, 1997. Available from: Electronic Embassy, http://www.embassy.org/ipc/-press/uruguay/00000016.html; Accessed: 3/6/02.

> "National Currencies Have Practically Disappeared from Circulation" (Press Release) (DN: IP/02/63; Jan. 15, 2002). Available on: Rapid (Commission of the European Communities, Brussels), http://europa.eu.int/rapid/start/welcome.htm; Accessed: 1/15/02.

> United Kingdom. Cabinet Office. *Tony Blair Calls for Greater International Action to Tackle Global Health Crisis* (Press Release) (CAB 117/01), May 8, 2001. Available at: http://www.nds.coi.gov.uk/; Accessed: 11/13/01.

S26 Securities and Exchange Commission (SEC) Reports

The Securities and Exchange Commission (SEC) requires various financial reports from companies selling stock on national exchanges. These reports vary in periodicity and content. The best known is the annual 10-K report, but there are, among others, 1O-Q's, 8-K's, and 10-C's. These reports are filed with the SEC; some are also sent to stockholders. The reports are available in many forms from a variety of government and commercial sources.

Include: Company Name, Date of Filing, Type of Filing. Publication city: Company, Publication date.

PAPER FORMAT

> Ford Motor Corporation. *Form 10-K Annual Report . . . FY Ended Dec. 31, 1991.* Detroit, MI, 1992.

MICROFORMAT

Include the micropublisher's name and the filming date in a note following the main part of the citation.

> Ford Corporation. *Form 10-K Annual Report . . . FY Ended Dec. 31, 1991.* Detroit, MI, 1992. (1992 Disclosure microfiche).

PEF SOURCES

> Merck & Co. (Record no. M419100000; Company Report). Available on: *Compact Disclosure* (CD-ROM). Nov. 1992.

VEF SOURCES

> Enron Corp. 4/02/01. 10-K. Available from: *SEC Edgar Database*, http://www.sec.gov/-edgar/searchedgar/webusers.htm; Accessed: 2/10/02.

> Enron Corp. 2/7/02. 8-K. Text from: *Full-Text Filings*. Available from: *Dow Jones Interactive*; Accessed: 2/10/02.

> Ford Motor Co. 3/22/01. 10-K. Text from: *Filings*. Available from: *Disclosure Global Access*, Thomson Financial; Accessed: 2/10/02.

> Merck & Co. 11/ 15/01. Form: 424B3. Text from: *Real-Time SEC EDGAR Filings*. Available on: *Hoover's Online*; Accessed: 2/10/02.

S27 *Serial Set*

The U.S. Serial Set is the official compilation of Congressional reports and documents. At one time nearly all government publications were issued as Congressional documents in the *Serial Set* and bear a Congressional number (e.g., 42nd Congress, H. Doc. 242). The bound volumes have been numbered consecutively since 1817.

To cite material in the *Serial Set* you should give the Congress, session, title, and number (e.g., 58-2, House Report 21). If available, also give imprint data. Inclusion of the *Serial Set* number is recommended and should be placed in a Note (Section 5.0). For examples of other congressional documents, consult *Quick Citation Guide to Legislative/Parliamentary Sources*.

> U.S. Senate, 50th Congress, 2nd Session. *Report on Indian Traderships* (S. Rpt. 2707). Washington: Government Printing Office, 1899. (Serial Set 2623).

> U.S. House, Select Committee on Small Business. *Organization and Operation of the Small Business Administration: A Report . . . Pursuant to H. Res. 46*. (H. Rpt. 87-2564). Washington: Government Printing Office, 1963. (Serial Set 12440).

> U.S. Senate, 23rd Congress. *Statistical View of the Population of the United States from 1790-1830 Inclusive* (S. Doc. 505). Washington: Duff Green, 1835. (Serial Set 252). (Library of Congress, American Memory). Available at: *A Century of Lawmaking for a New Nation*, http://memory.loc.gov/ammem/amlaw/lwsslink.html; Accessed: 2/9/02.

S28 Software

> U.S. Centers for Disease Control. *Epi Info: A Word Processing, Database, and Statistics System for Epidemiology on Microcomputers* (Software). By Andrew G. Dean et al. Version 5. Atlanta, GA, 1990. (HE20.7002:Ep 4.8).

> U.S. Environmental Protection Agency. *Hyperventilate: A Software Guidance System Created for Vapor Extraction Applications* (EPA 500-C-B-92-001) (Software). By Paul C. Johnson. Version 1.01. Washington: Government Printing Office, 1992. (Solid Waste and Emergency Response (OS-420)-WF) (EP1.8:H99).

> U.S. Federal Emergency Management Agency, Federal Insurance Division, Office of Risk Assessment, Risk Studies Division. *FAN: An Alluvial Fan Flooding Computer Program* (Software) (fan-prog.zip; 174 kb). Available at: http://www.fema.gov/-mit/tsd/dl_fnprg.htm; Accessed: 12/10/01.

S29 Translations of Non-English News Sources

The U.S. government has translated a wide range of non-english sources for use by researchers and the scientific community. These two series: The JPRS Reports and FBIS Reports have very different content and are both frequently cited by researchers.

S29a The *FBIS Reports* are translations of written and spoken media messages picked up by FBIS bureaus located throughout the world. These messages are usually translated from a foreign language into English, although occasionally the original television/radio transmissions are in English. The reports are grouped by geopolitical source and subject area. In citing an FBIS document, take the information about the original document from the paragraph heading.

NEWSPAPER ACCOUNTS

The citation should include: personal author, if any; title; an edition statement as to whether the translation is complete "text" or only "excerpts"; city and source; volume; date; and page number.

> Simurov, A., and V. Yanovskiy. "We Have Come To Know Each Other Better; the Peace March—82 Has Ended" (text). Moscow *Pravda* (July 30, 1982) p. 4. Translation by the Foreign Broadcast Information Service. *FBIS Daily Report—Soviet Union* Vol. III: 150; Aug. 4, 1982 (GPO microfiche; PrEx7.10: FBIS-SOV-82-150; pp. AA7-11).

> Mazari, Shireen M. "Pakistani Analyst Emphasizes Need for 'Strategic Cooperation' with Iran Islamabad" (Article ID: SAP20020207000065). FBIS Transcribed Text of *Islamabad: The News* (Internet Version in English) (Feb. 7, 2002). Text from: *Region—Near East and South Asia (FBIS-NES-2002-0207)*. Available from: World News Connection (NTIS), Bethesda, MD; Accessed: 2/10/02.

TELEVISION/RADIO BROADCASTS

The citation should include personal author, title, edition statement (as above), the source and language in which the message was broadcast, and the date of broadcast in Greenwich Mean Time (GMT). All of this information is given in a line (or more) which precedes the credit for the translation. This is followed by information describing the FBIS report in which the translation can be found, including SuDoc number if available.

MICROFICHE COPY

> Mnatsakonov, Edward. "The World Today" (text). Moscow Domestic Television Service in Russian (1445 GMT, Aug. 3, 1982). Translation by the Foreign Broadcast Information Service. *FBIS Daily Report—Soviet Union* Vol. III: 150; Aug. 4, 1982. (GPO microfiche; PrEx7.10:FBIS-SOV-82-150; p. H 14).

PAPER COPY

> "Destroyer Sent to Beirut" (excerpts). Rome Domestic Service in Italian (2200 GMT May 9, 1983). Translation by the Foreign Broadcast Information Service. *FBIS Daily Report—Western Europe* Vol. VII: 91; May 10, 1983; p. A7.

> Ho-sam, Kim. "DPRK Commentator Assails, Refutes US President's Mention of 'Axis of Evil'" (Article Id: KPP20020204000119). FBIS Translated Text of: P'yongyang Korean Central Broadcasting Station in Korean (1224 GMT, Feb. 4, 2002). Text from: *Region—East Asia. FBIS-EAS-2002-020*. Available from: World News Connection (NTIS), Bethesda, MD; Accessed: 2/10/02.

S29b The *JPRS Reports* are primarily translations of print media. The reports are grouped by geographic area with several articles in each report. Information on the original source is found in the paragraph heading for each translation. For the microfiche edition you will have to look at the first frame of the translation to find this information. You should include personal author (if any), the title (shortened if necessary), the city and source of the original document, volume, date, and page numbers. When an entire book is translated, you should include all of the following (if given): author, translated title, original title, place, publisher, and date.

The second part of the citation describes the JPRS series. You should include the area name and report number (if they are given), the JPRS report number, and the date of the translation. This information can be found on the title page, the bibliographic data sheet, or on the microfiche header. In citing a GPO microfiche edition (the most widely used), give the microfiche number, and the page numbers on the microfiche. Finally, your citation should include a note containing either the SuDoc number or the Readex entry number.

PERIODICAL CITATION IN THE GPO EDITION

Konstandinou, T. S. "PASOK Positions on EEC Membership Analyzed," Athens *Oikonomikos Takhydromas* 46 (Nov. 12, 1981) pp. 23-26. Translation by the Joint Publications Research Service. *West Europe Report No. 1885* (JPRS No. 79843; Jan. 12, 1982). (GPO microfiche; PrEx7.18:1885; pp. 25-35).

BOOK CITATION IN READEX EDITION

Subversion: Uruguayan Armed Forces Summary of Subversive Movements in Latin America (trans. of *La Subversion*). Montevideo: Joint Chiefs of Staff, Uruguayan Armed Forces, 1977. Translation by the Joint Publications Research Service. (JPRS No. 69596-1; Aug. 12, 1977). (1978 Readex microprint 12212).

S30 Treaties

Treaties are issued either as separate documents or as part of a series. Several large treaty series published by the U.S., the U.N., and the European Union are the most frequently cited. In addition, many treaties are now widely accessible on the WWW. Consult rules in Sections E1.0-E6.0 for help in citing in these sources.

S30a U.S. treaties are published in two forms: individually in *Treaties and Other International Acts Series (TIAS)* and compiled in *United States Treaties (UST)*. In both, they are arranged sequentially by TIAS number. You should cite the title, the parties, the date of signing, and the TIAS number. Other elements will depend on whether you are citing *TIAS* or *UST*.

Take the title from the first page of the treaty. Use the first form of agreement listed (e.g., treaty, convention, agreement), followed by a short title based on the subject matter. Since the U.S. is party to all treaties in these series, it is necessary to include only the other party in bilateral treaties and designate "multilateral" for multilateral treaties. If there are multiple dates of signing, give the first and last dates. Multilateral treaties may say "done at" rather than "signed." In any case, use the date on the cover page of *TIAS*.

TIAS CITATION

"Convention on Atomic Energy," Sweden, signed Jan. 27, 1981 and Feb. 23, 1981, *Treaties and Other International Acts Series 10099*.

UST CITATION

"General Agreement on Tariffs and Trade," done Mar. 10, 1955, Multilateral (TIAS 3437), *United States Treaties* 6, Pt. 5 (1955) p. 5815.

S30b For treaties published in the U.N. Treaty Series, specify the parties; the name or type of agreement; the place and date of signing; the U.N. registry number; the name of the series; volume; date; and page numbers.

Spain and Colombia Agreement on Nationality, signed at Madrid, June 27, 1979 (No. 19299). *United Nations Treaty Series* 1200 (1980) pp. 47-56.

Canada and United States of America Agreement on Air Quality (With Annexes), signed at Ottawa, Mar. 13, 1991 (No. 31532). Known as: Air Quality Agreement (Ottawa Agreement). Text from: *United Nations Treaty Series*. Available at: United Nations Treaty Collection; Accessed: 2/9/02.

S30c There are two classes of European Communities treaties: the treaties which established the EC (i.e., the basic law of the EC) and treaties between the EC and other parties.

ESTABLISHING TREATIES

Cite by name, date, and source. It is not necessary to specify the parties because it must be assumed that any EC member country has acceded to the treaty.

> Treaty Establishing the European Economic Community, signed in Rome on Mar. 25, 1957, *Treaties Establishing the European Communities* (FX-23-77-962-EN-C). 1978 ed. Luxembourg: Office for Official Publications, 1978.

TREATY COLLECTIONS

Treaties and agreements with other parties may be found in the *Collected Acts* and in other collections, such as the *Official Journal of the European Communities*. Cite a title composed of the form of agreement and the subject; if none is given on the treaty, create one and enclose it in brackets. The title should be followed by the names of the parties and the date and place of signing or "doing." Finally, you should cite the source.

> [Agreement on Trade] between the European Economic Community and the Swiss Confederation, done at Brussels, July 22, 1972, pp. 18-31. In European Communities. Council. *Collection of the Agreements Concluded by the European Communities, Vol. 3: Bilateral Agreements EEC-Europe* (1958-1975) (RX-23-77-590EN-C). Luxembourg: Office for Official Publications, 1978.

> *Treaty of Nice.* Text from: *Official Journal of the European Communities* C 80 (3/10/2001) pp. 01. Available from: *Eur-Lex,* http://europa.eu.int/eurlex/en/-treaties/index.html; Accessed: 1/5/02.

> "Treaty of Nice Amending the Treaty on European Union, the Treaties Establishing the European Communities and Certain Related Acts Declarations Adopted by the Conference Declaration on Article 111 of the Treaty Establishing the European Community" (Feb. 26, 2001), *Official Journal of the European Communities* C 80 (Mar. 10, 2001). Text from: *CELEX Database: Treaties.* Available at: Academic Universe, LexisNexis; Accessed: 2/13/02.

S30d Many other countries collect their own treaties in treaty series.

> Canada. External Affairs and International Trade. Fisheries: Exchange of Letters Between Canada and the European Economic Community. (EEC), Brussels, Jan. 1, 1984, In Force Jan. 1, 1984. Ottawa: Queen's Printer for Canada, 1989. (Treaty Series 1984, no.2). (Catalogue no. E3-1984/2).

S30e The full text of treaties will frequently be included in databases containing the full text of sources such as the *Official Journal of the European Communities*; consult examples in the *Quick Citation Guide to Legislative/Parliamentary Sources,* L4.1

> "Agreement between the European Economic Community and the Republic of Sierra Leone on Fishing off Sierra Leone." Text from: *CELEX* (Office for Official Publications of the European Communities, Brussels) (Text available in most official languages of the European Communities); Referenced: 2/5/92, 2:45 pm EST.

> "Recommendation of the EFTA Surveillance Authority No 68/00/COL of Mar. 24, 2000 on a Coordinated Programme for the Official Control of Foodstuffs," *Official Journal of the European Communities* L 274 (26/10/2000) pp. 0042. Text from: CELEX *Database: Treaties.* Available from: Academic Universe, LexisNexis; Accessed: 2/9/02.

> *European Convention for the Prevention of Torture and Inhuman or Degrading Treatment or Punishment.* Strasbourg, Nov. 26, 1987. Entry into force Mar.1, 2002. Available at: http://conventions.coe.int/Treaty/en/Treaties/Html/126.htm; Accessed: 2/9/02.

S31 U.N. Conferences

U.N. conference documents will be cited much like other U.N. documents: as *Official Records* (Fig. 2) or as masthead documents (Fig. 10). Consult the *Quick Citation Guide to Legislative/Parliamentary Sources,* L3.1-L3.2, for additional examples. The conference name, location and date are cited as the Issuing Agency. If "Official Record" appears as part of the title, it need not be repeated in the edition statement.

AS A MASTHEAD DOCUMENT

> U.N. Conference on Desertification, Nairobi, Kenya, Aug.29, Sept. 9, 1977. *Case Study on Desertification: Mona Reclamation Experimental Project Pakistan* (A/CONF.74/13). n.d. (Masthead).

AS AN OFFICIAL RECORD

> U.N. Conference to Consider Amendments to the Single Convention on Narcotic Drugs, 1961, Geneva, 6-24 Mar. 1972. *Official Records, Vol. I: Preparatory and Organizational Documents; Main Conference Documents; Final Act and Protocol . . . ; Annexes* (E/CONF.63/10). New York, 1974.

S32 *U.S. Government Manual*

The *U.S. Government Manual* is a product of the General Services Administration. However, since this title is a standard reference work, it is not necessary to include the name of the Issuing Agency. A simple citation to the item itself will suffice.

> *United States Government Manual, 1991/92.* Washington: Government Printing Office, 1991.

> "Department of State." In *United States Government Manual, 2001/02.* National Archives and Records Administration. Available from: GPO Access, http://www.access.gpo.gov/nara/nara001.html; Accessed: 2/10/02.

---

[1] "Rule 18—Electronic Media and Other Nonprint Resources," pp. 129-144. In *The Bluebook: A Uniform System of Citation.* 17th ed. Cambridge, MA: Harvard Law Review Assoc., 2000.

PART 2
Citation Rules for Physical Formats
(including Floppy Disks
and CD-ROMs)

0.0 BASIC RULES FOR FORM AND PUNCTUATION

This Section Includes:

* Where to Locate Information to Include in a Citation (Section 0.1).
* Capitalization Rules (Section 0.2).
* Punctuation Rules (Section 0.3).

* Abbreviations Rules (Section 0.4).

* Non-English Language Sources Rules (Section 0.5).

0.1 Where to Locate Information to Include in a Citation: Use the Internal vs. External Rule

Determining the content of a citation is a problem, especially when different versions, conflicting, and variable information are present on a single publication or source. The key to determining the most important information is to distinguish between information that is found in an internal source and information that is found in an external source.

Internal sources for citation information are always preferred over external sources. Thus, in the situation where contradictory information exists (on the title page, on the spine, and on the cover, for example), the title page version (an internal source) would be the one that should be used.

Table 11: Internal and External Sources of Information

Internal Sources are more integral to the publication and are the preferred source of information.	**External Sources** can be separated from the source being cited.
* Title page and its verso * Cataloging in Publication information * Bibliographic Data Sheet (Technical Reports) * Startup screen * Readme or .doc file * "About..." file * Surface of a CD-ROM—either as a logo or as text	* Cover (back, front, or spine) * Diskette or Microfilm box/holder, its cover or spine labels * Accompanying documentation, caddy inserts, user manuals * Diskette labels (especially if handwritten or you think it is a copy of a copy) * Microfiche header * Mailing labels, preface, or introductory material
Entries in an index, publishers catalogs, or on-line library catalog, or large databases such as *Worldcat* or *RLIN* can be used to clarify information. Ask a librarian for help if you are unsure.	

Other sources of information:

Microfiche, microfilm, or opaque microcards: Use the title on the title page frame of the microformat. Do not rely on the header (of microfiche or microcards) or the storage box (of the microfilm) for the title, since the form of titles on such sources is dictated by the space available and does not always agree with the title page. You must inform your reader that the document is on microform, usually by including this in a Note (Sections 3.3 and 5.3a) (Fig. 4).

The Cataloging in Publication (CIP): Provides the complete form of the title and should be used. It is typically located on the verso of the title page. This information is used for most indexes and catalogs (Figs. 9 and 10).

Bibliographic Data Sheets (included with technical reports): If the document includes a form titled "Bibliographic Data Sheet" or "Technical Report Documentation Page," use the title included on this sheet. This form is intended for indexers and is the title that will be used in most indexes and catalogs. Consult examples in the *Quick Citation Guide to Special Cases and Well-Known Sources,* Clearinghouse Documents, S6.

The "Suggested Citation": Many publications include a "Suggested Citation" on the verso of the title page. These suggest the information that should be included in a source citation. Use these to guide the content of your own citation. (Figs. 6 and 10).

Figure 4: Internal and External Sources of Information: The Microfiche Header

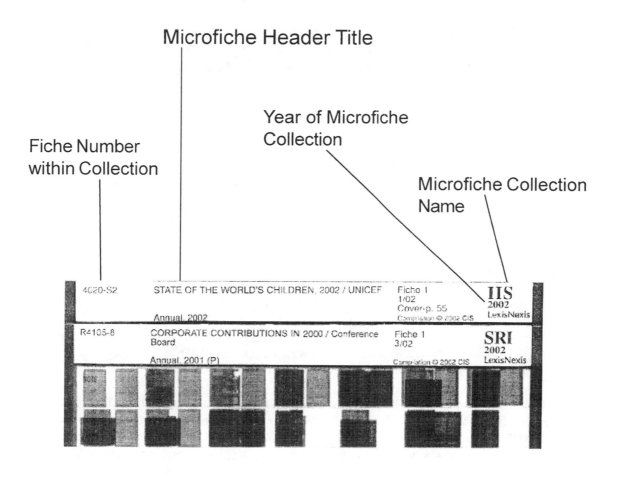

0.2 Capitalization Rules

➢ Capitalize all major words in each part of the citation, except articles, prepositions (of less than 5 letters), and conjunctions.
➢ Personal Authors: capitalize the first, middle and last names, and any initials.
➢ Notes and Edition: capitalize the first word.
➢ For Non-English Language publications: use the conventions for capitalization that are consistent with the language of the publication; if you are unfamiliar with the capitalization conventions of the language, use the capitalization as found on the title page, see also Section 0.5.

0.3 Punctuation Rules

➢ Follow the punctuation practices illustrated in Tables 3 and 10, and in the examples provided in the *Quick Citation Guides*.
➢ Brackets are used to tell the reader the information was not on the document, but was derived or deduced from some other source.
➢ Ellipses (…) indicate words were omitted.
➢ Series and Notes: enclose in parentheses.
➢ For Non-English Language publications, use the conventions for punctuation that are consistent with the language of the publication, see also Section 0.5.

0.4 Abbreviation Rules

➢ Choose a style for abbreviations and use it throughout or identify a style manual (e.g. the *Chicago Manual of Style*) and follow its rules (see *Appendix A: Style Manuals*) or follow your publisher or institution's style guidelines. Always use any abbreviations exactly as shown on the publication.
➢ Consult *Appendix D: Abbreviations* for a list of frequently used abbreviations; additional accepted abbreviations are included in the *Citation Rules* sections, as appropriate.
➢ Postal code abbreviations may be substituted for other state name abbreviations.
➢ Use standard abbreviations for dates, pages, volumes, issue numbers, and similar numbering devices.
➢ Geo/Political Designations: Use the most commonly accepted abbreviation for countries. Be consistent throughout bibliography.
➢ Issuing Agency acronyms and abbreviated forms: Some are well known by an acronym or an abbreviated form of their name (for example, UNESCO). Other abbreviated forms can be confused (for example, WTO can be confused by some readers as meaning the World Trade Organization or the World Tourism Organization); other organizations are better known within some contexts or disciplines (for example, E.U. (European Union) is well accepted in Europe, but less known in the United States); and finally some abbreviated forms are so little known, except by experts that they will leave your reader confused about the source. For these reasons, it is recommended that you use the full name of an organization or agency. You may elect to use abbreviated forms and acronyms and when doing so use the most commonly accepted standard abbreviation and be consistent throughout the bibliography.
➢ Legislative/Parliamentary Bodies—Consult Section 1.3b and use accepted abbreviations (see *Appendix D: Abbreviations* for the most frequently used).

0.5 Non-English Language Sources Rules

> ➤ Geo/Political Designation: Use the form consistently throughout as it would normally be found in the language you are using for the rest of your bibliography. Use translation forms included in the *Yearbook of International Organizations* (see *Appendix B: Standard Reference Sources for Governments and Organizations*). Do not change forms even when documents differ. This assures that all publications from the same country are grouped together in your bibliography.

> ➤ Issuing Agency and Legislative/Parliamentary Body: if the name is given (or is known) in multiple languages, select a single form and use it consistently. If the name is only given in a non-English language, use the form as it appears on the publication, regardless of the language of the rest of your bibliography. Note: you may create citations with parts in two languages, this is necessary to avoid non-standard translations of agency names.

> ➤ Do not translate titles, cite as given, even if you give the author and publisher data in your own language. You may add a Note (Section 5.4a) if you feel the language is not apparent to your reader.

> ➤ If a publication is bilingual or multilingual, it is not necessary to include all the languages of the work in your citation. In choosing the title follow the same rules used in choosing the language of the Issuing Agency (Section 1.0)

> ➤ If a PEF or VEF source allows you to select the language of your search interface, or to select titles in a specific language, cite those titles in the primary language of the bibliography. It is not necessary to indicate the language of the source you are citing, unless it will clarify the citation. For example, you may add a Note (Section 5.0) to indicate if the text is available in multiple languages.

1.0 AUTHORSHIP—Who is responsible for the content?

An author, of course, is responsible for the intellectual content of a publication. In most citation systems for non-government publications the Personal Author is given the first position to recognize this relationship to the content. *However, government and organization publications are used to communicate the official positions and work of a government or organization. For this reason, the Issuing Agency is considered the author of a government document and should be given the first position in any citation.*

By recognizing the Issuing Agency as the author of a government or organization publication you provide the reader, even in this electronic age, with important clues about the sources of the document.

Use the Issuing Agency as the first element in a citation to a government or organization document because:

1) It is important to recognize an Issuing Agency's role in guiding the content of a publication.

2) The Issuing Agency name serves as an important identification "tool" in on-line library catalogs and indexes, particularly for U.S. federal documents published prior to 1976.

3) Government and organization documents will be grouped together in your bibliography by Issuing Agency and alerts your reader immediately that additional library sources or the help of a librarian may be needed to locate the source in the library's documents collections or from an appropriate sales source.

4) Many government and organization documents are now being placed full-text on agency WWW sites. Search engines may not be able to locate these documents. The Issuing Agency name tells the reader which agency WWW site to search for "invisible/hidden" documents.

5) Research using government and organization documents/resources is bound by history and historically, indexes and library catalogs have listed the Issuing Agency rather than the Personal Author as a document's "author" (major indexes for government documents are listed in *Appendix B: Standard Reference Sources for Government and Organization Information*). While this pattern has changed since 1976, the Issuing Agency still provides the reader with important clues, even in this electronic age, about the source of a document that can be lost if not included as the first element in your citation.

Three types of authorship for government publications:

Issuing Agencies: Government Agencies and Organizations

Governments and organizations are organized into complex organizational hierarchies (bureaucracies) often depicted in an organizational chart. These agencies and departments issue publications and are considered the authors of most government publications.

Issuing Agencies: Legislative/Parliamentary Bodies

All governments and organizations have a Legislative/Parliamentary Body that produces a wide range of publications—laws, resolutions, directives, committee reports, documents, and hearings—that are frequently cited by researchers. Legislative/Parliamentary Bodies are one specific example of a government Issuing Agency. However, because these sources are frequently cited and because of their unique nature, some special rules are required.

Personal Authors

Although Personal Authors are frequently not credited for the publications of a government or organization, many more are being recognized for their contributions to the content of a publication. It is important to include this information, particularly if the publication itself names a Personal Author. This information, along with the Issuing Agency, will help the reader to locate the document and recognizes the role of the Personal Author and the Issuing Agency, respectively.

HOW TO BEGIN: The Issuing Agency of governments, organizations and their Legislative/Parliamentary Body are considered the author and given first position in citations to most government publications.

If the Issuing Agency is a:	Examples:	What to do:
Government	**National (Canada)** **State or Province (Ontario)** **Regional (Quebec River Basin Commission)** **Local (Toronto)**	**Begin the entry with a Geo/Political Designation (Section 1.1) followed by the Issuing Agency and its subsidiary bodies, as applicable (Section 1.2)**
International organization or IGO	**U.N.** **European Union**	**Begin the entry with the Issuing Agency (Section 1.2) (no Geo/Political Designation is required)**
Government's Legislative/Parliamentary Body	**U.S. Congress** **Pennsylvania. General Assembly** **United Kingdom. Parliament**	**Begin the entry with a Geo/Political Designation (Section 1.1) followed by the Legislative/ Parliamentary body and its subsidiary bodies, as applicable (Section 1.3)**
An Organization's Legislative/Parliamentary Body	**U.N. General Assembly** **European Union. Parliamentary Assembly.**	**Begin the entry with the Issuing Agency, followed by the Legislative/Parliamentary Body and its subsidiary bodies, as applicable (Section 1.3)**
Personal Author	**By John Smith** **Compiled by Susan Taylor**	**Include this information following the title proper (Section 1.4)**

1.1 Governments as Issuing Agency: The Geo/Political Designation

Basic Rules:

* For national, state, regional, and local government publications only.

* The most commonly accepted form of the government name (Iceland, not Republic of Iceland, for example) should be used.

* The most commonly accepted abbreviation (U.S. for United States, for example) or postal codes should be used; be consistent throughout your bibliography.

Recommended Form and Punctuation:

Follow the Geo/Political Designation with a period. Use commas to separate parts of the Geo/Political Designation:

U.S.
Pennsylvania.
New York, NY.
Canada.

Related Sections:

➢ Publishing Information (Section 4.0).
➢ Legislative/Parliamentary Body as Issuing Agency (Section 1.3).
➢ Personal Authors (Section 1.4).

Consult examples in the *Quick Citation Guides*.
Ask a librarian for additional help.

Care should be taken that sufficient information is given so that Geo/Political entities with similar names (e.g., Beaufort, NC and Beaufort, SC) are distinguishable. Distinguishing information may also be included in the Publishing Information part of the citation (Section 4.0).

New York, NY. Dept. of Transportation, Bureau of Highway Operations. *1982 Annual Condition Report on Bridges and Tunnels*. n.p., 1983.

Allentown, PA. Urban Observatory. *An Analysis of Tire Service Delivery for Master Planning in Allentown*. n.p., 1977.

1.1a Geo/Political Designation as Part of the Issuing Agency Name

If the country, state, or local government's name (or a form of the name), is in the Issuing Agency's name, it is not necessary to repeat the country's name as a separate element of the Issuing Agency.

Southwestern Pennsylvania Planning Commission. *The Plan for the 80s*. Pittsburgh, 1979.

Canadian Advisory Council on the Status of Women. *Women and Labour Market Poverty*. By Morely Gunderson, Leon Muszynski, with Jennifer Keck. Ottawa: The Council, 1990.

1.1b Geo/Political Designation for Regional Governments and Organizations

Because regional organizations and governments cross community, county, state, or country boundaries, the location of these organizations is found in the Publishing Information (Section 4.0).

> Colorado River Basin Salinity Control Forum. *Report on the 1990 Review: Water Quality Standards for Salinity, Colorado River System.* Bountiful, Utah, 1990.

> Sistema Económico Latinoamericano. *Canada, Latin America and the Global Economy : Old Challenges and New Opportunities.* Caracas: SELA, 1993

1.1c No Geographic/Political Designation Named

When no Geo/Political Designation is given in the internal sources of information (Section 0.1) scan mailing labels, the preface, introductory material, a library's on-line catalog (or other similar database), or a publisher's catalog for this information. If located in any of these or other external sources, enclose the information in brackets.

If reliable information cannot be located, begin the citation with the title.

> [Hong Kong.] *White Paper—The Development of Representative Government: The Way Forward.* Hong Kong: Government Printer, 1988.

1.1d Geo/Political Designation Name Has Changed

If the name of the country has changed over time, use the form of the name that was in use when the publication was issued. This will be the country name as it appears on the document. An example of such changes would be Rhodesia, now Zimbabwe.

1.2 The Issuing Agency

Basic Rules:

The Issuing Agency consists of the complete form of the agency name in the form of the organizational hierarchy from largest to smallest. It is not necessary to repeat information included in the Title (Section 2.0). Use the form shown on any internal or external source of information (Section 0.1).

Recommended Form and Punctuation:

A Government: Geo/Political Designation. Umbrella Department, Sub-Agency.
An Organization: Organization name, Umbrella Department, Sub-Agency.

Related Sections:
➢ Legislative/Parliamentary Body as Issuing Agency (Section 1.3).
➢ Issuing Agency as Personal Author (Section 1.4c).
➢ Citing Parts: Periodical Articles and Statistical Sources (Section 6.0).

Hint: Creating the Issuing Agency's Organizational Hierarchy

There are many ways to organize the work of a government or organization. Creating an organizational hierarchy can be challenging since the relationships of different offices to one another are not always clear. Look for the layout of department and subgroup names on an internal source of information to help you construct the Issuing Agency organizational hierarchy.

➢ **Geo/Political Designation or Organization Name:** Always begin with either the Geo/Political Designation or organization name, as appropriate (Consult Section 1.0).
  ➢ **Umbrella Department:** Most governments and organizations organize the work into several large departments, agencies or commissions. Occasionally this level can be omitted if the Sub-Agency is well known in its own right (Section 1.2a).
    ➢ **Sub-Agency:** Each Umbrella Department is typically divided further into smaller theme (Geological Survey) or task oriented agencies (Economic Statistics Division). Some sub-agencies are further divided into even more closely focused offices or divisions. Sometimes the structure can go down several subgroup levels. Usually no more than 3 are necessary (Section 1.2b).

Consult examples in the *Quick Citation Guides*.
To clarify organizational hierarchy or relationships, consult standard reference tools in *Appendix B: Standard Reference Sources for Government and Organization Information*, your library's on-line catalog, or a librarian.

1.2a An Issuing Agency Well-Known in Its Own Right

When an agency or sub-agency (within an "umbrella" department) is well known in its own right and does not need to be placed within the context of the umbrella department for adequate identification, the umbrella department can be omitted from the organizational hierarchy in the Issuing Agency statement. In these situations, the umbrella department may or may not be included on the document (Fig. 5).

U.S. Forest Service. *Taraghee Lodgepole: A Pioneering Effort in Deadwood Salvage.* Washington: Government Printing Office, 1979. (A13.2:T17).

1.2b Many Levels in an Organizational Hierarchy (The Rule of Three)

If the agency given on the document is composed of more than three bureaucratic levels, you may use only the "umbrella" department and the lowest level sub-agency given, if you feel this combination will provide sufficient identification. This approach is typically used when a sub-agency has a significant role within an agency and is well-known in its own right. When in doubt, use more levels rather than fewer to help your reader.

Note: Agency names become increasingly generalized as they move further down into the organizational hierarchy. Be sure to include the "umbrella" department for agencies with names such as the "Bureau of Statistics" or the "Economic Division," since agencies in several different departments may have similar names.

U.S. Dept. of Justice, Bureau of Justice Statistics. *Correctional Population in the United States, 1989.* Washington: Government Printing Office, 1991. (J29.17:989).

1.2c No Issuing Agency Named

When no Issuing Agency is given in the internal sources of information (Section 0.1) scan mailing labels, the preface, introductory material, a library's on-line catalog or other similar database, or from a publisher's catalog for this information. If located in any of these or other external sources, enclose the information in brackets.

If reliable information cannot be located, begin the citation with the title.

[Idaho. Dept. of Education.] *Fall Enrollment Report, 1982/83.* Boise, 1982.

U.N. Educational, Scientific, and Cultural Organization. [Secretariat. Sector for Programme Support]. *Organization of Unesco Secretariat Since 1946* (PRS.79/WS/47). Paris, 1979.

Figure 5: An Agency Known in Its Own Right: U.S. Census Bureau

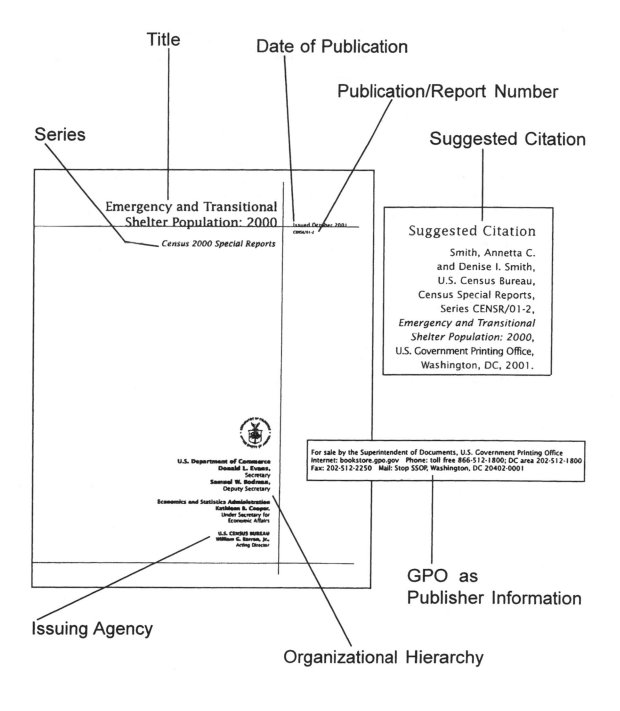

1.2d Multiple Issuing Agencies

Sometimes more than one government or organization may be instrumental in the production of a document as in a cooperative effort.

Variation: An Issuing Agency as Personal Author consult Section 1.4c.

If more than one agency is listed, but both are within the same government use the first one listed. This agency will be noted in the standard indexes as the Issuing Agency, and it will help your reader locate the document. The second agency need not be included in a note, unless you are unsure which agency should be considered the Issuing Agency. In this case, select one agency as the Issuing Agency and include the second in a Note (Section 5.0).

> U.S. Employment and Training Administration. *Environmental Protection Careers Guidebook.* Washington, 1980. (In cooperation with the U.S. Dept. of Energy).

If more than one agency is listed, but are within different organizations or levels of government use the agency that figures most prominently on the document or the first agency listed as the Issuing Agency. List the second agency in a Note (Section 5.0) since you cannot be sure which agency will be considered the author and which will be an alternative source for the publication.

> Oklahoma. Dept. of Agriculture, Crop and Livestock Reporting Service. *Oklahoma Agricultural Statistics 1981.* Oklahoma City, 1982. (Produced as a cooperative effort with the U.S. Dept. of Agriculture).

> Canada. Royal Commission on Electoral Reform and Party Financing. *Interest Groups and Elections in Canada.* Edited by F. Leslie Seidle. Toronto: Dundern Press, 1991. (Research Studies, v.2). (In cooperation with the Canada Communication Group).

> U.N. Economic Commission for Latin America and the Caribbean. *Transnational Bank Behaviour and the International Debt Crisis* (LC/G.1553/Rev. 1-P). Santiago, 1989. (Estudios e Informes de la Cepal 76). (Joint Publication of ECLAC and United Nations Centre on Transnational Corporations).

1.2e Issuing Agency and Publisher Included

When a source includes a government or organization publisher/printer, such as the Government Printing Office and an Issuing Agency you should include both in the citation—one as Issuing Agency, the other as the Publisher (Section 4.2). Organizations and governments are often inconsistent in identifying the publisher/printer; therefore the publisher/printer may be missing from an internal or external source of information (Section 0.1). In these cases, the Issuing Agency can be used as the Publisher. This occurs most frequently when the source includes a Personal Author (Section 1.4). Consult Section 4.2 for additional guidance. It is not necessary to repeat information included elsewhere in the citation.

> Jones, Nicholas A., and Amy Symens Smith. *Two or More Races Population: 2000* (C2KBR/01-6). Washington: Census Bureau, Nov. 2001. (Census 2000 Brief).

1.3 Legislative/Parliamentary Bodies as Issuing Agency

Basic Rules:

The Legislative/Parliamentary body as an Issuing Agency consists of the complete form of the Legislative/Parliamentary body name in the form of organizational hierarchy from legislative body to subsidiary body (from largest to smallest) (Fig. 6), any designation for a numbered session, a date (or range of dates) in years, months, or days, and a named location (if applicable) (Figs. 8).

Recommended Form and Punctuation:

Government: Geo/Political Designation. Legislative Body, Session Number. Legislative
            Chamber, Subsidiary Body.
Organization: Organization Name. Legislative Body, Session Number. Legislative Chamber.
            Subsidiary Body.

Related Sections:

➤ The Geo/Political Designation (Section 1.1).
➤ Issuing Agency as Personal Author (Section 1.4c).

Hint: Creating the Legislative/Parliamentary Organizational Hierarchy

Legislative/Parliamentary bodies are organized into organizational hierarchies similar to those of other government agencies (Section 1.1 and 1.2). Because the structure varies it can be difficult to develop a Legislative/Parliamentary body organizational hierarchy from largest to smallest. The follow example provides a basic framework.

➤ **Geo/Political Designation or Organization Name:** <u>Always</u> begin with the government or organization.

   ➤ **Legislative/Parliamentary Body:** Most governments and organizations have a law-making body. Occasionally this level can be omitted (Sections 1.3a and 1.3b) and frequently the session is numbered and must be included (Section 1.3e).

      ➤ **Legislative Chamber:** Typically the Legislative/Parliamentary Body is divided into multiple chambers (as defined by constitution, charter, or treaty); frequently a shortened form of the chamber name can be used (Section 1.3b).

         ➤ **Subsidiary Body:** Some legislative chambers are further divided into committees and subcommittees where much work is accomplished and from which many publications are generated. Sometimes the structure can go down several levels. Usually no more than three are necessary (Section 1.3b).

Consult examples in the *Quick Citation Guide to Legislative/Parliamentary Sources*.

To clarify legislative/parliamentary organizational hierarchy or relationships consult standard reference tools in *Appendix B: Standard Reference Sources for Government and Organization Information*, your library's on-line catalog, or a librarian.

Figure 6: Legislative Body as Issuing Agency: U.S. Congressional Hearing–Title Page

Title

READING & ACCOUNTABILTY:

IMPROVING 21ST CENTURY SCHOOLS

Issuing Agency

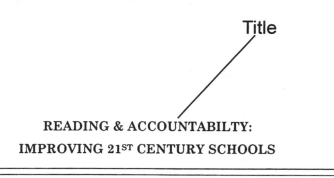

HEARING

BEFORE THE

COMMITTEE ON EDUCATION AND
THE WORKFORCE

HOUSE OF REPRESENTATIVES

ONE HUNDRED SEVENTH CONGRESS

FIRST SESSION

Date of Hearing

HEARING HELD IN MARIETTA, GEORGIA, FEBRUARY 20, 2001

Serial No. 107-2 —— Publication Number

Printed for the use of the Committee on Education
and the Workforce

Publishing Information

U.S. GOVERNMENT PRINTING OFFICE

75-503 pdf   WASHINGTON : 2002

For sale by the Superintendent of Documents, U.S. Government Printing Office
Internet: bookstore.gpo.gov Phone: (202) 512-1800 FAX: (202) 512-2250
Mail: Stop SSOP, Washington, DC 20402-0001

I

1.3a The Legislative/Parliamentary Body Well Known in Its Own Right

When a subsidiary Legislative/Parliamentary body is known in its own right, it does not need to be preceded by the legislative body.

> U.S. Office of Technology Assessment. *Competing Economies: America, Europe, and the Pacific Rim.* Washington: Government Printing Office, 1991. (Y3.T22/2:2Ec7).

1.3b Omitting Levels in the Legislative/Parliamentary Organizational Hierarchy (The Rule of Three)

You may omit a part of the organizational hierarchy if you are still able to provide adequate identification for the Legislative/Parliamentary Body within the organization or government. Care should be taken that sufficient information is given that the Legislative/Parliamentary Body can be identified, especially since organizational hierarchy can change frequently. It is not uncommon to use at least three levels of hierarchy in the organizational hierarchy.

Using a shortened form of a chamber or body name: If there is only one legislative body within an organization or government, you may use a shortened form of the name. For example, there is only one U.S. House of Representatives. The form U.S. House can be used because it cannot be confused with another body.

Omitting the legislative body: For example you may omit "Congress" or "Parliament" and use only the name of the legislative chamber, "U.S. House" or "U.S. Senate."

Variation: If, for alphabetizing purposes, you wish to keep all publications together, you may use "U.S. Congress. House." and "U.S. Congress. Senate."

> U.S. Congress. Senate. *Year-end Report of the 2nd Session of the 97th Congress* (S.Doc. 97-38). Washington: Government Printing Office, 1982. (Y1.1/3:97-38).

Omitting the subsidiary body: You may omit the names of subcommittees, but not the committee. Be sure the Issuing Agency for the publication is well-identified. Frequently publications of subcommittees are listed under the name of the committee in the standard indexes and are arranged in most libraries by committee, not subcommittee.

Variant forms of subsidiary bodies (Joint Committees and Conference Committees)

Joint committees are made up of members of both legislative chambers. Thus they do not strictly belong to either chamber. In this case you must include the full committee name and the Legislative/Parliamentary Body.

> U.S. Congress. Joint Economic Committee. *High Technology and Regional Development, Hearing, Mar. 1, 1982.* Washington: Government Printing Office, 1982. (Y4.Ec7:T22/4).

Conference committees are formed from members of both chambers. One legislative chamber issues the report. Include this chamber as the Issuing Agency. The internal sources of information, such as the cover/title page should indicate by layout which chamber is issuing the publication. Note: The words "conference report" are not part of the Title Proper (Section 2.1). In this example they are included to provide additional information, but not italicized as part of the title.

> U.S. House. *Authorizing Appropriations for Fiscal Years 1982 and 1983 for the Department of State, the United States Information Agency, and the Board for International Broadcasting*

Conference Report (H. Rpt. 97-693). Washington: Government Printing Office, 1982. (Y.1.1/3:97-693).

1.3c No Legislative Body Named

When no Issuing Agency is given in the internal sources of information (Section 0.1), scan mailing labels, the preface, introductory material, a library's on-line catalog or other similar database, or a publishers catalog for this information. If located in any of these or other external sources, enclose the information in brackets.

If reliable information cannot be located, begin the citation with the title.

1.3d Multiple Legislative/Parliamentary Bodies Named

When more than one Legislative/Parliamentary Body or subsidiary body (for example more than one committee) is identified as the Issuing Agency, use the committee with primary position/location on the title page.

If a second Issuing Agency or private company is named in the manner of a Personal Author (prepared by, compiled by), include the second agency following the title in the manner of a Personal Author (Section 1.4c).

1.3e Numbered and Dated Legislative/Parliamentary Body Meetings/Sessions

The meetings and sessions of many Legislative/Parliamentary Bodies are numbered. Frequently these numbered sessions correspond to specific dates. For example, the U.S. Congress meets in a two year session (called a "congress") that begins in odd-numbered years. Each year within a congress is called a session, and these are numbered the 1st session, and the 2nd session. This information can serve as a necessary means to verify and locate proceedings, debates, bills, acts, and resolutions since some publications reuse numbers beginning with every numbered meeting (Fig. 7). After the Legislative/Parliamentary Body statement, include as many of the following in the form found on the document:

> ➤ Any designation for a numbered session.

> ➤ A date (or range of dates) in years, months, or days.

> ➤ Meeting place (if it moves regularly) (Section 1.3g).

It is not necessary to duplicate information that is included as part of the Title Proper (Section 2.0) or as part of a Publication/Report number (Section 3.1). Consult Table 4 for additional guidance and examples in the *Quick Citation Guide to Legisltaive/Parliamentary Sources*.

Examples of Numbered Sessions	
U.S. Congress	101st Congress, 2nd Sess.
Pennsylvania. General Assembly	Session of 1992
Canada	34th Parliament, 3rd Sess.
U.N. General Assembly	46th Sess. 15th Sess., 864th Plenary Meeting

Vanuatu. Parliament, 3rd Parl., 1st Ordinary Sess., 2nd Mtg. *Summarized Proceedings, May 22-25, 1989*. n.p., [1989].

Council of Europe. Parliamentary Assembly, 42nd Ordinary Sess., Jan. 28-Feb. 1, 1991. "Report on Economic Reform in Central and Eastern Europe" (Doc. 6351), *Documents*. Strasbourg, 1991.

International Labour Organization. International Labour Conference, 69th Sess., 1983. *Report VII: Social Aspects of Industrialisation*. Geneva, 1983.

If the session or meeting number are not explicitly mentioned on an internal or external source of information (Section 0.1), but you can deduce them from other sources, such as a report number, include them in brackets.

International Atomic Energy Agency [General Conference, 27th Regular Sess.]. *The Agency's Budget for 1984* (GC(XXVII)/686). Vienna, Austria, 1983.

Sometimes Legislative/Parliamentary Bodies **and** their subsidiary body (committee, for example) will **both** number their sessions/meetings. In this case be sure to include the number following each, if it is not duplicating information supplied as part of the Title Proper (Section 2.0) or as part of a Publication/Report number (Section 3.1). If the numbered session is included in the title, it does not need to be repeated.

Note: Do not confuse the legislative/parliamentary session with the date of a conference (Section 2.1h) or hearing (Section 2.1g), which should follow the Title statement.

Canada. Parliament. 37th Parl., 1st Sess., Standing Committee on Human Rights, 1st Meeting.

U.N. Economic and Social Council, 1974 Sess. Economic Committee, 55th Sess.

Figure 7: Numbered Legislative Sessions: U.S. Congressional Bill

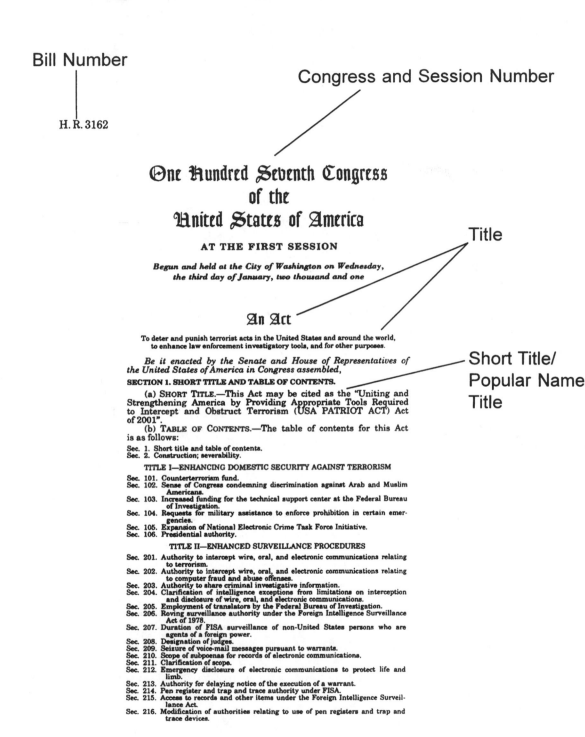

1.3f Location of Meeting/Session Named

Some organizations and IGOs meet in different places. If this is the case and a city is named as the meeting place, include it.

> U.N. Educational, Scientific, and Cultural Organization, Intergovernmental Council of the International Programme for the Development of Communication, 13th Sess., Paris, 17-24 Feb. 1992. *Final Report.* Paris, 1992.

1.4 Personal Authors

Basic Rules

Personal Authors are those who: write, compute, compile, edit, prepare, draw, or create the document's content. (Figs. 6 and 9). Do not include as Personal Authors those who: direct, supervise, order, or administer a document's content (for example, an agency director).

Recommended Form and Punctuation:

The Personal Author follows the Title Proper (Section 2.0). Use the form given on the document, including middle initials; preceded by a phrase indicating the author's role:

By Alice D. Schreyer.
Edited by Tom Jones.
Compiled by Sally J. Smith and John Edwards.

Related Sections:

➢ Issuing Agency (Section 1.0).
➢ Citing a Part (Section 6.0).
➢ Issuing Agency and Publisher Included (Section 1.2e).

Consult examples in the *Quick Citation Guides*.
Ask a librarian for additional help.

Hint: A Personal Author (compiler, editor, or translator) may take the primary position in a citation to a government or organization publication only when The Issuing Agency is included in the Publishing Information (Section 4.0). This recognizes the role of both Personal Author and the Issuing Agency. However, when a Publisher/Distributer is also included that differs from the Issuing Agency, the Issuing Agency must be included in the primary position in the citation (Sections 1.2e and 4.2d). Consult examples in the *Quick Citation Guide to Books and Monographs*, B1.3 and B4.4.

1.4a Honorary and Royal Titles and Degrees

Any title (for example, Mr. or Mrs.), including those of government officials (President, Representative, Member of Parliament), professions (Dr.), or academic degree (Ph.D, Dr.) should be omitted from the author's name, unless needed to distinguish between persons. For example, when the author is identified only as Mrs. Sam Smith the title must be included.

Titles such as Representative (Rep.) or Senator (Sen.) can be included, especially if needed to clarify in which chamber the member of Congress has spoken. Many legislative/parliamentary debate sources also identify a member by their district or political party. It may also be necessary to distinguish between two members with the same last name (Smith (NH) and Smith (OR), for example).

> Spelman, Caroline (Meridien). "Adoption Bill," United Kingdom. Parliament. *Hansard—House of Commons Debate,* 365:63 (Mar. 30, 2001) col. 1203.

> "Written Question E-1155/01 by Daniel Varela Suanzes-Carpegna (PPE-DE) to the Commission (Apr. 10, 2001). Tuna Steaks." *Official Journal of the European Communities* C 364 E (12/20/2001) pp. 51-52.

Consult the *Quick Citation Guide to Legislative/Parliamentary Publications* for examples. However, this information can be omitted if it is supplied elsewhere in the citation or if it is desireable for alphabetization purposes to omit it.

1.4b Multiple Personal Authors

Include up to three personal authors in the author statement. If more than three authors are mentioned, name only the first and include the others in "et al" or "and others."

> U.S. Dept. of Education, National Center for Education Statistics. *The 1990 Science Report Card: NAEP's Assessment of Fourth, Eighth, and Twelfth Graders.* By Lee R. Jones et al. Washington, 1992. (ED1.302:Sci1).

> Massachusetts. Division of Employment Security. *Occupational Profile of Selected Manufacturing Industries in Massachusetts 1980.* Prepared by Richard Subrant et al. Boston, 1981. (Occupation/Industry Research Publication 14).

> Organisation for Economic Cooperation and Development. *Japan at Work: Markets, Management and Flexibility* (81-89-01-1). By Ronald Dore and others. Paris, 1989.

Variation:

When multiple personal authors take the primary position, consult Section 1.2e examples for recommended form and punctuation.

1.4c An Issuing Agency as Personal Author

Sometimes a government agency will contract with a private company (or individual) to research a problem and produce a document. In a few instances government agencies may be responsible for providing research materials and documents for another agency (for example, the Congressional Research Service produces many background publications for members of Congress and Congressional committees). In these cases, the second Issuing Agency is named in the manner of a Personal Author.

Note: Do not confuse with publications with Multiple Issuing Agencies (Section 1.2d).

> U.S. Dept. of Housing and Urban Development. *Rehabilitation Guidelines 1982: 10 Guidelines on the Rehabilitation of Walls, Windows, and Roofs.* Prepared by National Institute of Building Sciences. Washington: Government Printing Office, 1983. (HH1.6/3:R26/8/982).

> Southwestern Pennsylvania Regional Planning Commission. *Directions in Housing Policies for Low and Moderate Income Families. . . .* Prepared by the Institute for Urban Policy and Administration, University of Pittsburgh. Pittsburgh, 1972.

1.4d Translator

If a document has been translated from its original language into another language, give credit to the translator or translating agency in a Note (Section 5.0).

Japan. Defense Agency. *Defense of Japan, 1991*. n.p.: Japan Times, Ltd., 1991. (Translated from the original Defense Agency White Paper by Japan Times, Ltd.).

1.4e Compilers and Editors

If a document has a compiler or editor, this information is included in the manner of the Personal Author, if no Personal Author is included.

If the compiler or editor is included in the primary position (see Hint) the abbreviations ed. (editor) or comp. (compiler) are used to show the author's relationship to the content and are inserted following the name. When citing part of a work including an editor, consult Section 2.3a.

Jones, Sally, comp. *Sticks and Stones: A Collection of Images from the Library of Congress Collections Depicting Women in History.* Washington: Library of Congress, 2001.

Smith, Sam, ed. *The Way of the Crime World* (DVD). Washington: The Federal Bureau of Investigation, 2002.

2.0 TITLE —What is the title of the source?

A document's title is often critical when locating a document in a library's on-line catalog, from a sales source, or even on the WWW. The title is the one element most likely to be found on every document. But even the title can be a problem. For example, the design of a document may present you with variations of the title (variations on the title page, cover, and spine), with several choices as to title (a series title, for example), or the title may be so long and rambling that it seems unnecessary to include it all. In addition, researchers are often faced with deciding on the correct arrangement of words and whether they are really part of the title at all, due to the layout and typefaces used by the publisher. Despite these difficulties, care should be taken to provide your reader with an accurate and complete title statement.

This Section Includes:

* Title Proper (Section 2.1).

* Subtitle (Section 2.2).

* Titles of Chapters or Other Book Parts (Section 2.3).

Related Rules:

➢ Series (Section 5.1).
➢ Citing Parts: Periodical Articles and Statistical Tables (Section 6.0).

Consult examples in the *Quick Citation Guides*.
Ask a librarian for additional help.

HOW TO BEGIN—When more than one title (not just title variations found on spine and cover, for example) is given on any publication, take care to clarify the relationship between these titles before completing your citation.

Definition	How to identify them?	Rules to follow:
Citing a Part—Parts of larger works including journal or periodical articles, a data table, or data extracted from a database.	* Volume numbers (Fig. 12) * Page numbers * Data Table header (Fig. 11)	Follow rules in Section 6.0. Consult examples in the *Quick Citation Guides*.
Citing a Series—Series are used to bring related publications together under a common title.	* The word "Series" as part the series title; may be numbered (Fig. 9) * A monograph or book-like publication	Follow rules in Section 5.1. Consult examples in the *Quick Citation Guides*.

2.1 The Title Proper

The Title Proper is the part of the title that precedes the Subtitle (Section 2.2) or any additional supplied information, such as a hearing date (Section 2.1g).

Basic Rules:

* Give as shown in internal sources of information (Section 0.1).
* Underline or italize to set off from rest of citation elements; use punctuation as given or insert to clarify.
* Follow capitalization rules (Section 0.2).

Recommended Form and Punctuation:

U.S. Environmental Protection Agency, Office of Research and Development, Office of Environmental Engineering. *Energy Alternatives and the Environment, 1980: Handbook.* Washington: Government Printing Office, 1981.

2.1a Title Well-Known in Its Own Right

When a title is well-known in its own right, or if the Issuing Agency information will appear in the Title or in the Publishing Information (Section 4.0) you need not include an Issuing Agency. Begin the citation with the Title.

Yearbook of the United Nations, 1998. New York: Dept. of Public Information, 2001.

Variation for U.S. Censuses: The citation should begin with the title of the Census and year see *Quick Citation Guide to Periodical and Statistical Sources*, P12-P13 and P19.

Variation: When you would like to keep such publications together in your bibliography, the Issuing Agency can be included.

2.1b Multiple Titles

Some sources may provide two titles—a Project Title and a Report Title, for example, or a named annual report. In these cases, use the Report Title. If in your judgment the Project Title or annual report provides significant information, it can be included in a Note (Section 5.0).

Food and Agriculture Organization. *Projet Pilote pour le Developpement Intégré de la Pêche Artisanale. Guinee. Conclusions et Recommandations du Projet.* Terminal Report. (Project Number: GUI/87/025/R01). (Readex UNDP Reports Microfiche).

United Nations Development Programme. *Making New Technologies Work for Human Development.* New York: Oxford Univ. Pr., 2001. (*Human Development Report* 2001).

2.1c Excessively Long Titles

One of the outstanding characteristics of many government documents is an excessively long title. You need not cite the complete title; do not, however, leave out words in the beginning of the title or any important descriptive words. Omitted parts should be indicated with ellipses (. . .). For example, *Explanatory Report on the Protocol Amending the Convention of 6 May 1963 on the Reduction of Cases of Multiple Nationality and Military Obligations in the Case of Multiple Nationality and Explanatory Report on the Additional Protocol to the Convention of 6 May 1963 on the Reduction of Cases of Multiple Nationality and Military Obligations in Cases of Multiple Nationality* may safely be reduced to:

Council of Europe. *Explanatory Report on the Protocol Amending the Convention of 6 May 1963 on the Reduction of Cases of Multiple Nationality and Military Obligations . . . and . . . on the Additional Protocol*. Strasbourg, 1978.

U.S. Senate. Committee on Energy and Natural Resources. *Abandoned Shipwreck Act of 1987: Historic and Prehistoric Sites . . . St. Johns River . . . Chattanooga National Park, Georgia*. Washington: Government Printing Office, 1987. (Y4.En 2:S. Hrg.100-434).

2.1d No Title

When no meaningful title exists or no title is given in internal sources of information (Section 0.1) such as masthead publications or computer printouts, you may create a title that indicates the document's primary subject within brackets. This is more informative for readers than no title at all and will not affect their ability to locate the document when other identifying information is also provided.

Montana. Dept. of Community Affairs. Division of Research and Information Systems. [Profiles: Pondera County] (Computer Printout). 3rd ed. Helena, 1978.

U.N. General Assembly, 37th Sess. Letter . . . 25 October 1982 from the Permanent Representative of Israel . . . [on the Attack on Credentials of the Israeli Delegation] (A/37/565). 25 Oct. 1982. (Masthead).

2.1e Date as Part of Title

If the title includes a date as a part of the title, include the date, even though it may seem to be repeating the Date of Publication (Section 4.3) (Figs. 4 and 10). Underline or italicize as part of the title.

Note: The Date of Publication may differ from the date in the title, particularly with statistical publications, annual reports or historical publications being published and distributed long after their date of origin.

U.S. Bureau of the Census. *Tiger/Line Precensus Files, 1990: New England* (CD-ROM). Washington, 1990. (C3.280:N42e/990/CD).

U.S. Dept. of the Treasury. *Daily Treasury Statement, March 23, 1992*. Washington: Government Printing Office, 1992.

New Zealand. Dept. of Statistics. *Inter-Industry Study of the New Zealand Economy, 1986-1987*. Wellington: The Dept., 1991.

2.1f Abbreviations and Numbers as Part of Title

When a title includes abbreviations and numbers, these should be included as part of the title. If necessary for clarification, add missing letters enclosed in brackets.

Many legislative/parliamentary materials include terms which are often abbreviated and are readily recognized by researchers. For example, bill 231 introduced into the U.S. Congress House of Representatives would include "H.R. 231" as part of its Title. The abbreviation and number must be included as part of the Title for complete and accurate identification in every citation (Fig. 7).

Always use the form included on the document. Consult the *Quick Citation Guide to Legislative/Parliamentary Sources* for examples.

2.1g Adding a Date to Clarify a Title

Some publications record a hearing, conference, or meeting that took place on a particular date and in a particular place. When this information is not part of the Title Proper (Section 2.1e) or Issuing Agency statement (Section 1.0) but is judged to be relevant to a specific meeting, conference, or hearing, include the information following the title. Since this information is being included to enhance the title, do not italize or underline the information.

U.S. Congressional Hearings: The actual date of a hearing is not usually included in the Title although it usually appears on the title page. When this occurs, the title should be enhanced with "Hearing" and the date (or dates). (Fig. 6).

> U.S. House, Committee on Education and the Workforce. *Reading and Accountability: Improving 21st Century Schools*, Hearing, Feb. 20, 2001. (Serial 107-2). Washington: Government Printing Office, 2002. (Y4.ED8/1:107-2).

Note: Dates can be included in the European DD/MM/YYYY form, if the month is included in word form (see below). Months can be abbreviated, using standard abbreviations. Whatever form is used, be consistent throughout bibliography. Consult Section 4.3.

> U.S. House. Select Committee on Aging. *Recent Trends in Dubious and Quack Medical Devices*, Hearing, 9 Apr. 1992. Washington: Government Printing Office, 1992. (Y4.Sm 1:102-71).

U.S. Census: The date of the census year should also be included in a title proper, to distinguish titles within a specific census year's publications. Consult *Quick Citation Guide to Periodical and Statistical Sources*, P12-P13 and P19 for examples. See also Section 2.1a variation.

2.1h Location of Hearing, Conference, Meeting, and Symposia Named

For symposia and conference proceedings, give the place and date of the meeting (or either, if both are not known) following the title. Do not repeat information that is part of Title. The location of the hearing need not be included, unless it will distinguish the source from others with similar titles--for example, a series of hearings held in different cities and on different dates, but published under a common title.

> U.S. Dept. of Energy, Technical Information Center. *Energy and Environmental Stress in Aquatic Systems*, Symposium, Augusta, GA, 2-4 Nov. 1977 (CONF-771114). Washington: Dept. of Energy, 1978. (Symposium Series 48). (EI.10:771114).

 Note: Distinguish between a legislative/parliamentary meeting called a conference (Section 1.3) and a subject or agency conference (see example above) without legislative/parliamentary mandates.

A legislative/parliamentary meeting called a conference

> International Labour Organization Conference, 69th Sess., 1983. *Report VII: Social Aspects of Industrialisation*. Geneva, 1983.

2.1i Titled Volume in a Set

When citing a particular volume within a set, follow the set title, with the volume number and title (if individually titled). If not individually titled, follow the set title with the volume number only.

See also: Citing Periodical Articles (Section 6.0) and Series (Section 5.1).

United States. Senate. *Proceedings of the United States Senate in the Impeachment of Trial of President William Jefferson Clinton.* Vol. 3, *Depositions and Affidavits.* (S. Doc. 106-4). Washington: Government Printing Office, 2000. (Y1.1/3:106-4/V.3).

2.1j Popular Name Titles

Many government and organization reports, laws, and regulations are given or become known by popular names, frequently taken after the name of the chair of the commission or body that produced the report or law. Many bills and laws frequently include a "short title." Consult the *Quick Citation Guide to Legislative/Parliamentary Sources*, L1.5 and L1.6 for additional guidance (Figs. 1 and 8).

When the popular name title is not included on an internal source of information (Section 0.1), it can be included in a Note (Section 5.0) or inserted following the title in parentheses if the popular name is known or included on an external source.

U.N. Education, Scientific, and Cultural Organization, International Commission for the Study of Communication Problems. *Many Voices, One World: Communication and Society, Today and Tomorrow.* New York: Unipub, 1980. (Known as the MacBride Commission Report).

2.2 The Subtitle

Sometimes an internal source of information (Section 0.1) will include a Subtitle which might distinguish a generic Title Proper or help differentiate similar titles. Using the Subtitle may also help explain to your reader the relevance of this title to your research. Use a colon or other punctuation to separate the title and subtitle. Include other punctuation as needed for clarification.

U.S. Executive Office of the President, Office of National Drug Control Policy. *National Drug Control Strategy: A Nation Responds to Drug Use.* Washington: Government Printing Office, 1992. (PrEx 1.2:D84/992).

Maryland. Sales and Use Tax Division. *Maryland Sales and the Use Tax Tip Number 11: Agricultural Exemptions.* Baltimore, 1990.

International Labour Organisation. *To the Gulf and Back: Studies on the Impact of Asian Labour Migration.* Geneva, 1989.

2.3 Titles of Chapters and Other Parts

Usually you cite a whole book, report, or study. However, on occasion, it may be more appropriate to cite only a chapter, a data table, or section of the whole work, such as an encyclopedia or handbook. When to cite the whole work and when to cite only a part will depend on the purposes of your bibliography. How to cite a part will depend on the nature of the whole.

Basic Rules:

When a citation to a chapter, section, data table, or other part of a book or monograph is needed, cite the book as a whole preceded by the chapter (or other part) being cited.

Describe the Chapter by Including:

* The Author of the Chapter or other part, if present.

* Title of the Chapter or other part and any Unique Identifiers (Section 3.0).

* The range of pages, as appropriate.

Describe the Source by Including:

* Begin with the phrase "In".

* The complete citation to the book (follow rules in Sections 1.0-5.0).

* Include an editor in the manner of a Personal Author (Section 1.4).

Recommended Form and Punctuation:

"Engineers," pp. 64-72. In U.S. Bureau of Labor Statistics. *Occupational Outlook Handbook.* 1992-93 ed. Washington: Government Printing Office, 1992. (BLS Bulletin 2400).

Related Section:

* Citing Parts: Periodical Articles and Statistical Sources (Section 6.0).

* *Quick Citation Guide to Books and Monographs*

2.3a Conference Proceedings

When a conference proceedings includes an editor, include the editor in the manner of a Personal Author (Section 1.4).

When citing a paper or section of a Conference Proceeding, be sure the Conference is well-identified (Section 2.1h).

> Moghissi, A. A. "Biological Half Life of Tritium in Humans" (IAEA-SM-232/65), pp. 501-507. In International Atomic Energy Agency. *Behavior of Tritium in the Environment: Proceedings of a Symposium*, San Francisco, 16-20 Oct. 1978 (STI/PUB/498). Edited by Samuel S. Tristy. Vienna, 1979. (Proceedings Series).

2.3b Data Table Headers

When citing a single data table in an volume largely consisting of data tables, the data table header serves as the "title of the chapter." If the data table header includes a number (i.e., Table no. 235: OECD Countries Income), you may include the data table number as part of the title, or insert it following the data table header. The two approaches are shown below (Fig. 11).

"No. 938—Magazine Advertising Revenue by Category: 1998 and 1999," p. 579. In *Statistical Abstract of the United States, 2000*. 121st ed. Washington: Government Printing Office, 2000.

"Reported Voting and Registration by Citizenship, Race, Hispanic Origin: November 1996 and 2000," Table A, p. 5. In U.S. Census Bureau. *Voting and Registration in the Election of November 2000*. By Amie Jamieson, Hyon B. Shin, and Jennifer Day. Washington: Government Printing Office, Feb. 2002. (Current Population Reports; Population Characteristics, P20-542). (C3.186:P20/542).

"Population Changes," Table 1, p.12. In Denmark. Danmarks Statistik. *Monthly Review of Statistics,* No. 6, June 1992. Copenhagen: Danmarks Statistik, 1992.

2.3c Paper or Written Testimony Included in Legislative/Parliamentary Publications

Many legislative/parliamentary committee publications record testimony, committee recommendations and other information that may be cited separately from the publication as a whole.

Park, Robert L. "The Muzzling of American Science," pp. 609-614. In U.S. House, Committee on Government Operations. *Computer Security Act of 1987,* Hearing 25, 26 Feb. and 17 Mar. 1987. Washington: Government Printing Office, 1987. (Y4.G74/7:C43/29).

Roberts, Steven V. "The Congress, the Press and the Public," pp. 183-198. In U.S. House. *Understanding Congress: Research Perspectives, The Papers and Commentary from "Understanding Congress: A Bicentennial Research Conference,"* 9-10 Feb. 1989 (H. Doc. 101-241). Washington: Government Printing Office, 1991. (Y1.1/7:101-241).

Council of Europe. Parliamentary Assembly, 42nd Ordinary Sess., Jan. 28-1 Feb. 1991. "Report on Economic Reform in Central and Eastern Europe" (Doc. 6351), *Documents.* Strasbourg, 1991.

Consult the *Quick Citation Guide to Legislative/Parliamentary Sources* for additional examples and the *Quick Citation Guide to Special Cases and Well-Known Sources* for the Serial Set, S27, Official Gazettes, S21, and Legislative Journals, S19.

2.3d Chapters or Parts of a PEF Source

Governments and organizations frequently compile collections of books, statistics, and other sources and distribute them in a PEF, such as a CD-ROM, DVD, or floppy disk. The collection of resources frequently is archived for retention or packaged for a specific group (for example, the business community). This approach results in a "collection" of documents compiled into a single source, typically with a search interface to search across the many documents. In this situation, the phrase "In" can be replaced with "Available on" (or an equivalent phrase). See also Citing Parts: Periodical Articles and Statistical Sources (Section 6.0) and Menu-Driven Interface in PEF Sources (The Rule of Three) (Section 6.2a).

Note: Be sure to include an edition or publication date that provides adequate identification for the particular issue of the PEF source, since many of these sources are issued regularly in order to update and change the content.

U.S. International Trade Administration. *A Basic Guide to Exporting, 1992* (ID number: IT Guide). Available on: U.S. Dept. of Commerce. Economics and Statistics Administration. Office of Business Analysis. *NTDB: National Trade Data Bank* (CD-ROM). Washington, Oct. 1992. (C 1.88:992/3/CD).

"Energy: The Atlantic and Western Accords." Available on: Canada. Investment Canada. *The Canadian Edge* (Floppy Disk). English software edition, Release 3.0. Ottawa, 1988.

Note: Some parts, such as statutory sections, a regulatory section, or a data table, may include individual section and part numbers that constitute a unique identification for the Part being cited. Be sure to include these section and part numbers as part of the Title of the part, to ensure that the reader will be able to locate the exact part being cited. This may be particularly important with Parts included on a PEF source. The reader may need this information to locate the Part that has been included on a PEF source. Consult the *Quick Citation Guide to Special Cases and Well-Known Sources* for examples of the *Code of Federal Regulations*, S7; for Official Gazettes, S21; and the Quick Citation Guide to Legislative/Parliamentary Sources, L1.7.

> "ADA Standards for Accessible Design: 28 CFR Part 36" (4.5 mb). Updated 7/1/94. Text from: *ADA Technical Assistance CD-ROM.* Washington, 2001.

2.3e A Chapter or Other Part in Non-Print Format

Add a medium/publication type information (Section 3.3) to help your reader, such as "microfiche" or "CD-ROM".

> Warner, J. S. "Determination of Petroleum Components in Samples from the Metula Oil Spill" (NOAA DR ERL MESA 4; microfiche). Boulder, CO: NOAA, 1976. In U.S. National Oceanic and Atmospheric Administration. *The Metula Oil Spill.* By Charles G. Gunnerson and George Peter. Washington: Government Printing Office, 1976. (C55.602:M56).

3.0 UNIQUE IDENTIFIERS—Is there any additional information to distinguish this source?

Government and organization publications frequently include a wide range of unique identifying numbers that are omitted or overlooked in other style manuals. However, these unique identifiers can provide your reader with additional information that will help locate the source.

Types of Unique Identifiers:

* Publication/Report Numbers (Section 3.1).
* Edition Statement (Section 3.2).
* Medium or Publication Type (Section 3.3).

Recommended Form and Punctuation:

The preferred order, if more than one unique identifier is present, is:

Issuing Agency. *Title: Subtitle* (Medium) (Report Number). By Personal Author. Edition Statement. Publishing Information, Date. (Notes).

Related Sections:

* Notes (Section 5.2).

Consult examples in the *Quick Citation Guides*.
Ask a librarian for additional help.

3.1 Publication/Report Numbers

Some documents have printed on the cover and/or title page a combination of numbers and letters that is a unique identifying number for that publication or report. Many of these numbers help researchers locate the publication in some indexes, library on-line catalogs, and library collections. Some organizations consistently include these numbers on many of their publications. Consult *Appendix C: Numbering Systems* for examples of the report numbering schemes of the major IGOs and for information on where the number is likely to appear on the document. All Publication/Report numbers should be taken exactly as they appear on the document. If more than one report number is present, include them all (Fig. 9).

> **Basic Rule:**
>
> If a publication includes a unique identifying number (report, publication, or printer's number, for example) include this information in parentheses following the Title Statement.
>
> **Recommended Form and Punctuation:**
>
> Publication/Report numbers should be placed in parentheses immediately after the Title Proper (preceding the Personal Author statement, if present). Only the Medium or Publication Type (Section 3.3) would precede this information, if included.
>
> **Related Sections:**
>
> ➢ Superintendent of Documents (SuDocs) Numbers (Section 5.3e).
>
> ➢ United Nations Sales Number (Section 5.3f).
>
> ➢ Government Depository Numbering Systems (Section 5.3g).
>
> ➢ Catalog Numbering Systems (Section 5.4d).
>
> Consult examples in the Quick Citation Guides.
Ask a librarian for additional help.

Do not confuse an agency report number with a library call number or other numbering systems.

Do not confuse an agency report number with a contract or grant number. Grant/contract numbers are not unique to a document, but are instead applied to every document which is a product of that contract or grant. Grant/contract numbers are usually indicated on the document by "Grant No. xxx" or "Contract No. xxx."

Publication/Report Numbers (Common Variations)

> U.S. National Center for Health Statistics. *Family Structure and Children's Health: United States, 1988.* (DHHS Pub. No. PHS 91-1506). Hyattsville, 1991. (Vital and Health Statistics Series 10: Data from the National Health Survey No. 178). (HE20.6209: 10/178).

> U.N. Economic Commission for Latin America and the Caribbean. *Reforma agraria y empresas asociativas* (LC/L.497). Santiago, 1988.

> U.S. Dept. of Defense. *Hazardous Materials Information System: HMIS* (CD-ROM). (DOD 6050.5-L). n.p., May 1991. (D7.32:May 1991).

> U.S. House, Select Committee to Investigate Covert Arms Transactions with Iran. *Report of the Congressional Committees Investigating the Iran-Contra Affair* (H. Rpt. 100-133; S. Rpt. 100-216). Washington: Government Printing Office, 1988.

> U.S. House, Committee on Education and the Workforce. *Reading and Accountability: Improving 21st Century Schools*, Hearing, Feb. 20, 2001 (Serial 107-2). Washington: Government Printing Office, 2002. (Y4.ED8/1:107-2).

Printer's Number (typically used with legislation—bills, acts, resolutions)

Sometimes a printer's number will be assigned to legislation and serves as a useful number for differentiating among bill versions and amendments. These should be included following the title. If they are not useful as location devices, they may be omitted. If you are unsure about their value, it is best to include them.

For additional examples consult examples in the *Quick Citation Guide to Legislative/Parliamentary Sources.*

> Pennsylvania. General Assembly, 1992 Sess. *Senate Bill 1806, An Act Regulating the Check Cashing Industry* . . . (Printer's No. 2310). Harrisburg, 1992.

3.2 Edition Statement

Sometimes a document will be revised and published more than once as different "editions." This may be necessary to update content, to provide a new printing after previous editions have gone out of print, or to indicate the difference between a draft or working version and the final complete edition. Since content is often different, it is important to provide the reader with exact information about the edition you used.

The edition statement may be in the form of a:

> ➢ Number –2nd edition, 3rd edition, etc.

> ➢ Revision statement—revised edition.

> ➢ Edition type—limited edition, original edition, interim edition, draft edition, preliminary edition, terminal report.

> ➢ Language edition—French language edition.

> ➢ Frequency—daily edition, quarterly edition.

> ➢ Format edition—braille, microfiche, electronic edition (Section 3.3).

> ➢ Version (Software) (Section 3.2d).

> ➢ Legislative/parliamentary numbering (Section 3.2c).

Basic Rules:

* Include the edition after the title, use the edition statement as given on the publication.

* The word "edition" can be abbreviated: ed.

* Numbered editions can use the number form (3rd rather than third).

Recommended Form and Punctuation:

The edition statement follows the Title Statement and ends with a period.

Related Sections:

> ➢ Reprint Note (Section 5.3h).

Consult examples in the *Quick Citation Guides*.
As a librarian for additional help.

3.2a Edition Information Included Elsewhere in Citation

See also Date as Part of Title (Section 2.1e).

If the edition is clearly indicated by words in the Title Statement or the Publication/Report number (Section 3.3), it does not need to be repeated as a separate element in your citation. Some words that indicate an "edition" as part of a title include: "draft," "preliminary," "final," "summary," "a year," etc. are an essential part of the Title Statement and should always be included, even if they are only present in the subtitle of the publication.

> U.S. Bureau of Land Managment. *Draft Environmental Impact Statement: Transcolorado Gas Transmission Project.* Washington: Government Printing Office, 1991. (I1.98:T 68/draft).

> U.S. Dept. of Housing and Urban Development. *Public Housing Development Handbook* (HUD Handbook 7417.1, Rev.1). Washington: Government Printing Office, 1980. (HH1.6/6:7417.1).

> U.S. President's Committee on Employment of People with Disabilities. Braille ed. *Workforce Recruitment Program.* Washington, 1997. (PREX1.10.19:W89/5).

> Ozark Regional Commission. *The Consolidation of the Southeast Arkansas Solid Waste Authority: A Final Report.* Little Rock, Ark., 1981.

> Canada. Royal Commission on the Future of the Toronto Waterfront. *Regeneration —Toronto's Waterfront and the Sustainable City: Final Report.* Ontario: Queen's Printer of Ontario, 1992. (DSS cat. no. Z1-1988/1-1992-E).

> European Communities. Commission. *Commission's Proposals to the Council [on] . . . Generalized Tariff Preferences . . . 1982 to 1985 . . .* (COM(81)422 final). Brussels, 1981.

> Organisation for Economic Cooperation and Development, International Institute for Refrigeration. *Draft Code of Practice for Frozen Fish* (53-69-01-3). Paris, 1969.

3.2b Limited Editions

Some documents are frequently printed in a very limited quantity. If you are aware of this, inform your reader, since it may affect location of the document. Any phrases not included on the publication should be enclosed in brackets.

> Illinois. Commerce Commission, Public Utilities Division. *Operating Statistics of the Telephone Companies in Illinois, Year Ended Dec. 1991.* [Limited ed.] Springfield, 1992.

3.2c Legislative/Parliamentary Editions

Editions are inherent in the work of legislative/parliamentary bodies and in the creation of regulatory law. Bills, masthead documents, and a variety of other materials are issued in editions or versions and have a wide range of edition statement formats that are important identifiers for readers. Note: The "edition" name or number may not appear on the source itself, but rather as part of an index or database entry information (Fig. 7).

Bill version editions include:

- Engrossed
- Enrolled
- House/Senate Version
- As passed by the House/Senate
- Version Date:
- Star Print—indicated by a small star on the lower left corner of the title page.

U.S. Senate. 97th Congress, 1st Sess. *S. Res. 148, Resolution . . . for a Moratorium . . . on the Commercial Killing of Whales.* Star Print. Washington: Government Printing Office, 1982.

Consult examples in the *Quick Citation Guide to Legislative/Parliamentary Sources.*

3.2d Software Versions and Releases

Government agencies can be the source of a great deal of highly specialized software. Software citations will usually include personal authors and may also reflect joint projects between more than one agency or department. Include the version number as an edition statement; software frequently goes through several releases or revisions.

Note: Do not confuse the software release (for example, frequently given in the format: version 1.1.3) with the operating system version (DOS, Windows, etc). The operating system version information may be included in a Note (Section 5.5d) or omitted.

If you have a version, as well as an edition, language version, or specific operating sytem version statement, include both in your citation to assist your reader in distinguishing between versions. When in doubt, include as much information as is present on the source.

U.S. Dept. of Housing and Urban Development. *Community 2020: HUD Community Planning Software* (CD-ROM). Developed with Caliper Corp. Version 2.0; Deluxe ed. Newton, MA: Caliper Corp., 1997.

It is not necessary to repeat information included as part of the title.

Landview IV: Federal Geographic Viewer (DVD). Washington: Bureau of the Census, Geography Division, 2002.

3.3 Medium and Publication Type

The medium describes the physical format of the publication (e.g., DVD, floppy disk, videocassette). The publication type describes the nature of the publication (e.g., poster, brochure, map). While style manuals differ on whether to include the medium at all,[1] it is important to include them in citations to government and organization publications. It will help your reader locate the source you are citing and in determining the quality of the document. In addition, your reader may also experience special challenges locating and using non-print materials. Generally, the reasons for indicating the medium or publication type in a bibliographic citation are that they may:

➤ Require special housing and may be placed in separate locations in libraries.
➤ Require special equipment for use.
➤ Be indexed only in special resources.
➤ Be in the form of ephemera (brochure, pamphlets), thus content may differ in quality and extent.
➤ Be formatted in a specific manner or intended for a specific audience (press release) or use (poster).

Electronic formats present unusual challenges. Many PEF sources begin as a floppy disk, CD-ROM or tape file and are served up to users via the WWW (making them a VEF source—see Sections E0.0-E6.0 for rules to cite such sources). Identify the medium and publication type as accurately as possible to allow your reader a chance to locate the source in the future.

Basic Rules:

Provide the medium or publication type of the source you used to identify for your reader the format and type of publication you have used. Do not duplicate information supplied elsewhere in the citation, such as the Title (Section 2.0) or Notes (Section 5.2).

Recommended Form and Punctuation:

Include the Medium or Publication Type in parentheses following the title. It is not recommended that this information be merged into parentheses containing publication/report numbers (Section 3.1).

Related Sections:

* Note Information for (Section 5.2).
* Special Notes for PEF Sources (Section 5.5).
* Notes for Microfiche, Microfilm, and Microprint Collections (Sections 5.3a-5.3c).

Consult examples in the *Quick Citation Guides*.
Ask a librarian for additional help.

Medium and Publication Type (Common Variations)

AUDIO CASSETTE

U.S. Dept. of Labor, Women's Bureau. *Legal Rights of Women Workers* (Audio-Cassette). Washington, 1976.

BROCHURE

Pennsylvania. Dept. of Community Affairs. *Financing Parks and Recreation Facilities in Pennsylvania* (Brochure). 4th ed. Harrisburg, 1992.

CD-ROM

Australia. Dept. of Defence. *Defence 2000: Our Future Defence Force, A Public Discussion Paper* (CD-ROM). [Canberra]: NetImpact Online, 2000.

CHART

Joint United Nations Programme on HIV/AIDS. *A Global View of HIV Infections* (Chart). Geneva, Switzerland: UNAIDS, 2001.

COMPACT DISC/DVD

Canada Council. *Here and Now: A Celebration of Canadian Music* (Compact Disc). Produced in cooperation with the Canadian Broadcasting Corp. et al. Ottawa, Ont.: Canada Council, 1995. (4 Discs).

FACT SHEET

German Information Center. *Germany's Contribution to the Gulf Effort* (Fact Sheet). New York: German Information Center, 1991.

FILM

U.N. Centre for Human Settlements (HABITAT). *Action in Rural Living Areas* (Film). Nairobi, 1976. (16mm., 15 min., col.).

FLOPPY DISK

U.S. Coast Guard. *Merchant Marine Examination Questions: Book #4 Deck Safety* (Book 04, Year 92, Pt. 1; COMDTPUB P16721.25A) (Floppy Disk). Washington: Government Printing Office, 1992. (TD5.57/2:4/992/Pt.1).

MIMEOGRAPHED DOCUMENTS (IN-HOUSE DOCUMENTS)

U.S. Dept. of Education. *Investigation into Adolescent Promiscuity* (Mimeo). n.p., 1977.

MIXED MEDIA

U.N. Educational, Scientific, and Cultural Organization, Programme on Man and the Biosphere (MAB). *Man and the Humid Tropics* (Slide-Tape). By L. Hamilton. Paris: UNESCO Press, 1979. (MAB Audio-visual Series 1).

PAMPHLET

U.S. National Park Service. *Redwood* (Pamphlet). Washington: Government Printing Office, 1990. (I29.2:R24/990).

POSTER

Canada. Indian and Northern Affairs. Quebec Region. *Quebec Indians* (Poster). n.p.: Indian Affairs and Northern Development, 1988.

REALIA (THINGS)

U.N. [Secretariat], Office of Public Information. *Flag and Map Kit* (Realia). New York, 1976. (Sales No. E/F 76.I.3).

VIDEOCASSETTE

European Commission. *The Euro is Here!* (Videocassette). Dubbed version. Luxembourg: Office for Official Publications, 2001. (VHS format; 15 minutes).

3.3a Medium or Publication Type Included Elsewhere in Citation

You need not indicate the medium or publication type when you include the information elsewhere in the citation, for example in the Title (Section 2.0) or in a Note (Section 5.2).

U.S. Occupational Safety and Health Administration. *OSHA CD-ROM* (OSHA A92-1). Washington, Oct. 1991. (L35.26:92-1).

4.0 PUBLISHING INFORMATION—Who is publishing, printing, or distributing this source?

The publishing information part of a citation, or as librarians call it, the "imprint," provides the facts of publication. The rationale for including these elements is to distinguish among titles and editions and, in the case of government information, to alert the reader to a potential source for an item. These are important clues for researchers who may be trying to locate the government publications you have included in your bibliography. Unfortunately, with many government publications, some (if not all) parts of the publishing information is frequently missing. Yet it is an important part of the citation and care should be given to identify as many parts as possible (Fig. 8).

Parts of the Publishing Information Statement:

* Place of Publication (Section 4.1).

* Publisher (Section 4.2).

* Date of Publication (Section 4.3).

Related Sections:

➤ Authorship (Section 1.0).

Consult examples in the *Quick Citation Guides*.
Ask a librarian for additional help.

The manner in which government and international organization documents are published varies from country to country and organization to organization. There are several common patterns. The government or organization:

➤ May have an official printer or publishing agency that can be assumed, unless otherwise indicated (for example, United States: Government Printing Office; European Union: Office for Official Publications).

➤ May have no official printer or publisher that can be assumed; practice will vary, but the government agency is frequently assumed to be the publisher (for example, Canada and Great Britain and many states and local governments).

➤ Has many branches in many locations and publishes from many different locations. The Place of Publication varies (for example, the United Nations).

➤ Has used (or uses) a commercial publisher (for example, UNESCO).

HOW TO BEGIN: The publications of some governments and organizations demonstrate a consistent place of publication and publisher. For this reason, it is possible to supply missing information when either a Place of Publication or Publisher is not provided or when both are missing.

	If the Publisher is:	If the Place of Publication is:
National Governments		
Canada	Varies	Ottawa:
United Kingdom	HMSO Stationer's Office	London:
U.S.	Government Printing Office (If named anywhere on the document as printer, publisher, or sales agent, use as Publisher.)	Washington, D.C.:
International Organizations		
European Union	Office of Official Publications	Luxembourg:
United Nations	Varies	Varies; typically, New York or Geneva
States (U.S.)		
State Governments	Frequently a printer or the agency itself	Assume the state capital, unless otherwise indicated
Local governments	Frequently a printer or the agency itself	Assume the community of the issuing agency unless otherwise indicated
Regional Organizations	Frequently a printer or the agency itself	Assume the city where the organization's headquarters are located unless otherwise indicated
For all other situations	**Consult Section 4.0 for specific rules**	**Consult Section 4.1 for specific rules**

4.1 The Place of Publication

Basic Rules:

* Identify the geo/political place where the publication was published/printed.

* Give the name of the place in full (i.e., city and country or city and state); Washington D.C. can be Washington, if there is no chance that it will be confused with Washington state from the context; supply complete information if a place is not well-known or can be confused with another place (Section 4.1a).

* Do not translate place names; use form as it appears on the document.

Consult *How to Begin* (Section 4.0) if the Place of Publication is missing to identify any missing information.

Recommended Form and Punctuation:

Use a comma between place names (e.g., a city and a state); use common abbreviations (e.g., postal codes). Be consistent throughout your bibliography.

Consult examples in the *Quick Citation Guides*.
Ask a librarian for additional help.

4.1a Place of Publication Included Elsewhere

It is not necessary to repeat information already included elsewhere in the entry. For example, when the Place of Publication (e.g., a state or country) is listed in the Issuing Agency statement (Section 1.0), it can be omitted from the Publishing Information statement.

Similarly, when information is missing from the entry (for example, a place can be confused with another of the same or similar name, or be little known, outside a state or country), include information (a state or country name, for example) to clarify.

If a multistate regional organization does not include both the name of the city and the state of publication elsewhere in the entry, this information should be added to the Place of Publication.

Delaware River Water Authority. *Watershed Study for Southeast New Jersey.* By Thomas Burnett. Philadelphia, PA, 1983.

Rhode Island. Dept. of Economic Development. *Rhode Island Basic Economic Statistics 1990/91.* 7th ed. Providence, 1991.

Triad Regional Planning Commission (NC). *Housing Restoration in the Central Piedmont Area.* Greensboro, 1976.

Figure 8: Publishing Information

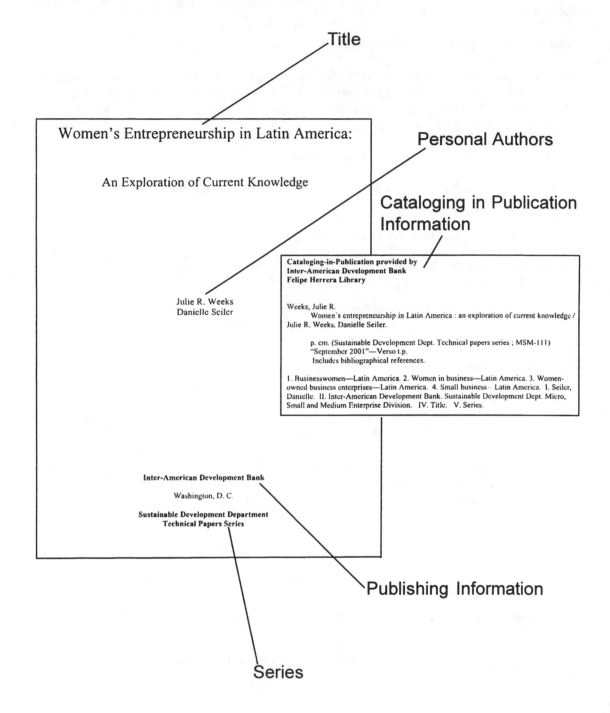

4.1b No Place of Publication

If you cannot locate a Place of Publication on an internal or external source of information (Section 0.1) or cannot make a *reasonable guess* by using sources such as *How to Begin* (Section 4.0) or your own knowledge of a government or organization's publishing practices, use "n.p." (no place).

Note: For many international organizations you cannot assume that a document comes from the headquarters city since international organizations have too many branches in too many locations. Do not *guess* at a place of publication.

If you make a *reasonable guess,* but have not found that information anywhere on the publication, insert the information in brackets to indicated it has been supplied.

> U.S. Dept. of Defense. *HMC&M: Hazardous Material Control & Management/HMIS: Hazardous Material Information System* (CD-ROM). n.p., Feb. 1992. (D212.16:Feb. 1992).

> U.S. Federal Insurance Administration. *In the Event of a Flood.* n.p., 1983.

> Canada. *A Consolidation of the Constitution Acts 1867 to 1982.* [Ottawa]: Dept. of Justice Canada, 2001.

> Canada. External Affairs and International Trade Canada. *Canada and the World Environment.* n.p.: Minister of Supply and Services Canada, 1992.

> U.N. Economic and Social Commission for Asia and the Pacific. *Handbook on Funding and Training Resources for Disability Related Services in Asia and the Pacific* (ST/ESCAP/541). n.p.: United Nations, 1989.

Note: for some special categories of publications such as working papers and documents from legislative/parliamentary bodies a place of publication and publisher may not be present, if they have been issued separately. In such cases, provide complete information as available on the source. Since many such sources are compiled in collections, your reader will be able to locate this source through other sources. (See Section 2.3c for an example of a working paper published as part of a collection.)

> Council of Europe. Parliamentary Assembly. *Report on Craftsmanship* (Doc. 4938). 20 July 1982.

4.1c Multiple Places of Publication

When a source includes more than one Place of Publication for the same publisher or Issuing Agency, use only one place. A general rule of thumb is to use the place in the country your publication will be published or distributed. For example, if New York and Geneva are offered, include New York if you will distribute/publish your work primarily in the United States.

4.2 The Publisher

National government and international organization publishing practices are not quite the same as those in the commercial sector. Strictly speaking, the agencies and organizations are the publishers since they alone have editorial control (Section 4.0). However, many governments also use printers or have a publishing agency (Consult *How to Begin*, Section 4.0) and the Issuing Agency has already been identified in the Authorship statement (Section 1.0). Therefore the publisher may frequently be included elsewhere in the citation and need not be repeated.

Basic Rules:

* Identify the source responsible for the publication/printing of the source.

* Give the name of the Publisher in full in the form given on the source, however, it is not necessary to repeat information included elsewhere in the citation.

* Do not translate non-English Publisher names, use the form as it appears on the document.

Consult *How to Begin* (Section 4.0) if the Publisher is missing for help identifying any missing information.

Recommended Form and Punctuation:

Use a colon between the Place of Publication and the Publisher. Use standard abbreviations for words such as company (Co.), limited (Ltd.), or incorporated (Inc.). Be consistent throughout your bibliography.

Related Sections:

* Authorship (Section 1.0).

Consult examples in the *Quick Citation Guides*.
Ask a librarian for additional help.

4.2a Publisher Information Included Elsewhere

If the Issuing Agency is also the publisher/printer, it is not necessary to repeat information already included elsewhere in the entry. If the name has already been given in full as the Issuing Agency, you may omit the name entirely and proceed with the Date of Publication (Section 4.3) (for example, Washington, 2001.), or use a phrase such as "The Department," "The Agency," or use the agency acronym or abbreviation, for example, the Department of Health and Human Services would become DHHS. Be consistent throughout the bibliography.

> U.S. National Defense University. *Afghanistan: The First Five Years of Soviet Occupation.* By Bruce Armstutz. Washington: NDU Press, 1986. (D5.402:Af3).

> Minnesota. Pollution Control Agency. *MEPA Hazardous Waste Compliance Guide.* St. Paul, 1991.

> Canadian Institute for International Peace and Security. *The Canadian Navy: Options for the Future.* By Robert H. Thomas. Ottawa: The Institute, 1992.

4.2b No Publisher Included

If you cannot locate a Publisher on an internal or external source of information (Section 0.1) or cannot make a *reasonable guess* by using sources such as *How to Begin* (Section 4.0) or your own knowledge of a government or organization's publishing practices, leave the element blank.

If you make a *reasonable guess,* but have not found that information anywhere on the publication, insert the information in brackets to indicate it has been supplied.

> Colorado. Bureau of Investigation. *Crime in Colorado: Uniform Crime Report.* Denver, 1990.

United Kingdom. Home Office. *The Response to Racial Attacks: Sustaining the Momentum.* n.p., 1991. (Second Report of the Inter-Department Racial Attacks Group).

Council of Europe. European Public Health Committee. *Family Planning.* Strasbourg, 1977.

World Bank. *The Education Finance Simulation Model* (Floppy Disk). n.p., 1987.

4.2c Multiple Publishers or Printers

Some governments have more than one major printer or distributer. When an alternative printer or distributer is indicated, use this instead of the primary printer or publishing agency. This will lead your reader more quickly to a source for purchase.

Note: For the United States—alternative printers/distributers to the Government Printing Office include NTIS or ERIC. Consult the *Quick Citation Guide to Special Cases and Well-Known Sources*, Clearinghouse Documents, S6 for examples.

Many PEF sources (such as a CD-ROM or floppy disk) include information about a software developer (the software is used to access the information or data contained on the CD-ROM or floppy disk; a government or organization is responsible for the data or information). The software developer need not be included in the bibliographic citation unless it is the only information indicating the source of the electronic format. Information about the software developer can be included in a Note (Section 5.5). Rather, include in the Publishing Information the publisher or printer responsible for printing/distributing the CD-ROM source itself; if not present, omit the Publisher Information.

U.S. Dept. of Commerce, Bureau of Economic Analysis, Regional Economic Measurement Division. *REIS: Regional Economic Information System* (CD-ROM). Washington, May 1991. (C57.24:991/CD/1).

4.2d Publisher, Issuing Agency, and Personal Author

When the publisher, an Issuing Agency, and a Personal Author are present, all should be included in the citation.

Canada. Federal Provincial Relations Office. *The European Community: A Political Model for Canada?* By Peter M. Leslie. Ottawa: Minister of Supply and Services Canada, 1991. (DSS. Cat. No. CP22-35/1991E).

4.2e Commercial Publishers

UNESCO Press publications are an excellent example of publications published by commercial publishers on behalf of governments and organizations, or in addition to the version published by the official government publisher. Such publications look like commercially published books (i.e., they are not photoreproduced, have a title page, are published in Paris, and have a UNESCO copyright). To distinguish them from other UNESCO publications which are not from UNESCO Press, you should use the Press as the publisher. In such circumstances, use the form of the publisher's name exactly as given on the publication. Be sure to include an Issuing Agency as the author (Section 1.0). This ensures the Issuing Agency is recognized in the citation.

U.N. Educational, Scientific, and Cultural Organization. *Biotechnologies in Perspective: Socio-Economic Implications for Developing Countries.* Albert Sasson and Vivien Costarini, eds. Paris: UNESCO Press, 1991.

U.S. Office of Management and Budget. *North American Industry Classification System.* Indianapolis, IN: JIST, 1999.

Great Britain. Minister of Transport. *Traffic in Towns, the Specially Shortened Version of the Buchanan Report.* By Collin D. Buchanan. Harmondsworth, Eng.: Penguin, 1964.

U.N. Institute for Disarmament Research. *National Security Concepts of States: New Zealand.* By Kennedy Graham. New York: Taylor and Francis, 1989.

<u>Variation</u>: Universities occasionally publish documents for state agencies as "university press books." This information should be included in the imprint statement.

North Carolina. Dept. of Cultural Resources. Division of Archives and History. *The Quest for Progress: The Way We Lived in North Carolina, 1870-1920.* By Sydney Nathans. Chapel Hill: University of North Carolina, 1983.

<u>Variation</u>: State data centers are cooperative enterprises between state governments and the U.S. Census Bureau. The reports should be cited as state reports, including issuing agency, title, report numbers, and imprint data.

Pennsylvania. State Data Center. *Pennsylvania Municipalities: Population and Per Capita Income Estimates* (PSDC88-19-90). Middletown, 1990.

Texas. State Data Center. *Final Population and Housing Counts for Texas Cities, Counties, SMSA's.* Austin, 1981.

4.2f Co-Published Sources

When a book is co-published by an organization or government and a commercial publisher, cite both if the government or international organization is not named as author. If the organization or government is used as the Issuing Agency (Section 1.0), the second publisher can be included in the Publishing Information.

U.S. Industry & Trade Outlook. New York: DRI/McGraw-Hill, Standard & Poor's; Washington, D.C.: U.S. Dept. of Commerce/International Trade Administration, 2000. (C 61.48).

U.N. Development Programme. *Investing in the Future: Setting Educational Priorities in the Developing World.* By Jacques Hallak. Paris: UNESCO International Institute for Educational Planning; Oxford: Pergamon Press, 1990.

4.2g Omitting Publishing Information

You may omit place and publisher for certain types of publications:

* Citing Parts: Periodical Articles and Statistical Sources (Section 6.0) and many other Special Cases (S6.0).

* Masthead publications (Section 5.3d; Fig. 10) and many other Legislative/Parliamentary sources—these publications are distributed to committees (not published) and can be located using other information included in the citation. Consult examples in the *Quick Citation Guide to Legislative/Parliamentary Sources*, L3.1

4.3 The Date of Publication

The publication or issue date may take the form of a year, a month, or a specific date, or an issue date and year (May 1989; Fall 1992). Be sure to use the form that will ensure that the item can be accurately identified.

Dates should be entered in the form MM/DD/YYYY. When the European style date is used (DD/MM/YYYY), to avoid confusion, use the standard abbreviations for months (e.g., 4 Aug. 1955). This form will be particularly prevalent on non-U.S. government and organization sources.

Do not mix styles within the same entry in a bibliography. Be consistent throughout your bibliography. Consult also Section 2.1g.

Some publications are issued (or reissued) frequently and a date and year may be necessary to accurately identify the source you are citing. When in doubt, use more information, rather than less.

Basic Rules:

* Identify the year of publication, to ensure adequate identification of the source cited.

* You may include a month or issue (e.g., Fall) if necessary to adequately identify a publication.

* Do not include information included elsewhere in the citation.

* Copyright date is indicated by a small case © prior to the date, it can be omitted from the citation.

Recommended Form and Punctuation:

Use a comma after the Publisher and prior to the Date of Publication. If a day and month is included with the year of publication, the month may be abbreviated and should be separated from the year by a comma.

Related Sections:

➢ Date as Part of Title (Section 2.1e).

➢ Issue Identifiers: Volume, Issue, Date (Section 6.4a).

Consult examples in the *Quick Citation Guides*.
Ask a librarian for additional help.

Using date stamps to establish a Publication Date

It is a common practice in some libraries to stamp documents with the date of receipt. If no other publication date is available you may use this date in your citation. Include this information in brackets preceded by the word "by". This will tell your reader that the document would have been published by that date. The brackets tell the reader you are supplying this information.

U.S. Dept. of Defense. *Radar Training Manual* (DATM 90-2-AX). Washington: DOD, [by 1975].

Rhode Island. Dept. of Business Regulations. *72nd Annual Report of the Banking Division.* Providence, [by 1979].

U.S. Environmental Protection Agency, Office of Toxic Substances. *Toxic Chemical Release Inventory: Title III-Emergency Planning and Community Right-to-Know Act of 1986* (CD-ROM). Washington, [by 1990]. (EP 5.22:T65/990).

4.3a Date Included Elsewhere

If a Date is Part of the Title (Section 2.1e), it is still necessary to include the Publication Date in the Publishing Information. Frequently dates in the title do not directly correspond to the Date of Publication, and this ensures complete information for your reader.

U.S. Dept. of State. *Soviet Active Measures, September 1983.* Washington: Government Printing Office, 1983. (Special Report No. 110). (S1.129: 110).

Maine. State Library. *Libraries in Maine 1990-91.* Augusta, 1991.

When a PEF source includes software, do not use the software copyright dates as the date of publication for the electronic source itself. This information may appear in a Note (Section 5.5).

4.3b No Date of Publication

If you cannot find a date of publication, use "n.d." (no date).

U.S. Dept. of Education, National Center for Education Statistics. *High School and Beyond: 1980 to 1986* (CD-ROM). Washington: Government Printing Office, n.d. (ED1.334:980-86/CD).

U.S. Forest Service, Pacific Northwest Region. *Forests for the Future: Growing New Forests in the Pacific Northwest* (6 Leaflets). n.p., n.d.

Illinois. State Board of Elections. *A Candidate's Guide for 1982 Elections.* Springfield, n.d.

Malawi. Office of the President. *Statement of Development Policies, 1987-1996.* Zomba: Government Printer, n.d. (With the Dept. of Economic Planning and Development).

4.3c Multiple Dates of Publication

Some publications may have several dates—an issuance date, a date of adoption (for a law, treaty, regulation), or the date an event took place (a hearing or convention for example), or a date of issuance (United Nations masthead publications, for example; Fig. 10). Be sure to use the date that best represents the date of publication or printing, not a date that represents the occurrence, effectiveness or legality of a publication's content. Consult Multiple Titles (Section 2.1b).

5.0 SERIES AND OTHER NOTES—What more can you add about this source?

Concluding many citations to government and organization sources is information often overlooked in many other citation style manuals: Series and Notes statements. These often provide important information that does not fit elsewhere in the citation.

Series:

Many government and organization publications are released in series—a group of publications, each with its own distinct title, but brought together under a series title. Some series include numbers for each of the unique titles in the series, others do not. Readers who are knowledgeable about specific series in their subject or discipline will want this information. It may also help the researcher locate a source more easily in a library or from a distributer. For rules, consult Section 5.1.

Notes:

Notes are a catch-all category in which you can place significant information which does not fit in other segments of the citation. Depending upon the specific data, notes may or may not be required. PEF sources (such as CD-ROMs and floppy disks) may require their own "special" notes due to their format. These are covered in a separate section in this chapter. For rules, consult Section 5.2.

5.1 Series

Series are used to connect publications on similar topics (the Current Population Reports Series provides summary analysis and reports of population growth and change in the United States) (Fig. 5); to identify publications of a certain type (the Water Resources Investigation Series brings together preliminary research findings); to group the major publications of an issuing agency (the Bulletins of the Bureau of Labor Statistics bring together a wide range of informational publications from the U.S. Department of Labor); or to group statistical publications derived from a specific dataset (the Vital and Health Statistics Series provides analysis of the National Health Interview Survey) (Fig. 9). Series can become quite important for organizing information produced by an organization or agency, for example, Eurostat, the Statistical Office of the European Communities, organizes its statistical publications into series called "themes" and "collections."

Historically, libraries and many finding tools listed government and organization publications by their series name only. For this reason, it is important that citations to historical publications (prior to 1976) include the series information as part of the citation. The series name and number (if applicable) can be an important shortcut in locating a document. Furthermore, some series titles and numbers are cited frequently by researchers, and including this information will ensure that you are providing your readers with information that is meaningful and useful. Series can be confused with *Citing a Part* (Section 6.0). And, they can be difficult to distinguish in some cases. Consult the *How to Begin* (Section 2.0) for guidance in distinguishing between a source's Title, Citing a Part, and Citing a Series.

Basic Rules:

* Identify the series title at the end of the citation. The citation should describe the distinct title in the Series (Fig. 9).
* Include a series number, if present; insert punctuation as needed to clarify; use standard abbreviations for numbered series (for example, no. 178).
* Do not duplicate information included elsewhere in the citation (Section 5.1a).

Recommended Form and Punctuation:

U.S. National Center for Health Statistics. *Family Structure and Children's Health: United States, 1988.* Washington: Government Printing Office, 1991. (Vital and Health Statistics Series 10: Data from the National Health Survey No. 178). (HE20.6209: 10/178).

Related Sections:

➢ Citing Parts: Periodical Articles and Statistical Sources (Section 6.0).

➢ Title (Section 2.0).

➢ Unique Identifiers: Publication/Report Numbers (Section 3.1).

Consult examples in the *Quick Citation Guides*.
Ask a librarian for additional help.

<u>Series (Common Variations)</u>

U.S. Census Bureau. *Sixty-Five Plus in the U.S.* By Frank B. Hobbs and Bonnie L. Damon Washington: Government Printing Office, 1996. (Current Population Reports; Special Studies, P23-190). (C3.186:P23/190).

European Union Foreign Direct Investment Yearbook (CD-ROM). Prepared by Eurostat. English ed. Luxembourg: Office for Official Publications of the European Communities, 2000. (Theme 2—Economy and Finance).

United Kingdom. Home Office. *Traffic Calming: the Reality of 'Road Rage.'* By Emma Marshall and Nerys Thomas. Nov. 2000. (Briefing Note 12/00).

Figure 9: Publication/Report Numbers and Series

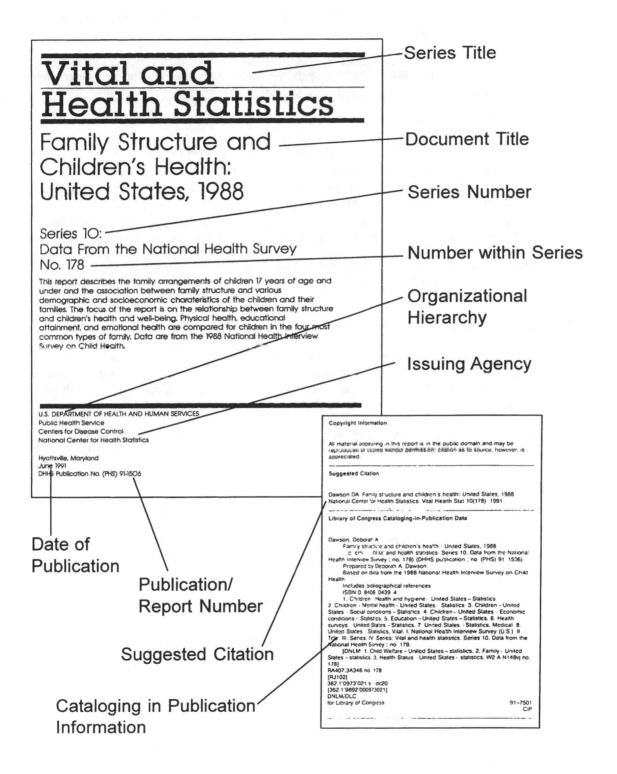

5.1a Series Number Repeated in Publication/Report Number

If a series number is given in the Publication/Report Number, do not repeat the report number (Section 3.1) in the Series Statement.

> U.S. Environmental Protection Agency. *Bioflocculation and the Accumulation of Chemicals by Floc-Forming Organisms.* By Patrick R. Dugan. (EPA-600/2-75- 032).Washington: Government Printing Office, 1975. (Environmental Protection Technology Series). (EP1.23/2:600/2-75-032).

5.1b Multiple Series Statements

If a document belongs to more than one series, cite all the applicable series.

> U.S. Census Bureau. *Voting and Registration in the Election of November 2000.* By Amie Jamieson, Hyon B. Shin, and Jennifer Day. Washington: Government Printing Office, Feb. 2002. (Current Population Reports; Population Characteristics, P20-542). (C3.186:P20/542).

> Food and Agriculture Organization of the United Nations. *Pesticide Residues in Food: Report of the 1976 Joint Meeting of the FAO Panel of Experts on Pesticide Residues and the Environment and the WHO Expert Group on Pesticide Residues,* Rome, 22-30 Nov. 1976. Rome: The Organization, 1977. (FAO Food and Nutrition Series No. 9; FAO Plant Production and Protection Series No. 8; World Health Organization Technical Report Series No. 612). (Published jointly with WHO).

5.1c Documents in Another Government or Organization's Series

If a document is prepared in cooperation with another government agency or organization (Section 1.2d), it may be part of a series belonging to that other government or organization. This may occur with state, local or regional publications that are prepared in cooperation with a federal government agency. If this is the case, it should be noted in either a Title or a Series statement.

> Florida. Dept. of Environmental Regulation. *Source, Use, and Disposition of Water in Florida, 1980.* By Stanley Leach et al. Tallahassee, 1983. (U.S. Geological Survey. Water Resources Investigation 82-4090).

5.2 Notes

Notes can be used to describe the physical format of a source, for example, microfiche or microfilm (Sections 5.3a-5.3b) or to provide a unique classification number, for example, SuDoc number (Section 5.3e). Generally, a Note can be used to include any additional information you believe will help the reader locate a particular source.

Types of Notes:

* Required Notes (Section 5.3).

* Optional Notes (Section 5.4).

* Special Notes for PEF Sources (Section 5.5).

Recommended Form and Punctuation:

International Telecommunications Satellite Organization. *IntelSat Report,* 1990-91. Washington, 1991. (1992 IIS microfiche 2090-S1).

Multiple notes can be included in enclosed in parentheses, separated by semi-colons.

Related Sections:

➤ The Series Statement (Section 5.0).

➤ Unique Identifiers: Medium and Publication Type (Section 3.3).

Consult examples in the *Quick Citation Guides*.
Ask a librarian for additional help.

5.3 Required Notes

Required notes help your reader locate your source more easily. They are listed here in their order of importance and, if multiple notes are needed, should be included in the citation in this order.

Basic Rules:

Two reasons for Required Notes:

* To help your reader find *precisely* the same material you have in hand.
* Assist your reader in locating or using the information source.

Related Sections:

➤ Unique Identifiers: Medium or Publication Type (Section 3.3).

5.3a Microfiche Collections

Some government and organizations began selling and distributing their publications in microfiche (or microfilm) in the early 1980s. In addition, commercial publishers distribute government and organization publications as part of microprint (used prior to 1990), microfiche or microfilm collections. These collections are frequently found in libraries; for ready access, documents from these collections should be identified as such. Be sure to describe the source using the title on the title page frame of the microfiche (Section 0.1) (Fig. 4).

<u>Government and Organization Microform Collections (Common Variations)</u>

When the microform's source is the government publisher/printer, the format can be included following the title, in the manner of the Medium and Publication Type Information (Section 3.3). The Publishing Information Section provides adequate identification for the microfiche.

> U.S. Bureau of Outdoor Recreation. *National Urban Recreation Study: Dallas Fort Worth* (Microfiche). Washington: Government Printing Office, 1977. (I66.24:D16).

> Delaware. Dept. of Natural Resources and Environmental Control. *Mosquito Control in Delaware* (Microfiche). Dover, 1989.

> Food and Agriculture Organization of the United Nations. *ESN-Nutritional Country Profile: Barbados* (Microfiche). Rome, 1989. (FAO Acc. No. 290723).

> Organisation for Economic Cooperation and Development. *Household Waste: Separate Collection and Recycling* (Microfiche) (97-82-09-1). Paris, 1983.

The U.S. Government Printing Office distributes bills and resolutions on microfiche; few institutions retain back files of these bills in paper form. Therefore, it is likely you will be citing, and your reader will be looking for, the microfiche edition. In order to facilitate locating the bill, you should include the fiche number and frame coordinates in a note.

> U.S. House, 102nd Congress, 1st Sess. *H.R. 205, A Bill To Amend the Social Security Act ...* Washington: Government Printing Office, 1991. (GPO microfiche 59, coordinate A3).

<u>Commercial Microfiche Collections (Common Variations)</u>

If you are using a document from a commercially produced collection, you must cite both the original document and the microfiche collection. The first part of the citation should contain a complete reference to the original paper document, taken from the title page frame of the microfiche. The information about the collection should be given in a note at the end. What information is given will depend on the organization of the collection—typically it includes the name of the collection and the year. Information should be taken from the microfiche header, when possible (Fig. 4). Common examples are shown below.

> U.S. Dept. of Health, Education and Welfare. *The Measure of Poverty*. Washington: DHEW, 1976. (1976 ASI microfiche 4006-3).

> U.S. Senate. *History of the Committee on Finance* (S. Doc.95-27). Washington: Government Printing Office, 1977. (1977 CIS microfiche S360-1).

> Nordic Medico-Statistical Committee. *Health Statistics in the Nordic Countries, 1988*. Copenhagen, 1990. (1990 IIS microfiche 2195-51).

> District of Columbia. Dept. of Employment Services. *Women in the Labor Force, Washington D.C. and Metropolitan Area 1989*. Washington, [by 1981]. (1991 SRI microfiche S1527-2).

> U.N. Economic and Social Council, 55th Mtg. *Agenda Item 5: The Problem of Mass Poverty and Unemployment in Developing Countries* (E/Res/1808). 10 Aug. 1973. Official Record, Annexes. New York, 1974. (Readex microfiche 1973).

> International Labour Office, World Employment Programme. *Education and Employment: A Synthesis*. By Jan Verslius (WEP 2-18/WP 19). Geneva, 1979. (WEP Research Working Papers in Microfiche 1978).

Vermont, Secretary of State. *Primary and General Elections Vermont 1980 Including Presidential Preference Primary.* Prepared by the Vermont Elections Project. Burlington: University of Vermont Agricultural Experiment Station, 1981. (1981 SRI microfiche S8115-1).

Philadelphia, PA, City Planning Commission. *Philadelphia Center City Walking Tour.* 1976. (Urban Documents Microfiche Collection PPA-0227).

Royal Canadian Mounted Police. *National Drug Intelligence Estimate, 1989, with Trend Indicators through 1991.* Ottawa: RCMP Public Affairs Service, 1991. (1992 *Directory of Statistics in Canada* 22279.002).

Variation: Some collections follow the organization of the source from which they were filmed. Greenwood Press has produced a microfiche collection of the holdings of the Senate Library. This collection uses the Senate volume number as an accession number. Since several documents may be found in one volume, you should also include the "tab" number for location on the microfiche.

U.S. Senate, Committee on Labor and Public Welfare. *Mine Safety Hearings*, 18-19, 24-27, 31 May 1949. Washington: Government Printing Office, 1949. (81st Congress Greenwood Press microfiche S. Vol. 908-1).

5.3b Microfilm Collections

Be sure to describe the source using the title on the title page frame of the microfilm (Section 0.1). Do not rely on the storage box for the title.

Great Britain. Foreign Office. *Foreign Office Files for Japan and the Far East: Series Three—Embassy and Consular Archives, Japan (Post 1945) (Public Record Class FO262), Detailed Correspondence for 1944-1957* (Microfilm). Marlborough, Wiltshire, England: Adam Matthew Publications, 1996. (7 reels).

Ireland. Central Statistical Office. *Census of Population of Ireland, 1981. Vol. 3, Household Composition and Family Units.* Dublin: Stationary Office, 1985. (*International Population Censuses*: Ireland Reel 1, 1981).

5.3c Microprint Collections

Be sure to describe the source using the title on the title page frame of the microprint (Section 0.1). Do not rely on the storage box for the title.

U.S. Dept. of Health, Education and Welfare. *Management by Objectives: Planning Where to Go and How to Get There.* By T. H. Bell. n.p., 1974. (1974 Readex non-depository microcard 01191).

U.N. General Assembly, 36th Session. *Preliminary List of the Provisional Agenda of the 36th Regular Session . . .* (A/36/50). 15 Feb. 1981. (1982 Readex microprint).

U.N. Economic and Social Council, 62nd Sess. *Resolution 2086 (LXII) Infringements of Trade Union Rights in Southern Africa* (E/Res/2086 (LXII). 23 May 1977. (Readex microprint).

5.3d Masthead Documents

Masthead documents are neither sales publications nor official records. They are documents printed and distributed in small quantities for U.N. officials and not meant for public distribution. However, they are readily available in many libraries and in electronic form. Thus, they are not difficult to find, but telling your readers they are Masthead documents will send them directly to an established category of U.N. documentation (Fig. 10). Consult the *Quick Citation Guide to Legislative/Parliamentary Sources*, L3.1 for additional examples.

Masthead Documents (Common Variations)

U.N. General Assembly, Preparatory Committee for the United Nations Conference on Environment and Development. *Protection and Management of Land Resources: Compilation of Proposals by Governments, 4th Sess.*, New York, 3 Mar.-2 Apr. 1992 (A/CONF.151/PC/105). 15 Jan. 1992. (Masthead).

> Food and Agriculture Organization, Food Preservation Study Group. *Study of Crop Losses in Storage, State of Zacatecas, Mexico 1965-1975.* By Hugo Perkins et al. n.p., 1976. (Masthead).

Figure 10: Notes: U.N. Masthead Documents

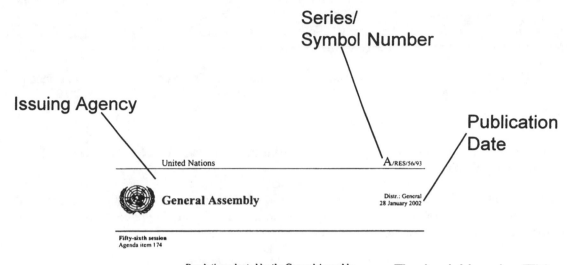

Series/
Symbol Number

Issuing Agency

Publication
Date

United Nations

A/RES/56/93

General Assembly

Distr.: General
28 January 2002

Fifty-sixth session
Agenda item 174

Resolution adopted by the General Assembly

Typical Header/Title

[on the report of the Sixth Committee (A/56/599)]

56/93.   **International convention against the reproductive cloning of human beings**

The General Assembly,

Recalling the Universal Declaration on the Human Genome and Human Rights,[1] adopted by the General Conference of the United Nations Educational, Scientific and Cultural Organization on 11 November 1997, in particular article 11 thereof, in which the Conference specified that practices which are contrary to human dignity, such as reproductive cloning of human beings, shall not be permitted and invited States and international organizations to cooperate in taking, at the national or international level, the measures necessary in that regard,

Recalling also its resolution 53/152 of 9 December 1998, by which it endorsed the Universal Declaration on the Human Genome and Human Rights,

Bearing in mind Commission on Human Rights resolution 2001/71 of 25 April 2001, entitled "Human rights and bioethics",[2] adopted at the fifty-seventh session of the Commission,

Noting the resolution on bioethics adopted by the General Conference of the United Nations Educational, Scientific and Cultural Organization on 2 November 2001,[3] in which the Conference approved the recommendations by the Intergovernmental Bioethics Committee towards the possible elaboration, within the United Nations Educational, Scientific and Cultural Organization, of universal norms on bioethics,

Aware that the rapid development of the life sciences opens up tremendous prospects for the improvement of the health of individuals and mankind as a whole, but also that certain practices pose potential dangers to the integrity and dignity of the individual,

---

[1] United Nations Educational, Scientific and Cultural Organization, *Records of the General Conference, Twenty-ninth Session*, vol. 1, *Resolutions*, resolution 16.
[2] See *Official Records of the Economic and Social Council, 2001, Supplement No. 3* (E/2001/23), chap. II. sect. A.
[3] United Nations Educational, Scientific and Cultural Organization, *Records of the General Conference, Thirty-first Session*, vol. 1, *Resolutions*, resolution 22.

01 47951

5.3e Superintendent of Documents (SuDoc) Numbers

A Superintendent of Documents (SuDoc) number is assigned to most U.S. documents published/printed by the U.S. Government Printing Office. They are used in many libraries as the publication's call number. The SuDoc number should not be confused with the Unique Publication/Report Number (Section 3.1). When known, it should be included in a citation, as it provides a valuable identifier for U.S. documents.

> U.S. Smithsonian Institution. *Through Looking to Learning: The Museum Adventure*. Edited by Thomas E. Lowderbaugh. Washington: Smithsonian Institution Press, 1983. (SI1.2:M97/6).

5.3f United Nations Sales Numbers

Note: For U.N. documents' Series/Symbols, consult Publication/Report Section 3.1 and *Appendix C: Numbering Systems.*

The UN Sales Number should be included in a note when there is no series/symbol number. The sales number may be found on the back cover or on the back of the title page. When both sales number and a series symbol are present, both should be included.

> U.N. Dept. of Public Information. *Basic Facts About the United Nations* (DPI/915). New York, 1987. (UN Sales No. E.88.1.3).

5.3g Government Depository Numbering Systems

Some publications of foreign governments are issued with a classification number assigned by the central depository distribution agency. If a document number is printed on the publication, or if you know the number from a government issued catalog, include this number in your citation. For example, Canadian depository numbers are frequently listed as: DSS Cat No.; U.S. documents are called Superintendent of Documents (SuDoc) Numbers (Section 5.3e); and other numbering systems are used by other governments.

> Canada. Treasury Board Secretariat. Administrative Policy Branch. Regulatory Affairs. *How Regulators Regulate*. Ottawa: Minister of Supply and Services Canada, 1992. (DSS Cat No. BT56-5/1992).

In Canada, the Canadian depository number can be closely related to its Catalog Numbering System (Section 5.4d). For example, some depository publications will use a catalog number as part of the Government Depository Numbering System.

> Wadhera, Surinder, and Jill Strachan. *Selected Infant Mortality and Related Statistics, Canada, 1921-1990*. Ottawa: Statistics Canada, Canada Centre for Health Information, 1993. (DSS Cat no. CS 82-549; Catalogue no. 82-549 occasional; Text in English and French).

If the material you are citing is part of an official census but this is not evident from the title, include this information as a note after the imprint information.

> Statistics Canada. *Mother Tongue: The Nation*. Ottawa: Supply and Services Canada, 1992. (1991 Census; catalogue no. CS 93-313).

5.3h Reprint Note

A reprint is similar to an Edition (Section 3.2) as it constitutes a new printing. A reprint note also provides your reader with information about the exact source you used. The publications of governments and organizations may be reprinted by commercial publishers. Infrequently, a government or an organization distributes documents which have not been issued or written by the agency itself or its sub-agencies. In these cases an agency has partially sponsored the writing or development of the document, and the government reprints and distributes the commercial publication.

For such documents, a citation to the item should include the personal author, title, edition, imprint, and series data, as applicable. Since there may be no straightforward indication that a government or organization had any connection with the production of the original document, a distribution, Superintendent of Documents (SuDoc) Classification (Section 5.3e), U.N. Sales Number (Section 5.3f), or Government Depository Numbering System (Section 5.3g) note should be added to alert your reader that the item is also a government or organization document.

<u>University Press Book Reprint</u>

> Shigo, Alex, and Karl Roy. *Violin Woods: A New Look*. Durham, NH: University of New Hampshire, 1983. (Distributed by the Government Printing Office; A13.2:V81).

<u>Commercial Publisher Reprint</u>

> Quirk, James, Katsuaki Terasawa, and David Whipple. *Coal Models and Their Use in Government Planning*. New York: Praeger, 1982. (Distributed by the Government Printing Office; NAS1.2:C63).

Consult Section 4.2e for additional information about commercial publishers for government publications.

<u>Reprints of Earlier Works</u>

The date of reprinting is not a necessary part of the citation unless the document has been reprinted by a different publisher. Include this data immediately after the original imprint information using the words "reprinted by . . . ."

> Colombia. Office of the President. *Policy of the National Government in Defense of the Rights of Indigenous People . . .* Bogata: Ministry of Indigenous Affairs, 1989. (Reprinted by Caja and Agraria, Incora, Indevena, 1992).

<u>Reprints of Non-Governmental Publications</u>

Government agencies sometimes reprint articles or other materials that first appeared as commercial publications. In these cases you should include a note citing the original document.

> Canada. Health and Welfare Canada, National Clearinghouse on Family Violence, Family Violence Prevention Division. *Child Maltreatment as a Social Problem: The Neglect of Neglect*. By Isabel Wolock and Bernard Horowitz. n.p., [by 1990]. (Reprinted from *American Journal of Orthopsychiatry* 54:4 (Oct. 1984) pp 241-253.)

<u>Reprints from Larger Works</u>

If the material being cited is from a larger work, even if it is from the same agency, this should be noted.

> Canada. Dept. of External Affairs. *The Canadian Political System.* By Eugene A. Forsey. Ottawa: The Dept., 1984. (Reprinted from *How Canadians Govern Themselves.* Canadian Unity Information Office, 1982.).

Note: A reprint may be identified as an Edition Statement following the title or as a note. Consult Section 3.1, as appropriate.

> Pennsylvania. Dept. of Education, Bureau of Curriculum and Instruction. *Han Hanh Duoc Gap.* Prepared by Bui Tri, Louisette Logan, and Fannette N. Gordon. Reprinted 1982. Harrisburg, 1980.

5.4 Optional Notes

Basic Rules:

- Optional Notes give information about the nature or characteristics of a document, as appropriate. They may be only marginally useful in locating the document.

Recommended Form and Punctuation: Consult Section 5.3.

Related Sections:

➢ Medium or Publication Type (Section 3.3).

5.4a Language

When the source is available in more than one language (i.e., you select the language you would prefer to use or it can be purchased in more than one language version) or if you feel the language is not apparent or it would help your reader to identify the language, include this information in a note (Figs. 3 and 12). Consult Sections 0.5, 5.5c and *the Quick Citation Guides* for additional guidance and examples.

> U.S. Dept. of Education. *MANAd.* By Elnora Mapatis. Washington: Government Printing Office, 1983. (Recounted in Hualapai).

> Texas. Dept. of Human Resources. *Chido en hogar de dia.* Austin, n.d. (Spanish).

> Canadian Advisory Council on the Status of Women. *We're Here, Listen to Us!: A Survey of Young Women in Canada.* By Janelle Holmes and Eliane Leslau Siverman. Ottawa: The Council, 1992. (DSS Cat no. LW31-35/92E; Issued in French under the title *J'ai des choses à dire, écoutez-moi*).

5.4b International Standard Book Number (ISBN)

Many government and organization publications destined for sale are given an International Standard Book Number (ISBN), usually located on the back cover or the back of the title page. This number may be helpful in identifying the publication, but it will not give the average user much help in locating it. Therefore, its use is optional.

> U.N. Economic Commission for Europe. *Learning and the Environment in Europe and North America: Annotated Statistics 1992.* New York: United Nations, 1992. (ISBN 92-1-116537-7).

5.4c Film and Video Characteristics

Film size, running time, and color or black and white may tell your readers if a film can be used for their purposes.

> U.N. Centre for Human Settlements (HABITAT). *Housing in Africa* (Film). Nairobi, 1976. (16mm., 15 min., col.).

5.4d Catalog Numbering Systems

If there is a catalog number that appears to be significant, include this in your citation as well. These can be useful in locating the document in a library's collection. Do not confuse catalog numbers with Publication/Report Numbers (Section 3.1). Catalog Numbering Systems can be closely related to Government Depository Numbering Systems (Section 5.3g). Include both when available.

> Australia. Australian Bureau of Statistics. *Transition from Education to Work.* Canberra: Australian Government Publishing Service, 1991. (ABS Catalog No. 6227.0).

5.5 Special Notes for PEF Sources

Notes for PEF sources can be used to provide information that does not easily fit into any of the categories described above. This information should provide additional information that will ensure the reader can identify the exact source cited.

Special Notes for PEF Sources will lengthen and complicate your citation considerably. For this reason, not all such notes are necessary and they may not be appropriate in some bibliographies and for certain readers. Use judgment in deciding whether to include these optional notes.

Basic Rules:

In addition to the Required Notes in Section 5.3, PEF sources may benefit from additional optional notes that are specific to these sources only.

These optional notes for PEF sources give your reader information about the physical format of the source or information about the format of the information or data.

Recommended Form and Punctuation: Notes may be grouped at the end of the bibliographic citation in a single set of parentheses separated by a semicolon; use the order that seems most appropriate to the note content; always conclude with the SuDocs number when present (Section 5.3e).

U.S. Bureau of the Census. Data User Services Division. *U.S. Imports of Merchandise: International Harmonized System Commodity Classification (HTSUSA) by Country, by Customs District* (CDIM-92-03) (CD-ROM). Washington, June 1992. (dBase format; C3.278:Im7/June 1992).

Related Sections:

➢ Medium or Publication Type (Section 3.3).

➢ Series and Other Notes (Section E5.0).

5.5a Data Format

The format (e.g., ASCII, Excel spreadsheet, dBase, compressed) of the data can be noted.

> U.S. Energy Information Administration. *CBECS: Commercial Building Energy Consumption Survey, Public Use Data Files, 1989* (Floppy Disk). Washington: Government Printing Office, June 1992. (Includes 16 files in ASCII format; E3.43/2-4:989).

5.5b Total Number of Disks in a Set

Include the total number of original disks. You may not be able to verify the total number of original disks in a set when disks have been copied from double-density to high-density disks or when an electronic source has been installed on a computer workstation. In these cases, the total number of disks should be omitted.

> U.S. Energy Information Administration. *World Energy Projection System (WEPS)* (Floppy Disk). Washington, Mar. 1992. (Files in Lotus spreadsheet format; 4 disks; E3.11/20-5:992/floppy).

5.5c Language

When the source in hand or on the computer screen is available in more than one language (i.e., you select the language you would prefer to use or it can be purchased in more than one language version), include a note indicating the available languages. Consult Section 0.5, 5.4a, and the *Quick Citation Guides* for additional guidance and examples.

> Statistics Canada. *National Income and Expenditure Accounts: First Quarter 1988* (13-001) (Floppy Disk). Evaluation diskette. n.p., 1988. (Statistics Canada Electronic Data Dissemination Time Series Data). (Text available in English or French).

5.5d System Requirements

When using an electronic source will require specific hardware or software, that information should be included. Typically, this information is included in accompanying documentation or in a "Readme" file.

> U.S. Energy Information Administration. *PC-AEO Forecasting Model (Annual Energy Outlook)* (DOE/EIA-M040 89) (Floppy Disk). Version 89C. Washington, 1989. (Lotus spreadsheet format; 3 disks; System Requirements: IBM PC or compatible; DOS 3.0 or higher 1MB RAM; 640K conventional and 768K expanded memory; hard disk drive with 4.5MB free memory; *Lotus 123*, 2.01 or higher; E 3.1/5:989).

5.5e Access Software Included

Many electronic sources include access software. Including this information in the citation helps the reader to know that this source provides access software. In addition, the user may be familiar with the particular software and, therefore, will know that they will be able to access and use the specific source cited. Provide the name of the software and the version.

> U.S. Dept. of Commerce, Economics and Statistics Administration, Office of Business Analysis. *NTDB: National Trade Data Bank* (CD-ROM). Washington, Oct. 1992. (2 disks; System requirements: IBM PC or compatible; 512KB memory; CD-ROM drive; *Microsoft Extensions*; DOS 3.1 or later; hard disk; EGA or VGA monitor; Includes Access software: *Browse* and *ROMWARE*; C1.88:992/3/CD).

5.5f Print Documentation

When known, the availability of print documentation should be noted. Precede the title and, if the paging is consecutive, the total number of pages with "Accompanied by:." Giving the number of pages helps your reader to know how helpful the documentation may be.

> U.S. National Center for Biotechnology Information. *Entrez: Sequences* (CD-ROM). Pre-release 6. Washington: Government Printing Office, July 1992. (GenInfo Compact Library Series). (Includes versions for Apple Macintosh and Microsoft Windows systems; Accompanied by: *User's Guide*, 29 pp.; HE20.3624:992/1/Pre.6/CD).

5.5g Clearinghouses and Distribution Agencies

When clearinghouses or distribution agencies are included as a source (for examples consult the *Quick Citation Guide to Special Cases and Well-Known Sources*, S6) include that information and location as a note. Include any unique Publication/Report Numbers (Section 3.1) provided.

> U.S. Energy Information Administration, Office of Energy Markets and End Use. *Oil Market Simulation: OMS* (DOE/EIA-MO28(90); Distribution category UC-98) (Floppy Disk). Washington, June 1990. (Lotus Spreadsheet format; System requirements: *Lotus 123*, version 2; Accompanied by: *Demonstration Disk* and *User's Manual*, 12 pp.; Available from: National Technical Information Service (NTIS), Springfield, VA (PB89-167886) or National Energy Information Center (NEIC); EI-231, Washington; E3.55:990).

6.0 CITING PARTS: PERIODICAL ARTICLES AND STATISTICAL SOURCES

Governments and organizations produce many many periodicals—sources published periodically, monthly, quarterly, or weekly, for example—whose titles do not change from issue to issue and whose contents include a variety of articles, stories, columns, editorials, speeches, notices, etc.

Governments and organizations are also inveterate collectors of statistics. They do so for many reasons—because they have been charged to do so, to explain and justify their existence, to gather evidence, and to inform and educate their clientele and members. With this wealth of statistical data collected, it is not surprising that they also publish many statistical sources periodically. Many print and PEF sources produced by governments and organizations are either entirely statistical in nature or include statistical tables. Thus, citing a statistical table is exactly like citing a periodical article.

This chapter describes how to cite periodically published sources, such as journals and newsletters, regardless of whether they include a statistical table or an article.

In citing periodical sources you must use both the title of the part and the title of the source or whole. If you cite only the title of the part (an article or data table, for example), the reader will not be able to locate your source. If you cite only the source, the reader will not be able to locate the particular part that you considered relevant to your topic.

Basic Rules:

Describe the Part:

* Author of the article or data table, if available (Section 6.1).

* Title of the article or data table header (Section 6.2).

Describe the Source:

* Title of the periodical or data table source (Section 6.3).

* Issue identification information (Section 6.4).

Recommended Form and Punctuation:

May, Michael M. "Nuclear Weapons in the New World Order," *Disarmament* 15:3 (May 1992) pp. 18-45. (Publication of the United Nations).

"Real Inventories , Sales, and Inventory-Sales Ratios for Manufacturing and Trade, 2001:III," *Survey of Current Business* (Jan. 2002) pp. 7-8.

Related Sections:

➤ For rules on how to cite a whole statistical volume, consult Sections 0.0-5.0.

➤ For rules on how to cite a periodical article or data table contained in a book or monograph, consult Titles of Chapters or Other Book Parts (Section 2.3).

➤ The Series Statement (Section 5.1).

Consult examples in the *Quick Citation Guide to Periodical and Statistical Sources* and the *Quick Citation Guide to Legislative/Parliamentary Sources.*
Ask a librarian for additional help.

6.0a Where to Locate Information to Include in a Citation to a Part: Use the Internal vs. External Rule

Apply the rules in Section 0.1. However, be aware that citing periodical articles and data tables presents unusual challenges and important information may appear on external sources, rather than internal sources. In such cases, use judgment in including this information in your citation. The goal is to provide enough information in your citation so that your reader will be able to locate the source (See "Purposes of the Citation"—Introduction, p.1). Any information supplied from sources such as indexes, on-line library catalogs, or databases such as *RLIN* or *WorldCat* should be enclosed in brackets.

6.1 Authors of the Article or Data Table (The Part)

Treat authors of articles or data tables exactly like Personal Authors (Section 1.4).

> Greenburg, Martin A., and Ellen C. Wertleib. "The Police and the Elderly (Pt. II)," *FBI Law Enforcement Bulletin* 52: 9 (Sept. 1983) pp. 1- 6. (J1.14/8:52/9).

6.2 Title of the Article or Data Table Header (The Part)

The title of the article or data table (Fig. 11) is distinguished from the title of the periodical source, by enclosing the article title in quotation marks. Follow rules for the Title Statement (Section 2.0) for additional guidance.

6.2a Menu-Driven Interface in PEF Sources (The Rule of Three)

Some PEF sources include a menu-driven interface that allows the user to select data or to generate a specific data table from a series of selections (frequently geographic area, time period, etc.). This approach may also be used with text or bibliographic databases when a PEF source includes a number of different sources, the researcher selects from a series of menus to reach the specific source or database to be searched.

In the case of data tables, these menu selections may appear as part of the data table header. When your menu choices do not appear as part of the table header or the order of the information presented reflects the hierarchy of the selections, rather than a more "logical" title, you should clarify the table content by "enhancing" the data table title with information on your menu choices by inserting the information in parentheses. In general, do not include more than three of those menu choices and use punctuation to clarify. Be sure the table header includes all of the important information so that the reader will be able to easily locate the exact data table you are citing.

If more than three menu choices are made or the table cannot be described by enhancing the title, consult Data Files and Datasets (PEF Sources) (Section 6.6).

When citing from such sources, insert the phrase "Data from:" (or equivalent phrase, see Section 2.3d) to indicate the source of the data.

"Detailed Race" (040 Pennsylvania, 161 Columbia Borough). Data from: *Census of Population and Housing, 1990: Summary Tape File 1C, United States Summary* (CD90-1C) (CD-ROM). Washington, Feb. 1992. (C3.282:990-1C).

"Metal Mining (SIC 1000): Pennsylvania, State Totals, 1988" (dBase format). Data from: U.S. Census Bureau. *County Business Patterns, 1988 & 1989* (CD-ROM). Washington, Mar. 1992. (C3.204/4:1988/89).

Figure 11: The Data Table Header Title

Data Table Header Title

Table A.
**Reported Voting and Registration by Citizenship, Race, and Hispanic Origin:
November 1996 and 2000**

(Numbers in thousands)

Characteristic	Total population				Citizens				Registered	
	Total	Citizen	Reported regis-tered	Reported voted	Percent reported regis-tered	90 percent C.I. (±)[1]	Percent reported voted	90 percent C.I. (±)[1]	Percent reported voted	90 percent C.I. (±)[1]
2000										
Total, 18 years and over ..	202,609	186,366	129,549	110,826	69.5	0.3	59.5	0.3	85.5	0.3
Race and Hispanic origin										
White.................	168,733	157,291	110,773	95,098	70.4	0.3	60.5	0.4	85.8	0.3
White non-Hispanic....	148,035	144,732	103,588	89,469	71.6	0.4	61.8	0.4	86.4	0.3
Black	24,132	22,753	15,348	12,917	67.5	1.1	56.8	1.2	84.2	1.1
Asian and Pacific Islander..............	8,041	4,718	2,470	2,045	52.4	2.7	43.3	2.7	82.8	2.9
Hispanic (of any race) ...	21,598	13,158	7,546	5,934	57.3	2.0	45.1	2.0	78.6	2.2
1996										
Total, 18 years and over ..	193,651	179,935	127,661	105,017	70.9	0.3	58.4	0.3	82.3	0.3
Race and Hispanic origin										
White.................	162,779	153,057	110,259	91,208	72.0	0.3	59.6	0.4	82.7	0.3
White non-Hispanic....	145,343	142,597	104,101	86,604	73.0	0.3	60.7	0.4	83.2	0.3
Black	22,483	21,486	14,267	11,386	66.4	1.2	53.0	1.2	79.8	1.2
Asian and Pacific Islander..............	6,775	3,865	2,210	1,741	57.2	3.0	45.0	3.0	78.8	3.3
Hispanic (of any race) ...	18,426	11,209	6,573	4,928	58.6	2.2	44.0	2.2	75.0	2.5

[1] This figure added to or subtracted from the estimate provides the 90-percent confidence interval.

Source: U.S. Census Bureau, Current Population Survey, November 2000 and 1996.

6.2b An Article in PEF Sources

Particularly with some PEF sources, you may need to cite an article or data table within a periodical contained on a PEF source. Such a citation includes an extra "Text from:" (or equivalent phrase) section. Consult Section 2.3d for additional guidance.

When cited with these sections in the citation, the reader has been supplied with enough information to locate this source in alternative formats, such as print or microformat, if necessary.

> "Standard Solicitation Documents Available on CD-ROM." Text from: *IRM Newsletter* (Mar. 1992). Available on: U.S. General Services Administration. *FIRMR/FAR: Federal Information Resources Management Regulation and Bulletins/Federal Acquisition Regulation and Circulars* (CD-ROM). Washington: Government Printing Office, July 1992. (GS12.15/2: July 1992).

6.3 Title of the Periodical or Source of the Data Table (The Source)

The Title of the Periodical or Source of the Data Table should be cited exactly as given and should be given in full. Follow rules for the Title Statement (Section 2.0) for additional guidance.

6.4 Issue Identification Information

The exact issue of the periodical or data table source must be well-identified for your reader, in order to distinguish between sources with the same name but different volume numbering and to help your reader identify an article quickly within a specific issue.

The Issue Identification Information Includes:

* Issue Identifiers: Volume, Issue, and Date (Section 6.4a).

* Page Numbers and Other Indicators of Length/Size (Section 6.4b).

Recommended Form and Punctuation: Volume: Issue (Date) Pages.

Use abbreviations as described in Sections 0.4, 6.4a, and 6.4b. For commonly used abbreviations consult *Appendix D: Abbreviations*. Due to variations in publishers numbering patterns, not all citations will include a Volume, Issue, Date, and Pages. Insert and omit punctuation as needed for clarity. Consult the *Quick Citation Guide to Periodical Articles and Statistical Sources* for examples.

6.4a Issue Identifiers: Volume, Issue, and Date

Governments and organizations use different numbering patterns to identify individual issues of a periodical (Fig. 12). The most typical:

➤ A volume (corresponding to a year).

➤ An issue (within that volume, often corresponding to a month or quarter).

➤ A date (typically a year corresponding to the volume number) (See Section 4.3 for additional guidance about the form of the date).

Occasionally, periodicals will include supplements (Vol. 23, Supp. 1, for example). When other variations are used, be sure to provide enough information to ensure your reader will be able to locate the article you have cited using the periodical title, volume, issue, and date. When volume and/or issue numbering is not available, be sure to include some indicator of date, such as a year or month, to help your reader distinguish between multiple issues of the same periodical.

Note: Issue identifiers in roman numerals can be converted, e.g., Vol. XXVI becomes Vol. 36.

6.4b Page Numbers and Other Indicators of Length/Size

Always include the exact length of the article or location of the data table by including page numbers. When page numbering is not consecutive, the non-sequential numbers may be omitted from the citation. Column numbers may be used instead of page numbers in some publications.

The page number should follow the Issue Identification information and be preceded by "pp." (for multiple page articles) or "p." (for single page articles). Precede a column number with "col."

Variation: When no page numbering is provided you may substitute the following to help the researcher understand the length/size/extent of the publication you have cited. Include at least one of the following, if provided by the electronic source:

* Size of the file (e.g., 2345 kb).

* The total number of lines or words (provided by the database), some systems also express this as "pages."

  "Green Taxation: 73% of Europeans in Favour of Eco-Taxes" *Europe Environment* 480 (June 27, 1996) (387 words). Text From: *General News (Newsletters)*. Available from: Academic Universe, LexisNexis; Accessed: 1/16/02.

6.5 Variations to Clarify the Issuing Agency of the Periodical (The Source)

In most libraries and for most non-government periodicals you need to know only the name of the periodical to find it. This is not always true for government periodicals. Libraries which keep government documents separate from the rest of their collection may also keep government periodicals separate from other periodicals. Further, the standard catalogs of periodicals do not include all government periodicals. Readers who are aware they are seeking a periodical published by a government or organization may be more successful locating the cited source in their own library.

6.5a Include the Issuing Agency

The Issuing Agency can be added as a Note (Section 5.0) that includes the name of the Issuing Agency, or some other indicator that the Source is a document, such as the SuDoc Number (Section 5.3e) or other agency number (Section 5.3g). Issuing Agency information can also be included before the title of the periodical in the manner of an Issuing Agency (Section 1.0). The need to identify the Issuing Agency occurs frequently with legislative/parliamentary materials with generic titles such as *Hansard* or *Official Journal*. Consult *The Quick Citation Guide to Legislative/Parliamentary Sources,* L2.1 and L4.1 for additional examples.

  Cantor, Norman F. "Why Study the Middle Ages?" *Humanities* 3:3 (June 1982) pp. 21- 30. (Issued by the U.S. National Endowment for the Humanities; NF3.11:3/3).

  "Non-governmental Organizations and the World Population Plan of Action," U.N. Secretariat. Dept. of International Economic and Social Affairs. Population Division. *Population Bulletin of the United Nations* 29 (1990) pp. 54-88. (ST/ESA/SER.N/29).

"Liquor Licensing Bill," Cook Islands. Parliament, 34th Sess. *Parliamentary Debates, Official Report (Hansard)* 6 (22 June 1988) p. 552.

6.5b Include Publishing Information.

Although a citation to a periodically published source does not typically include publishing information, this information can be included. Many government and organization publications include generic titles that have limited circulation or that are not well-known outside a country or discipline. In addition, some legislative/parliamentary publications have similar names and including a place of publication and/or publisher in a Note will help distinguish similar titles. These citations include the use of "In" in the manner described in Section 2.3.

"Science and Technology," pp. 628-656. In Council of Europe. Parliamentary Assembly, 33rd Ordinary Sess. *Official Report of Debates* Vol. III. Strasbourg, 1982.

"Violence," pp. 63-64. In Council of Europe. Parliamentary Assembly, 34th Ordinary Sess., 3rd Pt. *Orders of the Day: Minutes of Proceedings* 28th Sitting, 28 Jan. 1983. Strasbourg, 1982-1983.

Figure 12: Periodical Published by a Government Agency

Issuing Agency

Periodical Title

Issue Identification Information

Periodical Articles and Authors

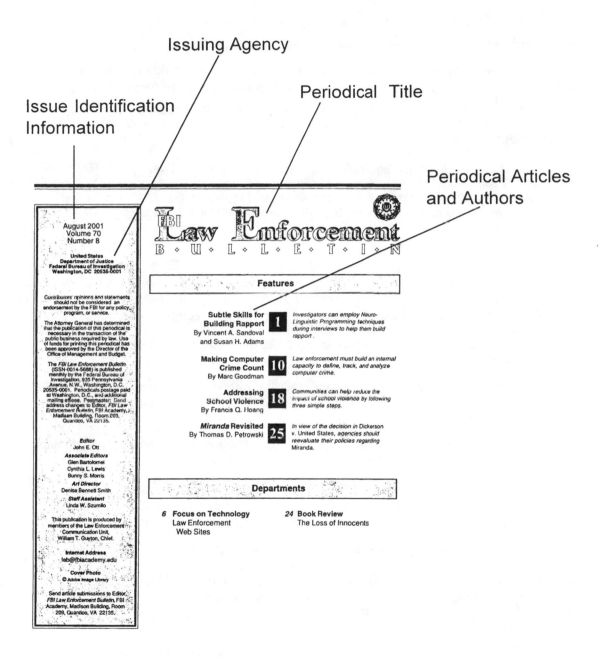

6.6 Data Files and Datasets (PEF Sources)

Many governments or organizations provide access to their statistical sources and large data sets on PEF sources. Most often the PEF source provides access to large datafiles that can be copied or from which data can be compiled or extracted for use with commercial data analysis software packages, including *Excel*, *SAS*, or *SPSSx*. This is an alternative to data tapes that must be mounted on larger computers.

6.6a Data Files

When a data file is made available on a PEF source, it is necessary to describe the data file and the PEF source providing the data file. Consult Section 6.4b and E2.1d for additional guidance.

> "Morpwk1.dbf" (dbase file; 185 kb). Available on: *U.S. Nuclear Regulatory Commission Licensed Operating Reactors, Status Summary Report NUREG-0020 Data* (Floppy Disk) 15:1 (Dec. 1990). (Y3.N88:15/v.15/#1).

> "Table 11: Death Rates for Suicide Among Persons 55 Years and Over by Sex, Race, Age: United States, Selected Years, 1980-86." (Four11.wk1; 9 kb). Available on: U.S. National Center for Health Statistics. *Health Data on Older Americans, United States: 1992* (Floppy Disk). Washington: Government Printing Office, 1992. (HE20.6209/4-4:3/1/floppy).

6.6b Datasets

When a data subset is created from a PEF statistical source from a PEF or your research relies extensively on data from such a statistical source, it is only necessary to indicate the source of the data, and the issue or release date. The phrase "Data from:" or "Compiled from:" (or equivalent phrases) indicates to the user that the data can be found on the electronic source cited.

> Data from: *International Financial Statistics* (CD-ROM). Washington: International Monetary Fund, July 2001.

> Data from: U.S. National Center for Health Statistics. *National Health Interview Survey, 1987-1992* (CD-ROM). Washington: Government Printing Office, 1993. (Access software on disk: SETS; HE20.6209:4/3).

> Data from: *World Development Indicators, 2001* (CD-ROM). 5th ed. Washington: World Bank, 2001.

Some commercial sources provide access to government or organization data that allows the user to create customized data subsets, to map, graph, or save the data for use in other software packages. If a single data table is being cited, consult Section 6.2a for guidance.

> Compiled from: *CensusCD 1980*. Version 2.0, New Brunswick, NJ: Geolytics, Inc., 1999.

Note: A citation to U.S. census data contained on a PEF source should include a complete title followed by the census year. Since some census data has been reissued, it is particularly important to include the date (including month or quarter, if included) in the citation. Consult Sections 2.1a and 2.1g.

> Compiled from: U.S. Census Bureau. *Census of Agriculture: State Data File, County Data File (Including U.S. Totals), 1987* (CD-ROM). Washington, Aug. 1990. (C3.277:Ag9/987).

> Compiled from: U.S. Census Bureau. *Census of Population and Housing, Summary Tape File 1A, 1990: Middle Atlantic Division (Vol. 2): New Jersey, Pennsylvania* (CD90-1A-2-2) (CD-ROM). Washington, 1992. (C3.282:990/CD90-1A-2-2).

Note: For alphabetization purposes the "Data from:" (or equivalent) phrase can be omitted at the beginning of the entry.

Consult the *Quick Citation Guide to Periodical Articles and Statistical Sources*, P12-P13 and P19 for examples.

---

[1] For example, "Publication Medium" Sec. 2.2.3, p. 34. In Janice R. Walker and Todd Taylor, *The Columbia Guide to Online Style*. New York: Columbia University Press, 1998 and "Computer Software and Manual Available on University Web Site" Entry 93, p. 4. In American Psychological Association. *APA Style for Electronic Resources*, Aug. 2001. Available at: http://www.apastyle.org instruct the researcher differently about whether to add or to omit a medium/format qualifier immediately following a title.

PART 3
Citation Rules for
Virtual Electronic Formats

Rules for Virtual Electronic Formats

E0.0 BASIC RULES FOR FORM AND PUNCTUATION

This chapter describes how to cite government and organization information and sources made available in a VEF (see Table 1 for a definition of VEF sources). These include sources available from agency and organization WWW sites; from government portals, such as *GPO Access* or the *U.K. Stationary Office Official Documents* WWW site; and from commercial database vendors, such as LexisNexis or Readex/NewsBank.

Citing VEF sources and information requires additional attention to detail because the presentation standards are not yet fixed. Thus agencies and organizations are "inventing" approaches for displaying their publications or for providing access to a dataset. At the same time they are moving quickly and using the WWW heavily as a dissemination medium. As this trend continues, more standards will develop, and, indeed, some agencies and organizations are becoming more sophisticated in providing authorship, title, and other elements of a good citation on their VEF sources.

Table 12: Common Types of VEF Sources

* The source appears as an exact electronic version of a print source. Such sources may include Publishing Information as described in Section 4.0, even though they are distributed as a VEF source (examples include PDF files) (Section E4.1).

* The source appears as a modified electronic version of a print source. Such sources typically include the titles of print publications, but may omit the formatting and graphics or illustrations of the original print source (examples include .TXT or .html or .DOC files). Many commercial vendors and portals provide access to government information in this format.

* The source is an entirely electronic source. Such sources may allow researchers to create their own specified data table by selecting criteria (geography or data items, for example). Often such sources can be displayed in or extracted in a variety of formats (Excel files, for example).

Detailed and complete citations to VEF sources is necessary because:

* Electronic sources can disappear, change, or be moved to other locations and addresses. For example, following the events of Sept. 11, 2001 many government WWW sites were taken down for security reasons[1]; and within minutes after President George W. Bush was sworn into office, the White House WWW page for the Clinton administration was moved to the National Archives and Records Administration (NARA) web site[2]. Although the changes are not preserved or documented, frequent users of the Census Bureau WWW (http://www.census.gov) site are aware that it has changed the design of its WWW site many times since its original debut.

* Access to electronic resources is becoming increasingly "controlled" by password, IP addresses, and other means. This means your reader may not have access to the exact version of the source and will need as much information as possible to locate an alternative avenue to the file/source you have cited. This is similar to print resources where complete information is needed because not all readers will be able to locate the same source in their own library, personal collection, or local bookstore. When you provide your readers with complete

citation information to any source (regardless of format) you give them the tools they need to seek out information in a location that is most accessible or convenient to them.

How to Begin

The *Quick Citation Guides* include examples of VEF sources along with sources in print, PEF, microfiche, microfilm, and many other formats. You will find the combination of these examples useful in creating your own citations because they illustrate the type of information that should be included, regardless of the form or format.

The rules for VEF sources build upon the Style Rules in Part 1.
Consult Part 1 rules as needed for clarification and for additional examples.

E0.1 Where to Locate Information to Include in a Citation: Use the "Internal vs. External" Rule

The advantage of the WWW is that you can hyperlink and embed links so that the structure of a "publication" may be entirely different than what we see with print or PEF sources. In addition, although publishing patterns have long ago been established for physical formats (most publications include a cover and title page that specify the Issuing Agency, the Title, and Publishing Information), this is not the case with VEF sources. For that reason, terms like title page or cover may only be useful if the electronic publication is a replica of a print publication (typically, in the the form of a PDF file).

Table 13: Internal and External Sources of Information for VEF Sources

Use sources of information as closely related as possible (usually in the same domain, directory, or subdirectory structure) to the source/file you are citing.	
Internal Sources	**External Sources**
• The file/source being cited. • A title page or cover replica—PDF files, for example. • A "parent page"--a group of files (one file per chapter, for example) may be hyperlinked from a "parent" page. • E-mail or Chat header or thread.	• An agency "splash" page or its home page. • A masthead, graphic, or information page, within the same subdirectory, directory or domain as the file/source you are citing. • A list of publications or directory index or other similar sources located within the same domain or directory. • Accompanying README files that provide documentation or user manuals.
Entries in an index, publishers catalogs, an on-line library catalog, or large databases such as *WorldCat* or *RLIN* can be used to clarify information. Ask a librarian for additional help.	

Follow all rules for Capitalization (Section 0.2), Punctuation (Section 0.3),
Abbreviations (Section 0.4) and Non-English Language (Section 0.5).

E1.0 AUTHORSHIP —Who is responsible for the content?

Governments, organizations, and their legislative/parliamentary bodies are responsible for the content of a VEF source and are considered the author and given the first position in the citation to these sources.

Basic Rules:

* Identify the government or organization responsible for the **content** of the source being cited, even when accessing information through a commercial vendor or portal.

* Commercial vendors and portals are included in the Source Information (Section E4.0).

* In some situations, the Electronic Source Address (URL) (Section E4.2) can replace the Authorship statement.

Recommended Form and Punctuation: Use form and punctuation described in Section 1.0.

Related Sections:

➤ The Source Information (Section E4.0).
➤ Citing Parts: Periodical Articles and Statistical Sources (Section E6.0).

Consult Section 1.0 and the *Quick Citation Guides* for examples.
Ask a librarian for additional help.

Table 14: Using the URL to Identify the Issuing Agency

It can be difficult to identify the Issuing Agency and Geo/Political Designation for a VEF source. When the source itself does not include any masthead, graphic image, or text to indicate the Issuing Agency, use the URL to help identify this information by locating a home page related to the source itself. It may be necessary to work backwards through the URL to an agency or organization's home page, in order to locate Issuing Agency information.

DON'T OVERESTIMATE the URL's ability to identify the Issuing Agency.

Many readers will not be familiar with the many acronyms and abbreviations that are used in URLs. In addition, frequently the Geo/Political Designation is not included.

Site Seeing on the Internet. Available at: http://www.ftc.gov/bcp/conline/pubs/online/sitesee/	The Federal Trade Commission (FTC) is identified as the Issuing Agency for this site. Consult *Quick Citation Guide for Books and Monographs*, Q1.10.
Digest of Education Statistics: 1999. Available at: http://nces.ed.gov/edstats	The National Center for Education Statistics (NCES) of the U.S. Dept. of Education is identified as the Issuing Agency. Consult *Quick Citation Guide to Periodical Articles and Statistical Sources*, P8.

Agenda Item 75: Draft Convention on the Elimination of the Discrimination Against Women (A/34/PV.17), Dec. 18, 1979 Available at: http://www.un.org/Depts/dhl/landmark/pdf/a34pv107e.pdf	The United Nations WWW site is identified. However, the URL does not identify the General Assembly, 34th Session as the "author" of this draft convention. It is recommended that this information be included. Consult *Quick Citation Guide to Legislative/Parliamentary Sources*, L3.2.
The *Congressional Record.* Available at: http://www.access.gpo.gov/su_docs/aces/aces150.html	The domain: access.gpo.gov identifies the U.S. Government Printing Office (GPO)—a portal to U.S. government information. The *Congressional Record* is made accessible by GPO Access for Congress and is an electronic supplier (Section 4.1), not an Issuing Agency. Consult *Quick Citation Guide to Legislative/Parliamentary Sources*, L1.1.
Meeting Minutes, August 23, 2001 Available at: http://www.IN.gov/legislative/interim/committee/minutes/RFSC48N.pdf	The URL domain identifies the Indiana government site, but the specific legislative committee is not well-identified and should be included in the Issuing Agency statement. Consult *Quick Citation Guide to Legislative/Parliamentary Sources*, L1.3.

E1.1 Governments as Issuing Agency: The Geo/Political Designation

Include the Geo/Political Designation as described in Section 1.1.

An agency logo (Fig. 3), graphic image, symbol, masthead, or text on an internal or external source (Section 0.1) may provide both the Geo/Political Designation and the Issuing Agency. (Section 1.2).

Use the form shown on the electronic source. For example, States of Jersey (also known as the Channel Islands). Consult Geo/Political Designation Name Has Changed (Section 1.1d) for additional guidance if appropriate.

> States of Jersey. *Report of the Review Panel on the Machinery of Government in Jersey.* Conducted by the MORI Local Government Research Unit Dec. 2000. (Known as: The Clothier Report). Available at: http://www.gov.je/pandr/clothier/clothier.htm; Accessed: 12/3/01.

In some circumstances, the Source Information (Section E4.0) may provide the Geo/Political Designation (Section 1.1). However, be sure the Issuing Agency (Section 1.2) is also identified as part of the Source Information, before omitting the Geo/Political Designation. When in doubt, include a Geo/Political Designation in addition to the Source Information.

E1.2 The Issuing Agency

When possible, create the Issuing Agency hierarchy as described in Section 1.2.

Use the form shown on an internal or external source of information (Section E0.1). For example, United Kingdom. HM Treasury—many library catalogs and indexes will list as United Kingdom. Treasury.

> United Kingdom. HM Treasury. *Delivering Economic Stability: Convergence Programme Submitted in Line With Stability and Growth Pact.* Dec. 2000. Available at: http://www.hm-treasury.gov.uk/mediastore/otherfiles/-DeliveringEconomic.pdf; Accessed: 12/3/01.

Note: Government agencies may use different forms of their name in print publications and in their VEF sources; they may also use different forms at different time periods. For example, the U.S. Bureau of the Census is now frequently listed as the U.S. Census Bureau. Use the form on an internal or external source of information (Section E0.1). If the form is similar, use the same form throughout your bibliography for alphabetization purposes. If the forms differ greatly or could be mistaken for another agency, use the form shown on the Source of Information (Section 0.1 and E0.1).

Organizations also use different forms of their names, for a variety of reasons. For example, the European Union and European Communities are both used and are both correct forms. Use the form present on an internal or external source of information (Section E0.1).

E1.2a Multiple Issuing Agencies/Co-Published with Another

Sometimes more than one government or organization may be instrumental in the production of a document as in a cooperative effort. Consult Multiple Issuing Agencies (Section 1.2d).

> *Egypt Human Development Report, 1998/99* (Project Document: EGY/96/012). Cairo: Institute of National Planning, 2001. (A Human Development Project with the United Nations Development Programme). Available at: http://www.undp.org.eg/Publications/-HDR/hdr-99.htm; Accessed: 1/31/02.

The WWW has produced new types of partnerships, in which governments and organizations "partner" with commercial businesses. The role of the commercial partner, if recognized on the WWW source, should be included in the citation.

> *A Basic Guide to Exporting.* Prepared by the U.S. Dept. of Commerce with the Assistance of Unz & Co. 1998 ed. Available at: http://www.unzco.com/basicguide/-index.html; Accessed 1/23/02.

E1.3 Legislative/Parliamentary Bodies as Issuing Agency

Consult the *Quick Citation Guide to Legislative/Parliamentary Sources* for examples.

Follow rules in Section 1.2 for constructing the Legislative/Parliamentary body organizational hierarchy, to the extent information is provided in the source being cited. Many organizations have begun to include this information on each source and, when visible or accessible, this information should also be included in the citation to assist readers who may need to locate an alternative source, if the electronic version is not archived or is archived at a different URL.

Legislative/Parliamentary sources from commercial sources should <u>always</u> include the Issuing Agency statement. Many of these sites have controlled access (by a password, IP address, for example) and your reader may have to seek an alternative source. The Secondary Source is included later in the Source Information part of the citation (Section E4.0) and does not identify the legislative/parliamentary body responsible for the content.

E1.4 Personal Authors

Personal authors are those who: write, design, program, edit, prepare, draw, conduct a survey, or create (for example, the author of a software program or image source) the VEF source's content. Do not include as personal authors those who: direct, supervise, order, or administer a VEF source's content (for example, a website administrator). Follow rules for recognizing a personal author as described in Section 1.4.

Note: Personal authors may appear in the first position in many citations to VEF sources because the publisher is both the Issuing Agency and the Source of Information, rather than the Government Printing Office or other official publisher (Consult Section E4.1 for additional examples).

Dean, Andrew G., et al, *EPI Info 2000: A Database and Statistics Program for Public Health Professionals Using Windows 95, 98, NT and 2000 Computers*. Version. 1.1.2. Atlanta, GA: Center For Disease Control, 2000. Available at: http://www.cdc.gov/-epiinfo; Accessed: 11/30/01.

Nanthikesan, S. *Trends in Digital Divide*. Nov. 2000. (*A Human Development Report 2001: Background Paper, no. 66*). Available at: http://www.undp.org/hdro/papers/-ocpapers/occ.htm; Accessed: 3/1/02.

E1.4a E-mail Messages

The Personal Author of an e-mail message can be found in the e-mail header, a signature file or other source.

Cheney, Debora (DLC@PSULIAS). Subject: Citing Electronic Formats (E-Mail). Message to: Elizabeth Montgomery (EBM@HARVARDA), Dec. 5, 1992.

Davis, J. Mike. Subject: *Chronic Disease Prevention CD-ROM* (E-Mail). Message to: GOVDOC-L Discussion List (GOVDOC-L@PSU.edu), Mar. 2, 1992. Available at: GOVDOC-L Discussion List, http://docs.lib.duke.edu/federal/govdoc-l/advsearch.html; Accessed: Mar. 3, 1992.

E2.0 TITLE—What is the title of the source?

The title of a VEF source can be located in a variety of places and for this reason it can be difficult to determine what title to include in your citation. However, the title serves as one of the most important parts of the bibliographic citation and care should be taken to identify the exact title of the source described in your citation. Electronic formats may undergo a variety of title changes and variations over time, and the title on the item or on the computer screen may actually help mark it for a specific date and time.

Basic Rules:

* Determine whether you are Citing a Part: Periodical Articles or Statistical Tables (Section E6.0), a Chapter or Other Book Part (Section 2.3), or a whole source; consult *How to Begin* (Section 2.0) for guidance.

* Give Title as shown on an internal source of information (Section E0.1).

Recommended Form and Punctuation:

U.S. Dept. of State. *Country Reports on Human Rights*. 25th ed. Feb. 2001. Available at: http://www.stategov/g/drl/rls/hrrpt; Accessed: 2/15/02.

Related Section:

➤ Citing Parts: Periodical Articles and Statistical Sources (Section 6.0 and E6.0).

Consult Section 2.0 and the *Quick Citation Guides* for examples.
Ask a librarian for additional help.

E2.1 The Title Proper

The Title Proper is the part of the title that precedes the Subtitle (Section 2.2) or any additional supplied information, such as a hearing date (Section 2.1g). Consult Section 2.1 for additional guidance.

E2.1a Title Well-Known in Its Own Right

When a title is well-known in its own right or if the Issuing Agency (Section E1.0) information will appear as part of the Title or the URL (Section E4.2), you need not repeat this information. The citation should begin with the Title.

> *Demographic Yearbook, 1995* [Selected Tables]. Available at: U.N. Statistics Division, http://www.un.org/-Depts/unsd/demog/index.html; Accessed: 2/1/02.

E2.1b Multiple Titles

If the title on an internal source of information differs from the title on an external source, use the internal title (Section E0.1). It is possible that title information will vary within the internal source; if so, use the title given on the page corresponding most closely to the URL or other internal source you will include with the Source Information (Section E4.0). Similarly, if there is no internal source of title information and the external sources vary, use the title given on the page corresponding most closely to the URL or other external source you will include with the Source Information (Section E4.0).

> *Census of Canada, 1996: Population and Dwelling Counts, for Canada, Provinces and Territories, 1991 and 1996 Censuses—100% Data.* Available from: Statistics Canada, http://www.statcan.ca/english/census96/table1.htm; Accessed: 2/20/02.

E2.1c Non-Traditional Title

A VEF source whose title is in a non-traditional format (form of a URL, for example) or encompasses a wide range of sources (an agency or organization home page, for example), or whose title cannot be identified, may require some additional information to explain a given source or "title." Any descriptive information that is supplied should be placed in brackets. When such titles are self-explanatory and include sufficient information to identify the issuing agency, the entries may be quite short.

> *Enviroene: Common Sense Solutions to Environmental Problems* [Home Page]. Available at: U.S. Environmental Protection Agency, http://www.opa.gov/envirosense; Accessed: 2/20/02.

> U.S. Office of the President. WWW.Whitehousekids.gov; Accessed: 12/15/01.

> *AIDS Economics* [Home Page]. Available: http://www.worldbank.org/aids-econ/; Accessed: 12/05/01.

E2.1d File Names as Titles

Many VEF sources, particularly image files (e.g., JPEG, GIF), zip files, or executable files (.exe), may not have a title beyond the file name. In such cases, use a directory listing or create a descriptive title and enclose the "title" in brackets to indicate it has been created and does not strictly exist.

Always include the exact file name in the Unique Identifier part of the citation (Section E3.0). Consult A Part Within a Part (VEF Formats) (Section E6.2b).

> United States Air Force. Air Combat Command. [*Vintage Aircraft*] (File name: Archive.zip; 3.88 mb). Available at: http://www2.acc.af.mil/gallery/zip.shtml; Accessed: 11/30/01.

> United States. Dept. of the Treasury. Bureau of Public Debt. [*One Hundred Million Dollar Graphic*] (Filename: Ccfn1.jpg). Available at: ftp://208.131.225.4:21/; Accessed: 11/30/01.

E2.1e Date of the Source

Most sources in any physical format (paper, microfiche, or CD-ROM, for example) will include Publishing Information (Section 4.0), including a Date of Publication, as part of the citation.

VEF sources are not "published" in the same sense and yet the date the publication was created, presented on the WWW, or modified, is important information for your reader. Frequently this information is missing and will continue to be omitted until WWW publishing practices become more standardized.

The date of the publication should follow the Title information. This may take the form of an Edition Statement (Section E3.2), a Date as Part of the Title (Section 2.1e), or it may follow the title in the manner of a Date of Publication (Section 4.3). The date may take the form of a year (2/2002), a month and year (Dec. 2001), or a specific day, month, and year (3/15/02). This information is distinguished from the Accessed: [date] (Section E4.3), which shows the date you used the source at the location designated by the Source Information (Section 4.0).

> *Argentina: Country Commercial Guide, 2002.* Available at: U.S. Census Bureau, Commercial Service, http://www.usatrade.gov/website/ccg.nsf; Accessed: 2/12/02.

> "Activity at Major Airports, 2000: Regional Trends" (D4662.xls). Data adapted from: *Regional Trends* 36, 2001 ed. (Datasets Theme: Transport, Travel, and Tourism). Extracted from: United Kingdom.HM Government. *StatBase.* Available at: www.statistics.gov.uk/statbase/mainmenu.asp/; Accessed: 2/11/02.

> *Top Decision Makers Survey: Summary Report* (Fieldwork: 19th February-20th May 1996), released Oct. 1998. Available at: European Commission, *Eurobarometer*, http://europa.eu.int/comm/dg10/epo/eb-top/index.html; Accessed: 2/21/02.

E2.2 The Subtitle

The Subtitle provides additional information to clarify and enhance the title. Consult Section 2.2 for additional guidance.

E2.3 Titles of Chapters and Other Parts

Usually when you cite a WWW source, you cite the whole source (possibly in the form of a WWW page, ending in .htm). However, frequently you may wish to cite a single chapter, data table, or section of the whole source. When to cite the whole work and when to cite only a part will depend on the purposes of your bibliography. How to cite a part will depend on the nature of the whole.

Consult Title of Chapters and Other Parts (Section 2.3) for additional guidance.

> "Chapter 4: Business Perspectives on Discrimination." In *Civil Rights Enforcement Efforts in North Dakota.* By the North Dakota Advisory Committee to the U.S. Commission on Civil Rights, Nov. 1999. Available at: http://www.usccr.gov/pubs/-nd/main.htm; Accessed: 1/16/02.

> "Chapter II: Current Issues in the World Economy" (397 kb file). In International Monetary Fund. *World Economic Outlook: Focus on Transition Economies.* Washington: 2001. Available at: http://www.imf.org/external/pubs/ft/weo/2000/02/pdf/chapter2.pdf; Accessed: 2/20/02.

E2.3a Conference Proceedings

Follow rules in Section 2.3a for citing a paper or section of a conference proceeding.

> Taylor, Brian D., and Michael Mauch. "Gender, Race, and Travel Behavior: An Analysis of Household-Serving Travel and Commuting in the San Francisco Bay Area, pp. 373-405. In *Women's Travel Issues: Proceedings of the 2nd National Conference* (Baltimore, MD, Oct. 1996). Available at: www.fhwa.dot.gov/ohim/womens/chap20.pdf; Accessed: 1/15/02.

E2.3b Data Table Headers

Follow rules in Section 2.3b for citing a data table in a statistical volume and Citing Parts: Periodical Articles and Statistical Sources (Section E6.0). Consult the *Quick Citation Guide to Periodical and Statistical Sources* for additional examples.

> "No. 938—Magazine Advertising Revenue by Category: 1998 and 1999." In *Statistical Abstract of the United States, 2000.* 121st ed. Available at: http://www.census.gov/prod/2001pubs/statab/sec18.pdf; Accessed 12/25/01.

"Kazakstan: Population of ... Cities of Over 100,000... Inhabitants," Table 8. In *Demographic Yearbook, 1995.* Available from: U.N. Statistics Division, http://www.un.org/Depts/unsd/demog/index.html; Accessed: 2/15/02.

E2.3c Paper or Testimony Included in Legislative/Parliamentary Sources

Many legislative/parliamentary committee publications record testimony, committee recommendations and other information that may be cited separately from the publication as a whole. Follow the rules in Section 2.3c for citing a part of a legislative/parliamentary publication.

Consult the *Quick Citation Guide to Legislative/Parliamentary Bodies* for additional examples.

E2.3d Parts of a VEF Source

In some circumstances you are citing part of a larger database (a speech within a database of speeches or a bill within a database containing the text of bills introduced into Congress). Frequently these databases are made available by a portal or commercial database vendor. When citing information from such a database, you should provide complete information about the database and the Source of Information.

A Part of a Database:

Some databases contain the full-text of a collection of sources—for example, speeches or press releases. When citing a single "part" within this database, include complete information about the Part, including any identifying numbers. Precede the name of the database with the phrase: "Text from:" or a similar phrase. Include Source Information (Section E4.0), as appropriate.

"Address by President Delors to the European Parliament Presenting the Commission's Programme for 1990" (Doc. number: 117/01/90:Speech/90/1; 1059 lines). Text from: Rapid (Commission of the European Communities, Brussels), http://europa.eu.int/-rapid/start/welcome.htm; Accessed: 1/20/90; 11:15 a.m. EST.

A Database Within a Collection of Databases

Many commercial database vendors and portals provide a single entry to many different databases (or files). When a source has been selected from a database within such a collection, you must provide your reader with information about, the source being cited, the database, and the Source Information (Section E4.0).

Use the phrase: Text from: (or an equivalent phrase) to describe the database. Use the phrase Available from: (or an equivalent phrase) to describe the Source Information.

U.S. House, 101st Congress, 1st Sess. *An Act to Provide Federal Assistance and Leadership to... Renewable Energy and Energy Efficiency Technologies....* Version 3, Sept. 23, 1989. Text from: *Bills.* Available from: Congressional Universe, LexisNexis; Accessed: 11/15/01.

Note: To provide your reader with as much information as possible, you may also include in parentheses any menu selections or database options you have selected as part of the "Text from:" phrase. Do not include more than three. It is not necessary to duplicate information included elsewhere in the citation.

U.S. Senate, Committee on Governmental Affairs. *Phony Identification and Credentials via the Internet* (S. Rpt.133), Feb. 4, 2002. Text from: *Publications (Reports)*. Available from: Congressional Universe, LexisNexis; Accessed: 2/11/02.

Consult the *Quick Citation Guides* for additional examples.

E3.0 UNIQUE IDENTIFIERS—Is there any additional information to distinguish this source?

Like print and PEF sources, VEF sources will often include unique identifying numbers that can provide your reader with additional information to help locate the source.

Types of Unique Identifiers:

* Publication/Report Numbers (Section E3.1).

* Edition Statement (Section E3.2).

* Medium or Publication Type (Section E3.3).

* File Description (name, size, and type) (Section E3.4).

Recommended Form and Punctuation:

Unique identifiers always follow the Title Statement (Section 2.0) and Personal Author (Section 1.4) and precede the Publishing Information (Section 4.0). The preferred order, if more than one is present, is:

Issuing Agency. *Title: Subtitle* (Medium) (Publication/Report Number). Edition Statement. By Personal Author.

Related Section:

➢ Series and Other Notes (Section 5.0 and E5.0).

> **Consult Section 3.0 for additional rules and the *Quick Citation Guides* for examples.**
> Ask a librarian for additional help.

E3.1 Publication/Report Numbers

Follow the rules for Publication/Report Numbers (Section 3.1). Since these numbers may be unique to each VEF source, they should be included in parentheses following the title. Do not confuse such numbers with the Superintendent of Documents (which are nearly never available on VEF sources) or a government depository numbering system (Section 5.3g) or the Series title and number (Section E5.0).

> *Mobile Food Vendors: Market Segment Specialization Program (MSSP)*. (Training 3149-119 (4/95): TPDS84082Y). Available from: *Fedworld*, http://www.fedworld.gov/-pub/is-mssp/foodvend.pdf; Accessed: 12/12/01.

> U.S. General Accounting Office. *U.N. Peacekeeping: United Nations Faces Challenges in Responding to the Impact of HIV/AIDS on Peacekeeping Operations*, Report to the . . . Committee on International Relations, House of Representatives (GAO-02-194). Washington, Dec. 2001. Available at: http://www.gao.gov; Accessed: 2/20/02.

> *Bush for President* (Committee ID: C00343509). Year 2001, April Quarterly Document. Display Image: 21990071691. Available from: U.S. Federal Election Commission, Transaction Query System, http://herndon1.sdrdc.com/cgi-bin/fecimg/?_21990071691+0; Accessed: 2/20/02.

Clinton/Gore '92 General Election Compliance Fund (Committee ID: C00268722). Disclosure Form 3P, Covering Period 10/01/2001 to 12/31/01. Available at: Federal Election Commission, Electronic Filing Report Retrieval, http://herndon2.sdrdc.com/cgi-bin/dcdev/forms/C00268722/25587/; Accessed: 2/21/02.

E3.2 Edition Information

Although the word is rarely used, new editions or versions of VEF sources are frequently issued under a variety of circumstances, including when data problems are discovered, when information within the source is updated (a "Last updated ..." note included on a page, for example), or when functionality or bugs are found in software or similar source (Version 3.1.2, for example).

In addition, the WWW has complicated the meaning of "edition" by introducing variant forms of the same source. A wide range of commercial and noncommercial "vendors" provide access to government and some organization information. Even the agencies and organizations themselves provide access to different "editions" of their publications and datasets.

Some examples of common variations of an "edition" include:

➢ The *CIA World Factbook* is available at a number of different WWW sites. Each provides a slightly different "user interface" to the same source.

➢ The World Bank makes its *World Development Indicators* database available on a CD-ROM edition, a WWW "edition" which includes only selected tables; and via a WWW interactive database.

➢ Sources such as ICPSR distribute a wide range of U.S. government datasets to its members and for a fee to those who wish to purchase their "edited" version of the data.

While the Title and Issuing Agency often remain the same, the Source Information (Section E4.0) or Publishing Information (Section 4.0) should differentiate these "editions." It is not necessary to repeat information that will appear in these parts of the citation.

Follow rules in Section 3.2 and include edition information after the title or report information. When it will clarify, add the word edition (release or revision, or other terms) in brackets, if not supplied.

NOTE: Do not confuse the edition statement about a VEF source's content with the version statements for DOS or Windows (or other operating systems). Information about the operating system can be included in the Note section of the citation (Section 5.5d).

Edition Statement (Common Variations):

U.S. Dept. of the Army. *Afghanistan: A Country Study.* Edited by Peter R. Blood. Research completed 1997. (U.S. Library of Congress. Federal Research Division. Country Studies Series). Available at: http://lcweb2.loc.gov/frd/cs/aftoc.html; Accessed: 12/10/01.

U.S. Small Business Administration. "Microloan Program." Updated 6/30/01. Available from: Small Business Administration, http://www.sba.gov/gopher/Financial-Assistance/slo4.txt; Accessed: 12/15/01.

Delaware. Dept. of Natural Resources and Environmental Control. *A Pollution Prevention Guide for General Business Practices: Three "R's" for the 90s—Reduce, Reuse, Recycle.* Last updated 12/17/1996. Available at: http://www.dnrec.state.de.us/del-busi.htm; Accessed: 12/10/01.

Council of Europe. Parliamentary Assembly, 2002 Ordinary Session, 1st Sitting (Jan. 21, 2002) *Report of Debate*. Provisional version. Available at: http://stars.coe.fr/index_e.htm; Accessed: 1/22/02.

U.N. Economic and Social Commission for Asia and the Pacific. *Asia and Pacific in Figures, 2000*. Data posted 13 June 2001. Available at: http://www.unescap.org/-stat/statdata/apinfig.htm; Accessed: 2/1/02.

E3.2a ICPSR Data Tapes

The Inter-University Consortium of Political and Social Research provides its member institutions with access to a wide range of social sciences data originally produced by government agencies. It is recommended that the ICPSR edition of a datatape be recognized in the citation. Two common situations are covered by the examples below. ICPSR typically provides "suggested citations" for its datafiles and these should be consulted for citation content.

U.S. Bureau of the Census. *Census of Population and Housing, 2000 [United States]: Summary File 1, States* (Computer File). 2nd ICPSR version. Washington, DC: Bureau of the Census [producer]; Ann Arbor, MI: Inter-University Consortium for Political and Social Research, [distributor], 2001. (Study 3194). Available at: www.icpsr.umich.edu; Accessed: 2/20/02.

U.S. Dept. of Justice, Bureau of Justice Statistics. *Law Enforcement Management and Administrative Statistics, 1987* (Computer File). Conducted by U.S. Dept. of Commerce, Bureau of the Census. ICPSR ed. Ann Arbor, MI: Inter-University Consortium of Political and Social Research [producer and distributer], 1997. (Study 9222).

E3.2b Partial or Selected Text Edition

Governments and organizations often place part of a publication on the WWW, while still continuing to publish the print equivalent or a PEF equivalent, such as a CD-ROM. When citing a VEF source that contains parts or selected text, this information should be included in the citation.

Two possible variations for including this information:

U.S. Dept. of Energy, Office of Environmental Management. *Closing the Circle on the Splitting of the Atom,* 1996. Selected text available at: http://www.em.doe.gov/-circle/index.html; Accessed: 2/1/02.

UNESCO Statistical Yearbook, 1999 [Selected Tables]. Available at: http://www.uis.unesco.org/en/stats/stats0.htm; Accessed: 1/25/02.

E3.2c Software Versions and Releases

Follow rules in Section 3.2d and 5.5e. Software editions can also be included as part of the Title Statement.

E3.3 Medium and Publication Type

For VEF sources the question of medium is often extraneous because the information may be included in the title, source name, or URL address. However, when this is not the case, as a courtesy, it is often useful to your reader to provide this information, since not all readers may be equally knowledgeable about the variety of electronic media available on the WWW.

The following phrases, and any equivalent, may be used when appropriate. However, any phrase that identifies the source format may be used. When the Title, URL, or file name includes adequate identification, the medium information need not be repeated.

- Audio File (.ram, .rm)
- E-Mail
- Home Page (.htm, .html)
- Image File (.gif, .jpg)
- Powerpoint file (.ppt)
- Software
- Sound File (.wav, .aiff)
- Video File
- Webcast

Medium or Publication Type (Common Variations):

President George W. Bush (News Photo Image). Available at: *Defenselink*, http://www.defenselink.mil/photos/Jan2001/010120-O-0000D-001.jpg; Accessed: 2/20/02.

U.S. Federal Emergency Management Agency, Federal Insurance Division, Office of Risk Assessment, Risk Studies Division. *FAN: An Alluvial Fan Flooding Computer Program* (fan-prog.zip; 174 KB) (Software). Available at: http://www.fema.gov/mit/tsd/dl_fnprg.htm; Accessed: 12/10/01.

"Bull with Frogs in Background" (wav-289 kb). Sound from: *Elephant Seal Vocalizations (Año Nuevo)*. Available at: California State Parks, http://cal-parks.ca.gov; Accessed: 2/21/02.

Postal Voting Forms—Federation (Image File). Taken from: *Bosnia Report Institute* (Published by The Bosnian), New Series no.5 (Aug. 1998). Available at: http://www.bosnia.org.uk/images/gifs/fed_v1.gif; Accessed: 2/20/02.

Council of Europe. Parliamentary Assembly. *TVMag: The Europeans* (Online TV Magazine) (*RealPlayer* required). Available at: http://assembly.coe.int/TVMagazine/-english/internet/europeen.ram; Accessed: 2/13/02.

"The European Anthem" (Audio file). European Commission. Audiovisual Library. Available from: Europa, http://europa.eu.int/comm/mediatheque/audio/select/hymne/-hymne2.rm; Accessed: 2/20/02.

Joint United Nations Programme on HIV/AIDS (UNAIDS). *Report on the Global HIV/Aids Epidemic—New HIV Estimates.* 27 June 2000 ed. (Powerpoint File). UNAIDS (Epi_core.ppt; 400 kb; 19 slides; also availabe in HTML format.) Available at: http://www.unaids.org/publications/graphics/index.html; Accessed 12/3/01.

News vs. Propaganda: The Gatekeepers' Dilemma: A Forum on the Media's Impact on Today's United Nations Anti-Descrimination Agenda, Dec. 6, 2001; 10:30 a.m-12:00 noon EST. (Webcast Archive) (RealPlayer required). Available from: United Nations, http://www.un.org/webcast/events/hrday/; Accessed: 2/20/02.

E3.4 File Description

For many sources, by including the file name, file size, and file type you will assist your reader; however, the information may be included elsewhere in the citation. It is not necessary to repeat information included elsewhere, unless doing so clarifies what is being cited.

E3.4a File Name

Frequently part of the Electronic Source Address (URL) (Section E4.2), but if not, it should be included.

> "Table I—Summary of Treasury Securities Outstanding, October 31, 2001" (opdm092001.xls), *Monthly Statement of the Public Debt of the United States, October 31, 2001*. Available from: U.S. Dept. of the Treasury, Bureau of the Public Debt, http://www.publicdebt.treas.gov/opd/opdhisms.htm; Accessed: 11/30/01.

E3.4b File Size

Include the file size, especially when citing large data sets or image files. This helps the reader understand the extent of the publication.

> Pine Grove, Inc. *AmortizeIT!* (Software) (amortiz.zip; 226 kb). n.p., Apr. 27, 1993. Available at: Small Business Administration. *Shareware Room*, http://www.sba.gov/library/-sharewareroom-financing.html; Accessed: 11/15/01.

> "Current Account Balances, 1970-2001 [Selected Countries and Country Groups]" (GIF; 78 kb), p. 155. In International Bank for Reconstruction and Development, *Global Economic Prospects and the Developing Countries, 2000.* Table from: *Power Tables*. Available from: Statistical Universe, LexisNexis; Accessed: 2/15/02.

E3.4c File Type

May be used instead of the file name, since some users will not recognize the file name extensions.

> "Table 1: Durable Goods, Manufacturers' Shipments and New Orders" (Excel File). Available at: U.S. Census Bureau. *Manufacturing, Mining and Construction Statistics*, http://www.census.gov/indicator/www/m3/adv/table1a.xls; Accessed: 1/29/02.

E4.0 THE SOURCE INFORMATION: Where would you locate this source?

VEF sources are not "published" in the same sense as print or PEF sources have been. Thus, the Publishing Information part of the citation (Section 4.0) becomes the Source Information in a VEF citation to reflect the WWW environment. The Source Information must be included to tell your readers where they can locate the source you have cited.

Parts of the Source Information Section of a VEF Citation:

* The Electronic Supplier (Section E4.1).

* The Electronic Source Address: the Uniform Resource Locator (URL) (Section E4.2).

* Accessed date: (Section E4.3).

Recommended Form and Punctuation: Precede the Source Information Section with the phrase "Available at:" (or a similar phrase) to signal to the reader that all subsequent information refers to the electronic supplier; then insert the Electronic Supplier and/or Electronic Source address; then, the Date Accessed, preceded by a semicolon (;).

Related Sections:

➤ Date of the Source (E2.1e)—be sure to include some indicator of the date of the source, as well as information about the supplier and the Accessed Date.
➤ PEF sources should include Publishing Information (Section 4.0).
➤ VEF sources that are equivalents of print publications in the form of PDF files (Section E4.1d).
➤ Parts of a VEF Source (Section E2.3d).

Consult the *Quick Citation Guides* for examples.
Ask a librarian for additional help.

E4.1 The Electronic Supplier

Identify the supplier of the VEF source. The most common are:

➤ Commercial database vendor (access controlled) (E4.1a).

➤ Government or organization WWW sites—freely available (Section 4.1b).

➤ Portals—freely available (E4.1c).

There is no need to repeat information included in Issuing Agency (Section E1.0), Title (E2.0), or the Electronic Supplier's Address (Section E4.2). However, when in doubt, always include more information rather than less since some suppliers are not well-known outside a discipline or a specific user community (Consult Table 14—Using the URL to Identify the Issuing Agency). In addition, URLs frequently use acronyms that may be confusing or unfamiliar.

E4.1a Commercial Database Vendor (Access Controlled)

Such sources control access to their databases by IP addresses, passwords, or other means. Your reader may not have access to this source. Therefore, include the name of the Commercial

Database, followed by the vendor name (for example, *Congressional Universe*, LexisNexis). The URL address should not be included with such entries, since users will not be able to access the database via this link in most cases, but rather will need to use their own password or university IP address.

Commercial Database Vendors (Common Variations):

➢ Available from: Congressional Universe, LexisNexis.

➢ Available from: AccessUN, Readex/NewsBank.

➢ Availabe from: SourceOECD.

Table 15: Is it AccessUN or is it the UN Documentation Centre?

As the world becomes increasing "connected," commercial database vendors are creating links to sources at freely available government and organization WWW sites (Section 4.1b). One example, *AccessUN*, Readex/NewsBank—an access-controlled source—links to many full-text PDF documents at the *UN Documentation Centre* (http:www.un.org/-documents/)--a freely available site. To complicate things, *AccessUN* also provides full text access to many UN documents in text format not available at the *UN Documentation Centre*. Normally, it would not make any difference where your reader started to locate a text. However, when access to the database source is controlled your reader should be alerted that they can locate the information elsewhere. Readex/NewsBank alerts their users with two different "notes." The following examples suggest recommended citation wording for such situations.

"The full text of this document is available elsewhere on the Internet. Readex/NewsBank is not responsible for content of Internet links."

U.N. General Assembly, 56th Session. *Children and Armed Conflict: Report of the Secretary-General* (A/56/342). 7 Sept. 2001. (Masthead). Available at: UN Documentation Centre, http://www.un.org/Docs/sc/reports/2001/852e.pdf; Accessed: 2/12/02.

"The full text of this document follows its citation."

U.N. General Assembly, 55th Session. *94th Plenary Meeting, 9 Mar. 2001* (A/55/PV.94). Official Record. Available from: AccessUN, Readex/NewsBank; Accessed: 2/12/02.

Readex/NewsBank is not the only vendor making these connections. Watch for other vendors that link to freely available information on the Internet. When they do, use wording in your citation to alert your reader, that they don't have to locate this source via an access-controlled source.

See the *Quick Citation Guides* for examples and Table 16: Portal to Portal.
Ask a librarian for additional help.

E4.1b Government or Organization WWW Sites: Freely Available

When governments and organizations place information on their freely available WWW sites that **cannot** be associated with a print equivalent through an internal or an external source (Section E0.1), the government or organization is effectively serving dual roles: as the Issuing Agency (Section E1.0) and as the Electronic Supplier; i.e., no publisher/printer is being used for this information or source. This multiple role needs only be recognized by including the following:

* The Issuing Agency (Section E1.0).

  Variation: The Issuing Agency may be combined with the Electronic Source Address, see the *Quick Citation Guides* for examples and Sections E4.1c and E6.5a.

* The Electronic Source Address (URL) (Section E4.2).

Note: Be sure a Date of the Source (Section E2.1e), Date as Part of Title (Section 2.1e), Edition Statement (Section 3.3) or some indication of the "age" or "currency" of the publication or when the page was last updated is included in the citation, as well as the Date Accessed (Section 4.3).

> "General Conditions in the Marketplace: Table 1—Selected Labor Market Indicators: Current Conditions, Annual Averages, 1948-2000." In U.S. Dept. of Labor, Bureau of Labor Statistics. *Report on the American Workforce 2001.* Available at: http://www.bls.gov/opub/rtaw/rtawhome.htm; Accessed: 12/12/01.

> United Kingdom. HM Treasury. *Budget 2001: Investing for the Long Term, Building Opportunity and Prosperity for All.* Available at: http://www.official-documents.co.uk/document/hmt/budget2001/hc279.htm; Accessed: 9/10/01.

> "Gross Domestic Product, Current Prices: All Countries" (csv file). Data from: International Monetary Fund. *World Economic Outlook (WEO) Database,* Sept. 2000. Available at: www.imf.org/external/pubs/ft/weo/2000/02/data/index.html; Accessed: 2/1/02.

E4.1c Portals: Freely Available

A number of freely available portals provide access to many different databases through a common search interface. These sources require a "Text From:" section in each entry to identify the specific database (Section E2.3d), as well as the portal as the Source of Information. Include the name of the Portal, followed by the URL address (Section E4.2). Portals which use passwords or other forms to control access to their content, should be cited in the manner of Commercial Database Vendors (E4.1a).

Note: Because some Portals are not well-known outside a discipline, it is advisable to include information about the portal provider in parentheses following the portal name, if the information is not included as part of the portal name.

Portals (Common Variations):

➢ Available from: GPO Access, http://www.access.gpo.gov/

➢ Available from: Thomas (Library of Congress), http://thomas.loc.gov

➢ Available from: American FactFinder (Census Bureau), http://www.factfinder.gov/

➢ Available from: Rapid (Commission of the European Communities, Brussels), http://europa.eu.int/-rapid/start/welcome.htm

> "The Comprehensive Test Ban Treaty: Strengthening Security for the U.S. and the World— Secretary Christopher, White House Fact Sheets,"*Dispatch* (U.S. Dept. of State) 7:34 (Sept. 16, 1996). Text from: *DOSFAN Archives.* Available from: Electronic Research Collection (University of Illinois, Chicago Library), http://dosfan.lib.uic.edu/-ERC/briefing/dispatch/1996/html/dispatchv7no38.html; Accessed: 2/15/02.

Table 16: Portal-to-Portal—"You are Now Leaving This Site…"

Increasingly portals are linking to each other as they each seek to provide specialized collections on their own WWW sites, but provide links to sources at other sites. One example is the relationship between GPO Access and Thomas (Library of Congress). Frequently searches will result in links to: "GPO PDF" versions of bills and other sources. In such cases, you should include "Available at: GPO Access" if you elect to cite the PDF version of the bill. Many portals indicate when you are leaving their own WWW site and connecting to another with the message "You are now leaving this site…" message.

Ask a librarian for help if you are unsure.

Variation: Some portals are well-known within some disciplines. When appropriate, the name of the portal (e.g., GPO Access) can be omitted from the entry and the URL only included.

Variation: Some portals are titled (e.g., GPO Access or Rapid). Other portals are not named, but are made available by an agency, organization, university or other non-commercial provider. In these circumstances the portal provider (the organization, agency, etc.) can precede the URL.

> U.S. Census Bureau. *County and City Data Book*. 1994 ed. Available at: University of Virginia, Geospatial and Statistical Data Center, http://fisher.lib.virginia.edu/ccdb/; Accessed: 1/28/02.

E4.1d VEF Equivalents of Print Publications (PDF Files)

When an entire document is presented as a PDF file, or as a series of PDF files, consult the title page and cover page images and treat as an internal and external source of information (Section E0.1). Complete the citation as given for a print source as described in Part 1. Add the Electronic Supplier (Section E4.1), the Electronic Source Address (Section E4.2), and the Date Accessed (Section E4.3).

Note: When the Electronic Supplier of a VEF source is included elsewhere in the citation, as part of the Issuing Agency statement or as part of the Publishing Information statement, for example, this information need not be repeated in the Electronic Supplier statement.

E4.2 The Electronic Source Address (URL)

Every Electronic Supplier has an Electronic Source Address that takes the form of a URL.

Table 17: What is a Uniform Resource Locator (URL)?

The URL serves as the "address" on the WWW for the source you are citing. It is made up of several parts.

Example: http://www.bls.gov/hom/homtoc.htm

http:	Protocol (Hypertext Transfer Protocol).
//www	World Wide Web server.
.bls	the Bureau of Labor Statistics server, where information/source is located.
.gov	the designation for a government WWW site, typically used for U.S. government sites; international organizations and state governments will have different designation.
/hom	the directory within the bls server containing the information/source.
/homtoc.htm	the file name for the information/source.

One variation on a URL is the PURL (Persistent Uniform Resource Locator). PURLs are stable links which consistently point to the source being cited. They should always be used in place of a URL.

If your source is spread across several files (i.e., WWW pages) always prefer the URL where much of the information for your citation appears, see Table 18—Which URL to Include.

Ask a librarian for additional help.

Several common situations arise with a URL and frequently you will need to make a judgment about which or how much of a URL to include. For example, you may choose the URL for the "home page" containing the links to several chapters, or the URL to the chapter itself. In addition, some database searches generate lengthy URLs that contain a .cgi script that are impractical to transfer to your bibliography. Your readers will have a hard time re-typing these URLs into their web browser, and they may not be persistent or permanent URLs for the sources you are citing.

The URLs in your citations should be as precise as page number references to a periodical issue, enabling your reader to find the relevant information with minimal effort, but such precision is not always possible.

In many cases a VEF source is completely contained in a single file ending in one of the common file types (.html, .htm, .pdf, .xls, etc.). In such circumstances you should include the complete URL all the way out to the file name and ending.

However, you will frequently be faced with situations in which you will need to exercise your judgment about which URL and how much of the URL to include in your citation. This will occur when, in your judgment, the URL for the source cited may change; when the URL includes a lengthy .cgi script; when you are citing only a part (a chapter, for example); or when the publication title and other key information is not included in the URL. In all circumstances follow the guidelines in Table 18.

Table 18: Which URL to Include?

The URL Should Point To (in order of preference):

* A specific chapter, data table, or other part if you are citing the part and the part is well-identified by a header, chapter title, or section heading.

* The whole work, if this provides the most reliable starting place and is the source of much of the information included in the citation.

* A WWW page providing the entry to the database or data extractor interface, when the database entries or data are generated by a search strategy or a series of menu selections. In these cases, be sure the citation (or the text of your own paper or publication) includes adequate information to allow your reader to duplicate or retrieve the source cited, typically in the form of "Text from:" (Section 2.3d).

* An agency, organization, portal, or commercial database vendor's home page.

E4.2a URL for a Commercial Database Vendor (Access Controlled)

Since access to many commercial sources and portals is limited by a library or other subscriber's licensing agreements, the database or source may be available only to certain groups of people (the students and faculty of a single University, for example). In these cases, the URL will not provide access for readers (unless they are members of the same group of authorized users). In these cases no URL is needed in the citation; the Electronic Supplier's Name (Section E4.1) is sufficient information.

When government information is accessed through a commercial database vendor (LexisNexis, for example), the URL of these secondary providers does NOT identify the Issuing Agency's role in producing the content of the publication. In these cases, always include a complete Issuing Agency statement for the VEF source. The commercial database vendor should be included in the Source Information part of the citation (Section E4.1).

E4.2b URL for Government or Organization WWW Sites: Freely Available

The citation to freely available WWW sites should be as specific as possible. In addition, the URL may replace the Issuing Agency statement because in some circumstances, a URL domain name and directory structure may provide an adequate Geo/Political Designation and Issuing Agency (Section E1.0).

In such cases, the citation may begin with the title as described in Section 1.2c or with a Personal Author (Section E1.4).

Use your judgment in such circumstances and be sure BOTH the Issuing Agency and Geo/Political Designation (if appropriate) are identified within the completed citation. URLs from freely available government or organization WWW sites usually (although not always) provide adequate identification. Consult Table 14—Using the URL to Identify the Issuing Agency.

> Washington [State]. Office of Trade and Economic Development. International Trade Division. *Why is Trade Important?* Last modified July 20, 2001. (Original source: *Foreign Exports and the Washington Economy*). Available at: http://www.trade.wa.gov/whyis.htm; Accessed: 12/10/01.

E4.2c URL for Portals: Freely Available

When government or organization information is accessed through a freely available portal (GPO Access, for example), the URL of these secondary providers does NOT identify the Issuing Agency's role in producing the content of the publication. In these cases, always include a complete Issuing Agency statement (Section E1.0) for the VEF source. The portal should be included in the Source Information part of the citation (Section E4.1).

E4.3 Date Accessed

The Source Information should conclude with the date you accessed the information or source. Since the contents of an on-line database or a VEF source can and do change without warning or notice, it is particularly important to record the date the database or source was used.

Including the date serves two main purposes:

➤ It informs your reader that the source/information existed on the specified date. Since VEF sources can be moved, changed, and edited, this provides a date stamp for the version you used as a source and its location on that date.

➤ It provides your reader with a rough sense of the date of the publication. Since the publication and issue date of many VEF sources are not apparent, the Date Accessed gives your reader some crude sense of when the information was created.

Precede the date with the word "Accessed:" (or similar phrase). The date should be in the form DD/MM/YYYY. For alternative forms of the date, consult Section 4.3.

E4.3a Time Accessed

For some databases and VEF sources, it may be important to also record the time (including "a.m." or "p.m." and the time zone) the database or source was accessed. This may be the case with economic indicators which can be adjusted or changed. Including the time accessed is optional and should only be included if it supplies information relevant to the source and its content. Time may be in either EST (Eastern Standard Time) or GMT (Greenwich Mean Time).

E5.0 Series and Note Information—What more can you add about this source?

Because so many publisher's series are well-known to researchers, governments and organizations continue to identify their VEF sources with these series titles. In some cases, the series serve as the primary point of access to individual titles in the series. For example, both the Census Bureau and the National Health Service list their series by series name. Thus, Series Statements should be added to VEF source citations in the manner described in Section 5.0.

Notes may be less prevalent when citing VEF sources as much of the descriptive information is not as relevant in this environment. Furthermore, government classification numbers are frequently irrelevant. When needed, Notes may be added in the manner described in Section 5.3.

Consult Section 5.0 for additional rules for Series and Notes and the *Quick Citation Guides* for additional examples.
Ask a librarian for additional help.

VEF Series (Common Variations):

FEC Reports on Political Party Activity for 1998-98. For immediate release, Apr. 9, 1999. (News Releases, Media Advisories). Available at: http://www.fec.gov/-press/ptype98.htm; Accessed: 2/19/02.

Little, Barbara, and Erik M. Seibert. *Guidelines for Evaluating and Registering Archeological Properties.* U.S. National Park Service, National Register, History and Education, 2000. (National Register Bulletin). Available at: http://www.cr.nps.gov/nr/-publications/bulletins/archeology/; Accessed: 2/21/02.

U.S. Census Bureau. *Mapping Census 2000: The Geography of U.S. Diversity* (CENSR/01-1) (28.8 kb). By Cynthia A. Brewer and Trudy A. Suchan. Washington: Government Printing Office, 2000. (Census 2000 Special Reports). Available at: http://www.census.gov/popular/www/cen2000/-atlas.html; Accessed: 2/21/02.

Great Britain. Dept. of Trade and Industry. *A World Class Competition Regime Department of Trade and Industry.* London: Stationery Office, 2001. (CM 5233). Available at: http://www.official-documents.co.uk/document/cm52/5233/5233.htm; Accessed: 2/28/02.

European Communities. European Parliament, Directorate-General for Research. *Teaching of Immigrants in the European Union.* By Léonce Bekemans. Luxembourg: European Parliament, Nov. 1997. (Working Paper: Education and Culture Series, EDUC100 EN). Available at: http://www.europarl.eu.int/workingpapers/educ/-pedf/100_en.pdf; Accessed: 2/13/02.

E6.0 CITING PARTS: PERIODICAL AND STATISTICAL SOURCES

The WWW is the perfect medium for government agencies to deliver their journals and magazines. Not surprisingly, a wide range of government and organization electronic periodicals are being delivered quickly via government and organization WWW sites, portals, and database vendors. The WWW is also the perfect medium for governments and organizations to deliver the plethora of data they collect and to provide new versions of the statistical data sources they have long published.

Therefore, you will be encountering and citing parts of government and organization VEF periodicals and data sources frequently on the WWW. Although the format and structure of most print periodicals and statistical publications have become standardized, the format and structure of electronic periodicals and statistical sources vary widely.

Researchers must be alert to the possibility that a given periodical article or data table may be part of a VEF source. If you cite only the article or data table, the reader may not be able to locate your source, or to be sure they have found the same source. If you cite only the source, the reader may not be able to locate the particular part that you considered relevant to your topic. Remember, as is the case with all VEF sources, you must include as much information as possible so that your reader can locate alternative electronic sources and formats if necessary.

Basic Rules:

<u>Describe the Part:</u>

* Author of the article or data table, if available (Section 6.1 and E6.1).
* Title of the article or data table header (Section 6.2 and E6.2).

<u>Describe the Source:</u>

* The Title of the Periodical or Data Table Source (Section 6.3 and E6.3).
* Issue Identification Information: volume, issue numbers, date (Section 6.4a and E6.4a).

<u>Describe the Source of Information (Available at):</u>

* Source of Information (Section E4.0).

Recommended Form and Punctuation:

Hoang, Francis Q. "Addressing School Violence: Prevention Planning Practice." Text from: *FBI Law Enforcement Bulletin* 70:8 (Aug. 2001) pp.18-22. Available at: http://www.fbi.gov/publications/leb/2001/aug01leb.pdf; Accessed: 1/15/02.

"Table 3.11: Real National Defense Consumption, Expenditures, and Gross Investment." Last revised 12/21/01. Taken from: U.S. Bureau of Economic Analysis. *National Income and Product Accounts Tables*, http://www.bea.doc.gov/bea/dn/nipaweb/index.asp; Accessed: 1/24/02.

Related Sections:

➢ Consult Section 6.0 for additional rules.
➢ For rules on how to cite a whole statistical volume consult Sections 0.0-5.0.
➢ Titles of Chapters or Other Book Parts (Sections 2.3 and E2.3).
➢ The Series Statement (Section 5.0 and E5.0).

Consult the *Quick Citation Guide to Periodical and Statistical Sources* and the *Quick Citation Guide to Legislative/Parliamentary Sources* for additional examples.
Ask a librarian for additional help.

E6.0a Where to Locate Information to Include in a Citation to a Part: Use the Internal vs. External Rule

Apply the rules in Section 0.1 and in E0.1. However, be aware that VEF periodical articles and data tables will present unusual challenges: important information may appear on external sources, rather than internal sources. In such cases, use your judgment about whether to include this information in your citation. The goal is to provide enough information for your readers to be able to locate the same source even if the URL has changed and they must find it in another location or format. Any information supplied from sources such as indexes, on-line library catalogs, or databases such as *WorldCat* should be enclosed in brackets.

E6.1 Authors of the Article or Data Table (The Part)

Treat authors, compilers, and editors of articles and data tables exactly like Personal Authors (Section 1.4 and E1.4).

E6.2 Title of the Article or Data Table Header (The Part)

Follow rules for the Title Statement (Section 2.0 and E2.0) for additional guidance.

Titles of electronic periodical articles and the headers of data tables may have non-traditional forms (Section E2.1c). Take care when determining the title of an article or data table. Screen layout may affect the way the title is read or viewed on the screen.

E6.2a Menu Driven Interfaces in VEF Sources (The Rule of Three)

Apply this rule to sources that include a menu-driven interface that allows the user to select a specific data table, to generate a customized data table or requires the researcher to select from a series of menus to reach the database search form (e.g., LexisNexis uses this approach in its databases).

If a table header includes all menu or item selections, use this information as the data table title. When the table header is incomplete (that is, your reader would not be able to create the same table by using the information in the data table header), "enhance" the title by adding the missing information in brackets. In general, do not include more than three of those menu choices.

> "P27A: Relationship by Household Type (Including Living Alone) (White Alone)—5 Digit ZCTA 16801." Dataset: *Census, 2000* (SF 1). Available from: American FactFinder (Census Bureau), http://factfinder.census.gov/; Accessed: 2/15/02.

If more than three selections are made, consult Section E6.6.

E6.2b A Part Within a Part (VEF Formats)

It is possible, particularly with some WWW-based periodicals and data tables, to cite a side-bar illustration, a chart, or an image contained within a VEF periodical article source. You may also want to incorporate a graphic, text or data table into your own work. In such cases, the periodical source should be recognized. While this can be done in the print environment simply by citing the page number on which the graphic appears, this approach is not adequate for VEF sources: it is also necessary to identify the VEF Source of Information (Section 4.0). To do so, your citation must include a "Text from:" or "Data from:" (or equivalent) section.

It is important to include these sections in the citation so that your reader has enough information to locate the source in alternative format, if necessary. Consult File Names as Titles (Section 2.1d).

> Fdbaby2a.jpg [picture of a graph indicating folic awareness]. Taken from: "Folic Acid Awareness," *FDA Consumer Magazine*, March-April 1999. Available at: http://www.fda.gov/fdac/features/1999/babyside.html; Accessed: 1/15/02.

> "Sources of Borrowed Capital for Owner" [Graphic; cap_o.gif]. Taken from: *Characteristics of Business Owners Survey, 1992*. Available at: http://www.census.gov/csd/cbo/; Accessed: 1/15/02.

Note: In the first example above, the .jpg image does not have its own "title" and has been enhanced with the "rollover" text provided on the WWW page. In the second example, the image has its own title.

Consult Titles of Chapters and Other Book Parts (Section E2.3) for additional guidance.

Variation: Unique Identification Numbers for Parts in VEF

Sometimes the best way to identify an electronic part is with a unique identifier such as a file name or record number. Be sure to include at least one of the following, if they are available:

- Record identification number;

- Exact file name (75FR23425.TXT)--be sure to include all the parts of the file name including the directory, subdirectory, file name and extension (e.g., .txt).

> "Movie Going Reaches 40-Year High," *Infomat* (11-002-XIE) Feb. 15, 2002. (Publications for a Fee). Available from: Statistics Canada, http://www.statcan.ca/; Accessed: 2/15/02.

E6.3 Title of the Periodical (The Source)

The Title of the Periodical should be cited exactly as given in full. Consult rules for the Title Statement (Section 2.0) and Citing Parts (Section 6.3) for additional guidance.

E6.4 Issue Identification Information

The exact issue of the periodical containing the article must be identified in order to distinguish between periodicals with the same name as well as to help your reader identify an article quickly within a specific issue. Issue Information may follow exactly the numbering of a print equivalent, or it may be in an entirely nontraditional format. Consult Section 6.4 for additional guidance.

E6.4a Issue Identifiers: Volume, Issue, and Date

Because the structure of periodical and data sources is not yet established, a wide range of methods are used to identify specific issues of periodicals that contain data tables and/or articles. Aside from helping your reader locate the information you have cited, the Issue Identification Information also lets your reader know the date (or currency) of the information. This is particularly important to users of statistical data tables.

Follow the rules in Section 6.4a for identifying any volume, issue, or, most importantly, date of the source cited.

> Philo, Greg. "An Unseen World: How the Media Portrays the Poor." Text from: *UNESCO Courier* (Nov. 2001). Available at: http://www.unesco.org/courier/2001_11/-uk/medias.htm; Accessed: 1/15/01.

> "Peace in the Middle East: A Role for Europe," *The Europeans,* Issue 26 (Apr. 2001). Available at: Council of Europe, Parliamentary Assembly, http://stars.coe.fr/-Magazine/te0401/index.htm; Accessed: 2/11/02.

Note: Do not confuse the date of the source, with the date of the data, since these may differ widely.

When other citation format variations are used, be sure to provide enough information to ensure that your reader will be able to locate the article or data table and the periodical title, using the issue identification information you have supplied.

"Interest in European Union News," *Eurobarometer* 55 (Fieldwork: Apr.-May 2001; Release: Oct. 2001) p. 66. Available at: The European Commission, http://europa.eu.int/comm/dg10/epo/eb/eb55/eb55_en.pdf; Accessed: 2/21/02.

The "Accessed:" information (Section E4.3) is also an important aspect of a citation to periodical source because older periodical and statistical soures are often "archived" at different locations and URLs or are removed from the original WWW site. The "Accessed:" information indicates that the source existed at the URL on that date.

Variation: Some journals will name individual issues or volumes of a periodical. Include this information in the manner of volume or issue number.

England, Lizabeth. "Socially Responsible Business: Doing the Right Thing," *Language and Civil Society: A Forum Electronic Journal,* The Business Ethics Volume. Available at: U.S. Dept. of State. Office of English Language Programs, http://exchanges.state.gov/forum/journal/index.htm; Accessed: 1/16/02.

E6.4b Page Numbers and Other Indicators of Length/Size

Many VEF periodicals will not include page numbering since hypertext document structure does not incorporate standard pagination. However, periodicals in PDF format will frequently include the page numbers; periodical articles accessed through portals and commercial databases also will frequently include the page numbers as part of the database entry. When present, these should be included in your citation.

Many legislative/parliamentary sources will include page numbers because they remain important for identification of specific parts or discussions. However, since sources such as the *Congressional Record* are widely available, variations will occur in the presentation of page numbers. You should sleuth out this information in each source so that your readers can locate the same text regardless of which system or format they elect to use.

Consult rules in Section 6.4b for additional guidance.

Variation: When no page numbering is provided, you may substitute the following to help the researcher understand the length/size/extent of the publication you have cited. Include at least one of the following, if provided by the electronic source:

* Size of the file (e.g., 2345 bytes or number of words).

* The total number of lines (provided by the database), some systems also express this as "pages."

Vourc'h, Ann, "France: Moving Towards 'Greener' Growth," *OECD Observer* (Feb. 15, 2002) (1436 words). Available from: http://www.oecdobserver.org; Accessed: 2/15/02.

Variation: When electronic sources provide page numbers which correspond to a print equivalent and "electronic" page numbers, always prefer the page numbers that correspond to the print equivalent. This is the most useful to researchers who may locate the source in print or microformats.

E6.4c A Part Within a Database

Commercial database vendors and portals can serve as an entry to several databases or sources. Some of these databases contain the contents of periodicals such as, *The Congressional Record* and other legislative/parliamentary sources or to a selection of statistical datasets, such as those provided by the U.S. Census Bureau.

Use the phrase "Text from:" or "Data from:" (or an equivalent phrase) preceding information about the specific database containing the article or data table.

> "Table 3: Statistics by Economic Sector, Subsector, and Industry Group—Bellefonte, PA" (Geography Quick Report). Data based on the: *Economic Census, 1997*. Available at: American Factfinder (Census Bureau), http://factfinder.census.gov; Accessed: 1/26/02.

Consult the *Quick Citation Guide to Legislative/Parliamentary Sources* and *Quick Citation Guide to Periodical and Statistical Sources* for additional examples.

Note: When the name of the database corresponds to the name of the source, it is not necessary to repeat this information. For example, if the database is named: *Congressional Record,* the "Text from:" is not necessary in a citation to a *Congressional Record* entry.

E6.5 Variations to Clarify the Issuing Agency of the Periodical (The Source)

For VEF sources it is still important that your reader be able to determine which government agency or organization is making the source you have cited available (Section E0.0). Since this information can be lost in citation to periodical or statistical sources, the variations described in Section 6.5 should be used with VEF sources as well.

E6.5a Include the Issuing Agency

The Issuing Agency can be included as part of the Electronic Supplier Information (Section E4.1a-c), as a Note (Section 5.0), or prior to the periodical or statistical source title. Consult the rules in Section 6.5a, and consult the *Quick Citation Guides* for additional examples.

> McDaniel, Lynda. "Ecotourism Takes Off in the Heart of Appalachia," *Appalachia Magazine Online* (May-Aug. 2001). Available at: Appalachian Regional Commission (Washington, D.C.), http://arc.gov/infopubs/appalach/mayaug01/ecointro.htm; Accessed: 1/15/02.

> Baucus, Max. "Doha and Beyond: The Role of Congress in a New Trade Round," *Economic Perspective* 7:1 (Jan. 2002) pp. 18-20. (An Electronic Journal of the U.S. Dept. of State). Available at: http://info.state.gov/journals/ites/0102/ijee/-ijee0102.pdf; Accessed: 2/15/02.

> "Table 10—U.S. International Transactions, by Area—Western Europe." Release Date: Dec. 12, 2001; Earliest Year Revised on Dec. 12, 2001: No Revision. Data from: Bureau of Economic Analysis, *U.S. International Accounts Data*. Available at: http://www.bea.doc.gov/; Accessed: 1/15/02.

E6.5b Include Publishing Information

Although VEF sources are not published in the traditional sense, they may be electronic versions of print publications—for example a PDF version of a print publication or an electronic database containing an electronic version of a print source. Consult rules in Section 6.5b and E4.1d for guidance in when to include publishing information in citations to VEF sources.

E6.6 Data Files and Datasets: Special Rules

Increasingly, governments and organizations are providing access to datafiles or the ability to create dynamically generated[3] files or data tables for your own research needs.

Basic Rules:

Describe the Data Table or Datafile (by including any or all):
➢ Data table header or file name, including file extension (.xls, for example).
➢ Data description (data items, geography, time period), enclose in parentheses if not part of data table header.
➢ Length/Size Indicators (Section E6.4b).

Describe the Dataset (Data from: or Extracted from:)
➢ Agency or Organization that produced the dataset.
➢ The name of the dataset.
➢ Date data last updated or date of the data—year, version, or edition.

Describe the Source of Information (Available at:)
➢ Source of Information (a commercial database vendor, portal, or freely available government or organization WWW site, or nonprofit organization), and electronic source address (URL), if appropriate.
➢ Include the name of the data generator (for example, *DataQuery)* (optional).
➢ Date Accessed.

Note: The Source of Information may be provided in the description of the dataset; do not repeat information already provided.

Related Sections:
➢ Menu Driven Interfaces in VEF Sources (The Rule of Three) (Section 6.2a).

E6.6a Data Files

Many WWW sites will generate a file or make files of data available to be used with commercial data analysis software. Sometimes these files are quite large and must be downloaded to your computer in the form of a .zip file. Until recently, these files were mostly accessible via FTP sites, but the prevalence of web browsers has resulted in a decrease in FTP sites. It is recommended that the full file name be used as the part title. The size of the file and a medium note are also highly recommended, if not already part of (or evident from) the citation (Section E6.4b). See A Part Within a Part (VEF Formats) (Section E6.2b) and Non-Traditional Titles (Section 2.1d) for additional guidance.

> AfghanistanUNSCAP.xls (Excel file; 37 kb). Data from: *Asia and the Pacific in Figures 2000.* Available from: United Nations, Economic and Social Commission for Asia and the Pacific (ESCAP), Statistics Division, http://www.unescap.org/stat/statdata/-apinfig.htm; Accessed: 2/7/02.

> ngdp_a.csv [Gross Domestic Product, Current Prices: All Countries] (47 kb). Data from: International Monetary Fund. *World Economic Outlook (WEO) Database*, Sept. 2000. Available at: http://www.imf.org/external/pubs/ft/weo/2001/03/data/ngdp_a.csv; Accessed: 2/1/02.

> cm02.zip [Committees 2001-02] (228 kb). Downloaded from: *Detailed Files Covering 2001-2002 ... and 1993-94 (Committees).* Available from: Federal Election Commission, http://www.fec.gov/data; Accessed: 2/20/02.

When a data file or other source was originally in a PEF format (e.g., floppy disk, CD-ROM), but is now accessible via the WWW (i.e., has become a VEF source) the citation should describe the Source Information (Section 4.0) you used to access the data.

> U.S. National Center for Health Statistics. *International Mortality Data Base: Death Rates.* Washington: Government Printing Office, 1995. (Contains 256 Lotus spreadsheets). Available at: Indiana University Bloomington, Government Publications Dept., Floppy Disk Project, http://www.indiana.edu/~libgpd/mforms/floppy/floppy.html; Accessed: 4/20/02.

Note: Optional Special Notes used for PEF Sources (Section 5.5) can be included, if appropriate.

E6.6b Dynamically Generated Data Files and Datasets

The WWW is increasingly providing researchers with the flexibility that was once only possible with customized programming to analyze and produce datasets based on their specific needs. The number of WWW sites that allow users such flexibility continues to grow and these sites will become even more sophisticated and important to researchers in the future.

Most sources allow the user to select from a series of menus until all of the contents of a data table have been specified. Most sources then generate a data table with a header (i.e., title for the table). Because of the way datasets have been programmed by their producers, data from the exact same dataset can be presented quite differently. For examples of periodical citations from two different electronic sources that appear quite different, see *Quick Citation Guide to Legislative/Parliamentary Sources*, Congressional Record, L1.1.

Dynamically Generated Data Tables and Files (Common Variations):

> "Egypt, 1994-1995." Data from: *U.S. Imports and Exports of Merchandise: Historical Summaries, 1989-1999.* Available at: University of Virginia, Geospatial and Statistical Data Center, http://fisher.lib.virginia.edu/trade/; Data extracted: 1/28/02.

> "Beverages, Spirits, and Vinegar Imported Through Washington, D.C." Data from: U.S. Census Bureau. *U.S. Imports and Exports History, 1994-1998.* Available at: Government Information Sharing Project, http://govinfo.library.orst.edu/; Accessed: 1/30/02.

> "Unemp[loyment] Rate-Civilian Labor Force-Black Female." Data extracted: 2/5/2002, 4:48 p.m. EST. Data from: *Labor Force Statistics from the Current Population Survey* (Series ID: LFS21000032). Available at: U.S. Dept. of Labor, Bureau of Labor Statistics, *Most Requested Statistics*, http://www.dol.gov/data/home.htm; Accessed: 2/11/02.

> "Current Labor Force Data: Mobile, AL." Data from: U.S. Dept. of Housing and Urban Development. *State of the Cities Data Systems (SOCDS).* Available at: http://socds.huduser.org/index.html; Accessed: 1/29/02.

> "Consumer Price Index—All Urban Consumers: Energy (U.S. City Average)" (Series ID: CUSR0000SA0E; seasonally adjusted). Data extracted on 2/5/02. Data from: *Consumer Price Index (All Urban Consumers)—Current Series*, using *Create Customized Tables (Multiple Screens)*. Available at: Dept. of Labor, Bureau of Labor Statistics, *Consumer Price Indexes*, http://www.bls.gov/cpi/home.htm; Accessed: 2/23/02.

Variation: Researchers who use data from a large dataset typically cite only the dataset. This same approach can be used for interactive WWW sites. This is particularly appropriate when more than three menu choices are required to select data from a dataset. When this information does NOT appear in a table header, the citation may be to the whole dataset. Ensure the reader can locate the dataset and the "search/menu engine"—this often requires several parts to your citation.

Labor Force Statistics from the Current Population Survey. Data generated using: Create Customized Tables (Multiple Screens). Available at: U.S. Dept. of Labor, Bureau of Labor Statistics, http://www.dol.gov/data/; Accessed: 2/7/02.

World Development Indicators Database, 1996-2000 [Selected Data]. Data generated using DataQuery. Available at: http://www.worldbank.org/data/dataquery.html; Accessed: 1/28/02.

Data from: *IPUMS-USA* (Minnesota Population Center, University of Minnesota). Data generated using the IPUMS Extraction System (Integrated Public Use Microdata Series—IPUMS-98, Oct. 1997). Available at: http://www.ipums.umn,edu/usa/index.html; Accessed: 2/2/02.

Note: For alphabetization purposes the "Data from:" (or equivalent) phrase can be omitted at the beginning of the entry.

---

[1] For a list of WWW sites that were removed or changed following Sept. 11, 2001, see Office of Management and Budget, *Access to Government Information Post September 11th*. Published on: 02/01/2002. Available at: http://www.ombwatch.org/-info/2001/access.html; Accessed: 3/4/02.

[2] Wiggins, Richard, "Digital Preservation: Paradox & Promise," *Library Journal NetConnect Supplement* (Spring 2001) pp. 12-17. Available from: LexisNexis; Accessed: 3/4/02.

[3] The term "Dynamically Generated Tables/Files" comes from the U.S. Census Bureau. They provide *Suggested Citation Styles for Our Internet Information* at http://www.census.gov/main/www/citation.html where this phrase is used to describe tables generated "on the fly."

Appendices, Glossary, and Index

Appendix A: Style Manuals

No citation style manual provides extensive examples and rules for citing government and organization information or for addressing the unusual challenges that researchers encounter when citing these sources. The style manuals below are the most frequently used by researchers and the form and punctuation described in each of these manuals can be used with the examples in this manual. The content of the citation would remain the same, the form and punctuation would differ. Many documents librarians have also developed style manuals for government information resources and these are available on their library WWW pages. *Always ask a librarian for help if you are unsure how to cite government and organization information sources.*

Clark, Suzanne M., Mary Lynette Larsgaard, Cynthia M. Teague. *Cartographic Citations, A Style Guide*. Chicago: ALA, 1992.

Gibaldi, Joseph. *MLA Style Manual and Guide to Scholarly Publishing*. New York: Modern Language Association, 1998.

Li, Xia, and Nancy Crane. *Electronic Style: A Guide to Citing Electronic Information*. Westport: Meckler, 1995.

The Chicago Manual of Style. 14th ed. Chicago: University of Chicago Press, 1993.

Patrias, Karen. *National Library of Medicine Recommended Formats for Bibliographic Citation*. Bethesda: National Library of Medicine, 1991. (Available from NTIS, Springfield, VA, PB91-182030).

Patrias, Karen. *National Library of Medicine Recommended Formats for Bibliographic Citation: Supplement, Internet Formats*. Bethesda: National Library of Medicine, 2001. Available at: http://www.nlm.nih.gov/pubs/formats/internet.pdf; Accessed: 2/23/02.

Publication Manual of the American Psychological Association. 5th ed. Washington: APA, 2001.—Includes *APA Style for Electronic Resources*, Aug. 2001. Available at: http//www.apastyle.org; Accessed: 2/23/02.

Shields, Nancy E., and Mary E. Uhle. *Where Credit Is Due: A Guide to Proper Citing of Sources, Print, and Non-Print*. 2nd ed. Lanham, MD: Scarecrow Pr., 1997.

Slade, Carole, William Giles Campbell, and Stephen V. Ballou. *Form and Style: Research Papers, Reports, and Theses*. 9th ed. Boston: Houghton Mifflin, 1994.

Style Manual for Political Science. Washington: American Political Science Association, Committee on Publications, 2001.

Thibault, Danielle. *Bibliographic Style Manual*. Ottawa: National Library of Canada, 1998 (Cat. No. SN3-247-1989E).

Turabian, Kate L., John Grossman, and Alice Bennett. *A Manual for Writers of Term Papers, Theses and Dissertations*. 5th ed. Chicago: University of Chicago Press, 1996.

A Uniform System of Citation. 17th ed. Cambridge, Mass.: Harvard Law Review Association, 2000.

Van Leunen, Mary-Claire. *A Handbook for Scholars*. Rev. ed. New York: Oxford University Press, 1992.

Walker, Janice R., and Todd Taylor. *The Columbia Guide to Online Style*. New York: Columbia University Press, 1998. Available at: http://www.columbia.edu/cu/cup/cgos/idx_basic.html; Accessed: 2/23/02.

For additional help citing government and organization sources

Furuta, Ken. *Government Documents Search—DocsCite*. Updated Feb. 2001. Arizona State University Libraries, July 2000. Available at: http://www.asu.edu/lib/hayden/govdocs/docscite/docscite.htm; Accessed: 2/23/02.—A forms-based interface to create citations for government documents in MLA and APA styles.

Sheehy, Helen. *Government Publications*. In: *Information Literacy and You: Citing Your Sources*. Available at: The Pennsylvania State University Libraries, http://www.libraries.psu.edu/crsweb/infolit/andyou/infoyou.htm; Accessed: 2/23/02.—Sample citations in APA, Turabian, Chicago, MLA, and Garner/Smith (2nd ed.) styles.

Uncle Sam: Brief Guide to Citing Government Publications. Last updated: Dec. 7, 2001. Available from: Government Publications Dept., The University of Memphis, http://exlibris.memphis.edu/govpubs/citeweb.htm; Accessed: 2/23/02.

U.S. Census Bureau. *Suggested Citation Styles for Our Internet Information*. Available at: http://www.census.gov/main/www/citation.html; Accessed: 2/23/02.

U.S. Library of Congress. *Citing Electronic Resources* [citation examples for the sources on the Library of Congress website]. Last updated 11/20/00. Available at: http://memory.loc.gov/ammem/ndlpedu/resources/cite/; Accessed: 2/23/02.

U.S. National Archives and Records Administration. *Citing Records in the National Archives of the United State*s. Revised. Washington, Nov. 1997. (General Information Leaflet, no. 17). Available at: http://www.nara.gov/publications/leaflets/gil17.html; Accessed: 2/27/02.

Many database providers include examples and guides for citing sources available on their WWW sites:

"Citation of Electronic Resources." Text from: Government Information Sharing Project Disclaimers and Citations. Available at: http://govinfo.kerr.orst.edu/disclaim.html; Accessed: 2/23/02.

Citing Electronic Data Files. Available from: Inter-University Consortium for Political and Social Research, http://www.icpsr.umich.edu/ORG/citation.html; Accessed: 2/23/02.

Citing References from LexisNexis Academic Universe. Accessed: 2/23/02.

General Principles for Composing Citations to Electronic Formats of Government Information. Available from: State Capital Universe, LexisNexis; Accessed: 2/23/02.

How to Cite Electronic, Print, and Microfiche Congressional Publications. Available from: Congressional Universe, LexisNexis; Accessed: 2/23/02.

How to Cite United Nations Documents and Publications. Available from: Readex/NewsBank; Accessed: 2/23/02.

How to Cite InfoTrac and Galenet Sources. Available from: Thomson/Gale, <u>http://www.galegroup.com/customer_service/citing.htm</u>; Accessed: 2/23/02.

Appendix B: Standard Reference Sources for Government Information
United States

American Statistics Index (ASI). Bethesda, MD: Congressional Information Service.

Andriot, John. *Guide to U.S. Government Publications*. McLean, VA: Documents Index.

AskEric (ERIC Database). U.S. Department of Education, http://www.askeric.org/; Accessed: 2/27/02.

CIS/Index to Congressional Publications. Bethesda, MD: Congressional Information Service.

CIS Index to Unpublished U.S. House of Representatives Committee Hearings, 1833-1954. Bethesda, MD: Congressional Information Service.

CIS Index to Unpublished U.S. Senate Committee Hearings, 1823-1968. Bethesda, MD: Congressional Information Service.

CIS Index to U.S. Executive Branch Documents, 1789-1909: Guide to Documents Listed in the Checklist of U.S. Public Documents, 1789-1909, Not Printed in the Serial Set. Bethesda, MD: Congressional Information Service.

CIS Index to U.S. Executive Branch Documents, 1910-1932: Guide to Documents Not Printed in the U.S. Serial Set. Bethesda, MD: Congressional Information Service.

CIS Index to U.S. Senate Executive Documents and Reports. Bethesda, MD: Congressional Information Service.

CIS U.S. Congressional Committee Hearings Index, 1833-1969. Bethesda, MD: Congressional Information Service.

CIS U.S. Congressional Committee Prints Index, 1830-1969. Bethesda, MD: Congressional Information Service.

CIS U.S. Serial Set Index. Bethesda, MD: Congressional Information Service.

Congressional Universe, Dublin, OH: LexisNexis.

Foreign Broadcast Information Service Electronic Index. New Canaan, CT: Readex/NewsBank.

Index to U.S. Government Periodicals. Bethesda, MD: Congressional Information Service.

Monthly Catalog of U.S. Government Publications. Washington: Government Printing Office. Now available 1994-to date as the *Catalog of Government Publications* at: http://www.access.gpo.gov/su_docs/locators/cgp/index.html; Accessed: 2/27/02.

U.S. Bureau of the Census. *Census Catalog*. Washington: Government Printing Office. Available at: http://www.census.gov; Accessed: 2/27/02.

U. S. Congress. *Official Congressional Directory*. Washington: Government Printing Office. Available at: http://www.access.gpo.gov/congress/cong016.html; Accessed: 2/27/02.

United States Government Manual. Washington: Government Printing Office. Available at: http://www.access.gpo.gov/nara/nara001.html; Accessed: 2/27/02.

U.S. Government Printing Office. *List of Classes of United States Government Publications Available for Selection by Depository Libraries.* Washington: Government Printing Office. Available at: http://www.access.gpo.gov/su_docs/-fdlp/pubs/loc/index.html; Accessed: 2/27/02.

U.S. National Technical Information Service (NTIS). *Government Reports Announcements and Index.* Springfield, VA: NTIS. —Available 1990-to date at http://www.ntis.gov/search.

State, Local, Regional

Index to Current Urban Documents. Westport, CT: Greenwood Press.

State Legislative Manuals on Microfiche. Boulder, CO: Numbers and Concepts.

Statistical Reference Index (SRI). Bethesda, MD: Congressional Information Service.

Statistical Universe, Dublin, OH: LexisNexis.

International

Documentos Oficiales de la Organización de los Estados Americanos. Washington: Organization of American States.

FAO Documentation. Rome: Food and Agriculture Organization of the United Nations.

Hajnal, Peter I. *International Information: Documents, Publications, and Electronic Information of International Governmental Organizations.* 2nd ed. Englewood, CO: Libraries Unlimited, 1997.

AccessUN (Index to the United Nations Documents and Publications). Available from: Readex/NewsBank.

Index to International Statistics (IIS). Bethesda, MD: Congressional Information Service.

Roney, Alex, and Stanley Budd. *The European Union: A Guide Through the EC/EU Maze.* 6th ed. London: Kogan Page, 1998.

United Nations. Dag Hammarskjöld Library. *United Nations Documentation: A Research Guide.* Available at: http://www.un.org/Depts/dhl/resguide/.

UNDOC. New York: United Nations.

UNESCO List of Documents and Publications. Paris: UNESCO.

Yearbook of International Organizations. Munchen, Germany: K.G. Saur.

Worldwide Government Directory, with International Organizations. Washington: Keesing's Worldwide.

Foreign

Most countries have a listing of their publications. For the most complete and current list of these catalogs consult:

Guide to Official Publications of Foreign Countries. 2nd ed. Chicago: American Library Association, Government Documents Round Table, 1997.

Law, Gwillim. *Administrative Subdivisions of Countries: A Comprehensive World Reference, 1900 through 1998*. Jefferson, NC: McFarland, 1999.

American Library Association, Government Documents Roundtable. *Guide to Country Information in International Governmental Organization Publications*. Bethesda, MD: Congressional Information Service, 1996.

Appendix C: Numbering Systems

Organization	Example	Place
United Nations— Series/Symbol Number 　Note: Do not confuse with 　U.N. Sales Numbers 　(Section 5.3f).	A/37/565 See examples at L3.1. Varies See examples at L3.2.	On masthead documents in the upper right corner of the first page (Fig. 10). On *Official Records*, either upper right corner or under title on cover page (Fig. 2). On Secretariat and other documents may be on back of title page.
European Communities	ST/ CA-22-77-613-6A- C See example at L3.1.	Any or all of the following: back cover, back of title page, bibliographic slip, or cataloging in publication on last page. Often preceded by Kat./Cat./.
Organisation for Economic Cooperation and Development (OECD)	21-82-06-1	Lower left corner of back cover, small type in parentheses, or last frame of microfiche.
Organization of American States (OAS)	OEA/SER.L/V/11. 61	Usually on title page; sometimes also on spine.
Food and Agriculture Organization (FAO)	ADCP/REP/80/11	On title or cover page.
International Atomic Energy Agency (IAEA)		
Documents:	INFCIRC/306	On upper right corner of first page.
Publications:	STI/PUB/498	On back of title page for whole publications.
	IAEA-SM-232/65	On first page of article for individual articles.
United Nations Education, Scientific, and Cultural Organization (UNESCO)	PRS.79/WS/47	On lower left or upper right corner of first page; used on documents only, not on UNESCO Press publications.

Appendix D: Abbreviations

The list below provides some commonly used abbreviations found in government and organization publications. In addition to these, consult Section 0.4 Abbreviations Rules and additional accepted abbreviations included in the citation rules. *The Chicago Manual of Style* (14th ed. Chicago: University of Chicago Press, 1993) also provides an extensive list of "Abbreviations" as do many other style manuals listed in *Appendix A: Style Manuals.*

Chapter=Chpt.
Column=Col.
Command Paper=Cmd. or CM
Compiler=Comp.
Congress=Cong.
Department=Dept.
Document=Doc.
Editor=Ed.
Hearing=Hrg.
Her (His) Majesty's Stationary Office=HMSO
House Document=H. Doc.
House Executive Document=H. Ex. Doc.
House Executive Report= H. Ex. Rpt.
House of Common=H.C.
House of Representatives=H.R.
House Report=H. Rpt.
Kilobytes=kb or KB
Megabyte=mb or MB
Meeting=Mtg.
Member of Parliament=M.P.
No Date=n.d.
No Place=n.p.
Number=No.
Pages=pp. or p.
Parliament=Parl.
Part=Pt.
Representative=Rep.
Section=Sec.
Senate Document= S. Doc.
Senate Executive Document S. Ex. Doc.
Senate Executive Report=S. Ex. Rpt.
Senate Hearing=S. Hrg.
Senate Print=S. Prt.
Senate Report =S. Rpt.
Senate=S.
Senator=Sen.
Session=Sess.
Volume = Vol.

Glossary

A

Act: a piece of legislation that has been approved by one chamber of the U.S. Congress. An Act becomes a Public Law after it has gone through the legislative process and is signed by the President. Consult the *Quick Citation Guide to Legislative/Parliamentary Sources* for examples.

Agency Report Numbers: unique numbers assigned to published documents. These numbers are alphanumerical and are usually located in the upper or lower corners of the cover and/or title page (Figs. 5, 6, 9, 10). Consult *Appendix C: Numbering Systems* for examples.

Agricultural Experiment Station/Agricultural Extension Service: agencies established by the U.S. Department of Agriculture, in cooperation with states, counties, and universities, to serve agricultural and rural communities. Consult the *Quick Citation Guide to Special Cases and Well-Known Sources*, S1 for examples.

B

Bibliographic Data Sheet: a form on the front or back of technical reports, but also found in other document types. The standard sheet contains information on authors, title, date, sponsoring and performing agencies, contract number, report number, subject headings, and abstract. Consult *Where to Locate Information to Include in a Citation* (Section 0.1).

Bill: the most common form by which legislation is introduced in the U.S. Congress and state legislatures. In Congress all bill numbers are prefixed by H.R. or S. for House of Representatives or Senate, respectively. Consult the *Quick Citation Guide to Legislative/Parliamentary Sources* for examples.

C

Catalog: (v.) the process by which a library describes the physical makeup and intellectual contents of a book.

CIP (Cataloging in Publication): initial cataloging provided by the publisher when a book is printed. This information is usually located on the back of the title page and frequently is labeled "CIP." Consult *Where to Locate Information to Include in a Citation* (Section 0.1).

Clearinghouses: organizations established primarily to provide copies of reports to individuals and groups. See also: NTIS and ERIC. Consult the *Quick Citation Guide to Special Cases and Well-Known Sources*, S6 and Section 5.5g for examples.

COM-Docs: a class of documents submitted by the European Union Commission to the Council of Ministers. These may be reports, proposals for action, etc. They were not indexed and were difficult to obtain until 1983 when the EC began to issue them on microfiche with an index. Consult the *Quick Citation Guide to Legislative/Parliamentary Sources,* L4.4 for examples.

Commercial Database Vendor: a commercial company that provides access to a computer file or a database containing text or bibliographic records for a fee. Access to the database or information is typically controlled by password, IP address, or other methods (Section E4.1a).

Commercial Publisher: a commercial company that prints and sells print or other physical formats such as microfiche, microfilm, or microprints. Some government and organization publications are sold by commercial publishers and serve as an alternative source or the only source for some publications (Section 4.2e).

Committee Prints: written for Congressional committees, these publications provide background information on a piece of legislation or on a specific topic (Section 1.3b).

Computer File: a machine-readable file that may contain text, numbers, or images.

Conference Committee: a committee, composed of House and Senate members, which attempts to eliminate disagreements between Congressional chambers by reaching a compromise on a piece of legislation (Section 1.3b).

Conference Report: a report issued by a conference committee.

Contract Number: a series of numbers assigned to publications contracted for a government. These numbers are usually alphanumeric but are not necessarily unique to a document. Therefore, they are not considered valid citation elements. See Clearinghouses.

Cooperative Publication: documents which are jointly written and funded by more than one governmental or intergovernmental entity.

D

Documents: congressional publications covering a variety of materials. Documents include committee activities, reports, communications to Congress from the President and other executive agencies, miscellaneous items from patriotic groups, annual reports to Congress, and reports from individual legislative fact-finding missions. Consult the *Quick Citation Guide to Legislative/Parliamentary Sources* for examples.

E

Electronic Bulletin Boards (EBB): a computer system accessible to telecommunications connections that can serve as an information and message system.

Ellipses: a form of punctuation (. . .) which indicates the omission of information. In citations, ellipses are usually employed when shortening title data.

E-Mail: a message transmitted between sender and receiver via a communications network (Section E1.4a).

ERIC (Educational Resources Information Center): a national network of 16 clearinghouses funded by the National Institute of Education. Frequently publications available from ERIC deal with education and are identified by an agency report number beginning with ED. Consult the *Quick Citation Guide to Special Cases and Well-Known Sources*, S6 and Section 5.5g for examples.

European Union: an economic, social, and, sometimes, political union of Western European countries—France, Belgium, Denmark, Germany, Greece, Ireland, Italy, Luxembourg, the Netherlands, and the United Kingdom, Spain and Portugal.

External Sources of Information: see Internal Sources of Information.

F

FBIS: see JPRS and FBIS.

File Formats: many PEF and VEF sources are made available in a wide range of file formats that allow the researcher to use the information and data in the file in different ways. Some of the most common are graphic file formats (.gif and .jpg) used for pictures, photographs, and other graphic images; zip files (.zip) use to transfer large files across the internet; data formats (.csv, .xls) to give the user flexibility using the data and information with commercial software packages; and hypertext files (.htm and .html) to allow imbedded links and formatting for files on the internet. In addition audio, sound and video files are increasingly available via the WWW. Files may also be transferred in common word processing formats (.doc, .txt, and .wp) and presentation formats (.ppt). See also .PDF files and consult Sections 5.5a, E2.1d, E3.3-E3.4 for guidance.

Frame: an individual page in a microform. In microfiche the location of the frame is occasionally designated by an alphanumeric code (e.g., C5).

FTP Site: the location of a machine-readable file that can be transferred from one computer to another over a network such as the Internet.

G

Geo/Political Designation: the geographical or political designation that precedes the government name (e.g., U.S., Pennsylvania, New York, NY, Canada) consult Section 1.1 and E1.1 for rules.

Gopher Server: a network address that includes access to a Gopher program.

Government Document or Information: is information in any format produced by or for a governmental body or by international or intergovernmental organizations (IGO). The See *Introduction*, p. 1 for further discussion.

GPO (Government Printing Office): the printer to the U.S. Congress and the major federal printer/distributor. The GPO is the agency responsible for the federal depository system, maintaining the SuDoc system and issuing the *Monthly Catalog of U.S. Government Publications.*

Grant Number: see Contract Number.

H

Hearing: usually a public meeting held by a Congressional committee to investigate a bill, to provide legislative oversight, or to gather background information on a particular issue. Also, the written testimony and discussion from such a meeting. Consult the *Quick Citation Guide to Legislative/Parliamentary Sources* for examples.

HMSO: The official printing agency for Great Britain.

I

ICPSR (Inter-university Consortium for Political and Social Research): a consortium, located at the University of Michigan, that provides to its members (largely academic libraries), computer tapes of data collected for or useful for political or social science research (Section E3.2a).

Imprint: see Publisher Information.

Internal and External Sources of Information: to determine the content of a citation select information from internal sources such as the title page and prefer this information over sources that appear on external sources such as a book cover. Consult Section 0.1 and E0.1 for additional guidance and examples.

Internet: an international network that connects similar smaller networks creating a national electronic highway that allows the user to access a wide variety of databases, FTP sites, and e-mail addresses.

ISBN (International Standard Book Number): a unique multidigit number which publishers assign to books. It is frequently used as an ordering and verification number by booksellers (Section 5.4b).

Issuing Agency: the government agency responsible for the official position and content of a government or organization publication. Typically included in the primary position, rather than a Personal Author (Section 1.0 and E1.0).

Item Numbers: numbers used by depository libraries to select federal publications. These numbers appear in the *Monthly Catalog of U.S. Government Publications,* preceded by the depository black dot. Since there is not necessarily a direct title to item number correspondence, these numbers are not included as citation elements.

J

JPRS (Joint Publications Research Service) and FBIS (Foreign Broadcast Information Service): translating agencies of the Central Intelligence Agency that monitor print and broadcast media worldwide.

L

Loose-leafs: publications issued in a notebook format, which allows for easy updating. Frequently, pages are dated either at the top or at the bottom. Consult the *Quick Citation Guide to Special Cases and Well-Known Sources,* S18 for examples.

M

Masthead Documents (formerly mimeos): preliminary records of the U.N. General Assembly, Economic and Social Council, Security Council, and the Trusteeship Council. Many of them are later reissued as U.N. official records (Fig. 10). They are identified by a series/symbol number and by the lack of a sales number or an official record designation (See *Appendix C: Numbering Systems*). The banner at the top of a publication contains the basic bibliographic information needed to complete a citation (e.g., title, volume numbers, etc.) is commonly found on a title page. Consult Section 5.3d and the *Quick Citation Guide to Legislative/Parliamentary Sources,* L3.1 for examples. See U.N. Official Records.

Microfiche, Microfilm, Microprint: many government publications are preserved and distributed on a number of different microformats. Consult Section 5.3a, 5.3b, and 5.3c for information on how to include this information in your citation. See Readex Microprints.

Mimeograph: a document produced internally, usually by photocopying. Often identifiable by its type face (Setion 3.3). See Masthead Documents (formerly mimeos).

N

NTIS (National Technical Information Service): a clearinghouse established within the U.S. Department of Commerce to distribute all forms of scientific, technical and government-contracted reports. Consult the *Quick Citation Guide to Special Cases and Well-Known Sources*, S6 for examples.

O

Official Gazettes: a periodical publication issued by a foreign government that is used to inform the public of government actions such as new laws and regulations. Consult the *Quick Citation Guide to Special Cases and Well-Known Sources*, S21 for examples.

On-line Library Catalog: a database containing records representing titles owned by a library; the on-line catalog can be reached via a telecommunications connection. See Catalog (v.).

Ordinances: laws of a municipality, passed by a municipal council or its equivalent. Such laws usually govern zoning, safety, building, noise, etc.

P

Parliamentary Body: used here to designate international groups which meet, debate, and pass resolutions, but which do not have legislative power (e.g., the U.N. General Assembly; Council of Europe. Parliamentary Assembly; European Parliament).

Parliamentary Papers: a collection of governmental reports from executive and parliamentary agencies, which are gathered together and republished under the auspices of the parliament. They generally appear as a numbered series.

PDF File: a file format frequently used by organizations and governments for VEF of print formats. Sources in PDF format typically can be cited exactly like a print source because they are a page image of what was originally a print source (Section E4.1d). Consult the *Quick Citation Guides* for examples of sources in .pdf file format. PDF files require Adobe *Acrobat* to be viewed. See File Formats.

Periodical: a title published at specified intervals (e.g., weekly, monthly). Consult the *Quick Citation Guide to Periodical Articles and Statistical Sources* for examples and Section 6.0 and E6.0 for rules relating to these sources.

Physical Electronic Format (PEF): those electronic formats that have a physical form which can be held in our hand and is used, viewed, or listened to using some form of technology. See *Table 1—Physical Electronic Formats (PEF) and Virtual Electronic Formats (VEF)* for examples.

Popular Name: many government reports, laws and regulations are given or become known by a popular name (Section 2.1j).

Portals: provide access to many different databases and sources through a common search interface (Section E4.1c). Some are freely available (e.g., *GPO Access* and *Thomas)* while access is controlled to others. See Commercial Database Vendors.

Printer's Number: a number assigned by a printer when publishing documents. The number may be item specific or may be assigned to a number of documents printed on a particular day.

Therefore, it is not usually considered a valid citation element (Section 3.1 and Legislative/Parliamentary Editions, Section 3.2c).

Publication: material reproduced and distributed through formal means. This term is also used by some international organizations for works created especially for public sale (as opposed to documents or working papers). These works look like commercial press books and are treated as such by some libraries.

Public Law: the official name of a piece of legislation passed by the U.S. government. Each Public Law has a P.L. number designating the Congress and chronological order of passage (e.g., PL 97-235). Consult the *Quick Citation Guide to Legislative/Parliamentary Sources* for examples.

Publishing Information: the facts of publication—place of publication, publisher, and date of publication or copyright. Also called the "imprint" by bibliographers and librarians (Section 4.0). For VEF sources, the publisher information will also include Source Information—who is providing access to the sources (Section E4.0).

R

Readex Microprints: collections of government documents done by the Readex Corporation. Until 1982 the medium was micro-opaque cards; now they are on microfiche. UN Readex is filed by series/number; US Readex is filed by *Monthly Catalog* entry number. See Microfiche, Microfilm, and Microprints.

Readme: a computer file frequently found on CD-ROMs, floppy disks, or EBBs that typically contains useful or necessary information, such as installation instructions, and that may not be available in print documentation or other sources.

Regulations: laws promulgated by executive agencies. They usually deal with the details of administering laws of legislative bodies. Consult the *Quick Citation Guide to Special Cases and Well-Known Sources*, S7 for examples.

Reports, Congressional: publications from a Congressional committee which recommend certain action, usually relating to a piece of legislation. Congressional reports present the committee's view of the legislative intent of a law. Consult the *Quick Citation Guide to Legislative/Parliamentary Sources* for examples.

Reprint: the republication of a document with no physical changes. Frequently, both the original and reprinting dates are listed on the document (Section 5.3h).

Resolution: a form of legislation in the U.S. Congress. Simple resolutions are designated by H. Res. or S. Res.; concurrent resolutions by H. Con. Res. or S. Con. Res.; joint resolutions by H. J. Res. or S. J. Res. Consult the *Quick Citation Guide to Legislative/Parliamentary Sources* for examples.

RLIN (Research Libraries): a large fee-based bibliographic database containing the records from major research libraries. Can be used to locate additional information or sources. Ask your documents librarian for information on how to access this database in your library.

S

Sales Catalogs: for some international organizations, these are the only listings of the publications of the organization. They may contain indexes—by subject, title, author— and/or they may be organized broadly by subject. They are usually available free from the agency or from its sales agent.

Serial Set: the official compilation of Congressional reports and documents. Each volume in the set is numbered on the spine of the volume. The set began in 1817. Consult the *Quick Citation Guide to Special Cases and Well-Known Sources*, S27 for examples.

Series: a group of publications each with its own distinct title brought together under a common series title (Section 5.0).

Series/Symbol Number: a number assigned to a document by the UN. It indicates the issuing body, the type of document, and its place in the series.

Slip Law: the first official publication of a U.S. Statute, issued as an unbound pamphlet. Slip laws give the text of a law, references to other statutes amended by the law, and a brief history of the bill's passage into law.

Software: a machine-readable program that allows a user to manipulate, use, view, or analyze text, data, or images also in a machine-readable format.

Sponsoring Agency: see Issuing Agency.

Star Print: a reprint of a piece of legislation, ordered because of typographical errors in the original publication. It is designated by a star in the lower left corner of the bill.

State Data Centers: institutions sponsored in cooperation with the U.S. Bureau of the Census and state governments. The objective of these centers is to provide census data more efficiently to groups, businesses, and individuals (Section 4.2e).

Stock Number: a twelve-digit number used by the GPO for ordering purposes. Because stock numbers have only recently appeared in indexes and have not been assigned to all GPO documents, they are usually not included in a citation.

SuDoc (Superintendent of Documents) System: an alphanumeric numbering system used by most federal depository libraries to classify federal documents. The system is arranged hierarchically by issuing agency (Section 5.3e).

T

Technical Report Documentation Page: see Bibliographic Data Sheet.

Title Page: usually the first printed page in a book or document. Information found on the front of a title page includes author, publisher, and title. The back of a title page contains the date and place of publications. With some documents the title page and cover may be the same.

U

U.N. Official Records: final records of the sessions of the UN. There are generally three types of official records: meetings record (verbatim or summary); supplements (reports, background material, etc.); and annexes (usually administrative information). Some official records do not fall into any of these classes. Consult the *Quick Citation Guide to Legislative/Parliamentary Sources*, L3.2 for examples.

Uniform Resource Locator (URL): the URL serves as the "address" on the WWW for the source you are citing. Consult *Table 17—What is a Uniform Resource Locator (URL)?* and Section E4.2 for examples.

University Press Books: books published by universities. Occasionally, university presses produce documents for the government (Section 4.2e).

V

Virtual Electronic Format (VEF): those electronic sources that do not have a physical format but rather are accessed via the Internet. They are read, viewed, or listened to on our computer or other electronic device. Consult *Table 1—Physical Electronic Formats (PEF) and Virtual Electronic Formats (VEF)* for examples.

W

WorldCat: a large fee-based bibliographic database containing the records from libraries. Can be used to locate additional information or sources. Ask your documents librarian for information on how to access this database in your library.

Index

Entries beginning with a number refer to Part 2 (rules on physical formats). Entries beginning with an "E" refer to Part 3 (rules on VEF). Entries beginning with B, L, P, S refer to bibliographic citation examples in the *Quick Citation Guides*. Italicized entries are reserved for examples of bibliographic citations that lack any textual explanations.